The Politics of Land Reform in Chile, 1950–1970

Written under the auspices of
The Center for International Affairs
Harvard University

The Politics of Land Reform in Chile, 1950–1970

Public Policy, Political Institutions, and Social Change

Robert R. Kaufman

Harvard University Press   Cambridge, Massachusetts   1972

To Madeleine

Preface

Most case studies in political science attempt, not always successfully, to straddle the general and the particular. On the one hand, the researcher is required, quite rightly, to "justify" his study in general terms, to show how "his" case is relevant to broader propositions about political behavior and why his study should be of interest to a larger scholarly community which is, for the most part, disinterested in the details of the particular case itself. On the other hand, in many instances, the decision to study a particular country is often inspired as much by a fascination with the details of the case as it is by a more general frame of reference, and this fascination may well influence research decisions, the manner in which the material is presented, and the various themes which are emphasized. So it is with this study of the Chilean land reform. It has been designed as a project which can contribute to and be evaluated in terms of interests which extend beyond Chile itself. At the same time the reader is entitled to know something of the more personal, particular objectives and dilemmas which drew me toward an examination of the Chilean scene and which affected the way this study was conducted.

When this project was begun in 1965, one of Chile's principal attractions was that it appeared to offer a "success story" rare in Latin America—a story of "democratic reform," initiated by a well-organized reform party and pursued within a constitutional framework. The most striking fact I found on my arrival in Chile was that this experiment seemed to be going remarkably well. Not only was the reform government implementing its program with great political skill, but the "extremist" elements of right and left were behaving far differently from the way many accounts of Chilean (and Latin American) politics had led me to expect. Leftists were supporting a moderate reform effort, rather than attempting to obstruct it; and, more striking still, the rightists who were opposed to the reform were conducting their opposition with unanticipated flexibility. And all of this was in a country with one of the most "rigid" rural social systems in Latin America—a country where many observers felt that "democratic" land reform would be impossible. Here, it seemed to me, was a good illustration of the way in which change could be achieved through a reformmongering process and of the way in which strong, relatively institutionalized political parties could support such efforts.

Since 1965 a great deal has changed, both in Chile and in my evaluation of the Chilean situation. First, much of the élan and optimism which had accompanied the Christian Democratic electoral victories disappeared. Next, opposition and conflict within the Christian Democracy and between that party and its competitors began to intensify. Then, after a series of electoral defeats, the Christian Democratic government was in 1970 replaced by a coalition dominated by Chile's two Marxist parties. Little of this, I hasten to confess, was seen clearly by me in 1965, and much of the ensuing period in which I examined the Chilean situation involved a struggle to understand events as they occurred, to account not only for the rather surprising "successes" of the Christian Democratic administration, but also for its increasingly apparent failures. In the course of this struggle it became necessary for me to readjust my perspectives and to rethink some initial assumptions.

Some of the product of this rethinking can be found integrated into the analysis presented below. In particular, the difficulties encountered by the Christian Democrats, in spite of their relative success in dealing with the left and the right, prompted me to look again at the social parameters within which this struggle occurred. Although I by no means abandoned my initial propositions about the importance of reformmongering or political institutionalization, it became increasingly clear that the constraints placed on these strategies and structures by Chile's urbanized, semimodern social order would have to be more carefully explored. The result of this exploration will, I hope, raise some new questions about the nature and impact of social modernization in Latin America.

There are, however, two other problems which have been less tractable within the framework of this volume. One of these lay in the desire to "keep up with events." Precisely because this study was an analysis of a contemporary, unfolding process, this proved to be a difficult task. It was rendered even more difficult by the victory of the Marxist parties in 1970, for this event raised important questions about which attributes of the Chilean system were "lasting" or "temporary." Rather than succumbing to the temptation to forecast, anticipate, or update the book to account for what might happen under a Marxist regime, it seemed best to terminate the analysis at the end of the Christian Democratic period. Although a few minor changes were made in the text after September 1970, almost all of the material — along with comments on the moderation and "incrementalism" built into the Chilean system — was written before that time and has been left unqualified. It remains to be seen whether subsequent events will prove the analysis valid or invalid.

The final problem is in the realm of the values which underlie my research, especially my concern about the relationship between "political democracy" and "social justice" in developing countries. My personal orientation is a liberal one, based on the hope, if not the certainty, that the goals of a more equitable and abundant social order can be attained within a humane and pluralistic political framework. The Chilean case raises serious questions about the degree to which this is possible, even within a highly institutionalized constitutional system. Yet the difficulties of drawing lessons from the Chilean experience are enormous. It is by no means clear that the defeat of the Christian Democrats and the victory of the left imply the failure of "democratic reform" in Chile, or that the Chilean system as a whole is not moving in the direction of a more desirable sociopolitical order. Nor is it at all certain that an authoritarian regime can attain these objectives more quickly, or indeed, whether these objectives can be attained at all.

Many of these problems are not treated explicitly in the text. The main focus of the book, rather, is on the factors which contribute to the scope, pace, and peacefulness of the reform, the forces which maintain the overall stability of the Chilean system, and the prospects of appeasing or accommodating new mass groups as they begin to enter politics. These are questions which, at least in principle, can be answered in the same way by persons

Preface

with quite different visions of a just society. After five years of studying the Chilean situation, though, I am less certain than ever about the kinds of changes which are, from a larger value perspective, both desirable and possible. This uncertainty can be read between the lines of almost every page in the book.

I would like to acknowledge those institutions and individuals who contributed to making the study less limited than it might otherwise have been. The initial research for this project was financed by the Henry L. and Grace Doherty Charitable Foundation during 1965–66. The Institute for the Comparative Study of Political Systems (ICOPS) published earlier versions of Chapters 2 and 5 as a monograph, *The Chilean Political Right and Agrarian Reform,* and has kindly permitted me to reprint portions of that monograph within this book. Additional research and the basic draft of the book were completed while I was a Research Fellow at the Center for International Affairs, Harvard University, during 1967–68.

Among the many individuals who contributed to this manuscript, I am grateful for the hospitality, candor, and cooperativeness of the many Chileans whom I met and interviewed while I was in Chile, and for the help of my colleagues at the Center for International Affairs and at Douglass College, who have vastly furthered my education in political science. I am also indebted to Terry McCoy, who read and commented on the manuscript; to the Center's Editor, Mrs. Marina S. Finkelstein; and to Mrs. Roberta Weber and Mrs. Ruth Bennett who typed the manuscript. Special thanks must also go to Samuel P. Huntington, both for his personal counsel and support and for the intellectual inspiration he provided. Finally, my wife has contributed to the completion of this project in so many tangible and intangible ways that it is impossible to enumerate all of them here. That this book is dedicated to her is a measure of both her contribution and my gratitude.

Contents

Introduction

Throughout Latin America peasants are entering politics, up-
setting the balance between established social forces that had
once been the exclusive competitors for governmental power.
Traditional rural ties are disintegrating. New "populist" spokesmen are emerging. Claims are being made for an extension of
the franchise, for expansion of governmental services, for a
broadening of educational opportunities, and, most important,
for redistribution of income and property.

The demands of these groups, to be sure, are proving far more
limited than had once been anticipated. Contrary to the expectations widely shared at the time of the Cuban upheaval, social
revolution is not necessarily the inevitable alternative to peaceful
reform. Even so, social reform is still the order of the day for
those societies which hope someday to become integrated national
communities. One of the most important of these reforms must
be directed toward reducing the extreme inequities of a land
tenure system that has permitted the owners of vast estates to
monopolize wealth and authority, leaving the remaining majority
of the rural population powerless and impoverished. Although
failure to institute such measures may or may not bring revolution, such failure will almost certainly lead to acts of insurrection
in the countryside and to more and bloodier coups d'etat in the
executive mansions of the hemisphere.

This study is, in part, a description of the land reform issue
as it emerged in Chile during the 1950s and 1960s. Following
the lead of Albert O. Hirschman[1] and Charles Anderson,[2] it
attempts to go beyond a discussion of the "desirability of change"
and the "obstacles to change" to focus on the manner in which
at least some changes have actually been made. It illustrates a
process that Hirschman has termed "reformmongering." The
book focuses on efforts by successive Chilean governments to
pass and implement land reform legislation. It attempts to map
the kinds of conflict that surround the emergence of the land

1

reform issue, the timing and nature of the involvement of various social groupings, and the building of coalitions in support of various types of change. Such casework is necessary to gain an understanding of both the difficulties of, and the potential for, reform that exists in Latin America.

In addition to the descriptive and historical objectives of the study, however, certain characteristics of the Chilean political system make it possible to link the discussion of land reform to some broader issues of comparative politics. Specifically, the Chilean case provides an opportunity to ask two larger questions. What is the impact of prior social change — urbanization, limited industrialization, and the emergence of new, nonagricultural social forces — on the prospects for rural structural reform? To what extent do well-developed representative institutions—parties and interest groups — facilitate the adjustment of the political system to new social demands?

The first of these questions refers to an aspect of Chilean society that is becoming increasingly characteristic of Latin America as a whole. More and more, rural communities and peasants are being displaced by the growth of cities and by the emergence of new, "urban," functional groupings. The countries of Latin America have attained a "middle level" of modernization, which distinguishes them not only from the more advanced nations of North America and Western Europe, but also from the more traditional societies of Asia and Africa. Chile, with more than two-thirds of its population now classified as "urban," is one of the Latin American countries farthest along this road; but at least ten other countries in the hemisphere follow closely behind. By 1970, more Latin Americans lived in cities than in the countryside.[3]

These developments have not diminished the importance of the land reform issue in Latin America. On the contrary, the needs of a growing urban population have placed increasing strains on inefficient agrarian structures, strains which have, from an economic point of view, increased the urgency of land reform measures designed to raise rural productivity. In most countries, including Chile, moreover, peasants are still the largest single occupational grouping — a grouping which provides an important base of potential support for governments willing to undertake rural reform. Nevertheless, in an urban context land reform will be subject to different political imperatives and will have a quite different political impact than when it takes place within more rural settings. Since the impact of urbanization is complex, no simple thesis about these differences can be advanced. What can be stated is that for those who desire massive alterations of traditional rural social structures, urbanization is by no means an unmixed blessing. In the process of social modernization, new groups and cleavages are introduced into the political situation which, in some ways, both increase the political difficulties of achieving a land reform and reduce its potential impact on the society as a whole.

The second analytical question treated in this case study — the impact on reform of relatively well-developed representative institutions — is suggested by that portion of political development theory which has placed special emphasis on the significance of "political" organizations in the process of social change.[4] Specifically, this study follows the work of Samuel P. Huntington, who stresses the existence of a dialectical tension between the "political" and "social" aspects of the modernization process.[5] Huntington suggests that as industrialization, increased communications, and economic development raise the level of political participation within a society, political stability will depend on the capacity of that society to develop linking organizations (parties and interest groups) which can channel political activity and build political consensus. Whether this will in fact occur in a given society is entirely problematical, for older institutions can decay as well as develop under the impact of increased mass demands and the pressures of newly participating groups.[6] In this respect the timing of the emergence of parties is of critical importance: "A society which develops well organized political parties while the level of participation is still relatively low (as was largely the case in India, Uruguay, Chile, England, the United States, and Japan) is likely to have a less destabilizing expansion of political participation than a society where parties are organized later in the process of modernization."[7]

Obviously, a case study cannot, by definition, be considered a test of such a hypothesis. Its acceptance or rejection can only come through the systematic consideration and comparison of many cases. Case studies can, however, be useful for illustrating such broader theoretical propositions and, more important, for refining them in the light of the evidence uncovered.

The case of the Chilean land reform is well suited for these tasks; for Chile is, as Huntington suggests, a country in which political organization has "kept pace" with accelerating social change and political participation. Chile has attained not only a relatively high degree of *social* modernization, but it has reached a level of *political* development quite unusual for Latin America. In other large Latin American countries, such as Argentina, Brazil, and Colombia, the emergence of middle sector groups and factory workers during the first quarter of the twentieth century led to the collapse of constitutional structures, to the emergence or reemergence of military strongmen, and at times, to widespread, anomic violence. In contrast, Chile's parliamentary system tended to survive and adapt to the demands of new urban social forces. To be sure, this transition did not occur without some institutional discontinuities, and the adaptation made by the Chilean system was by no means complete. But by the time the Chilean peasantry began to appear on the political scene in the 1950s, Chile's political system was characterized by a tradition of relatively free elections, by a strong, independent legislature, and by one of the most durable multiparty systems in Latin America — a system of political institutions presumptively capable of mediating the tensions associated with rural change. In contrast to politically less developed countries confronted with similar challenges, the politics of land reform in Chile provides the opportunity to observe a two-way flow of influence, from polity to society as well as the other way around.

In the following pages these analytical themes about the impact of urbanization and political development are woven into the descriptive-historical objectives of the case study. In keeping with the latter objectives, subsequent chapters are organized partially along chronological lines. The first section of the book traces the sociopolitical setting of the land reform issue, the emergence of the issue itself, and the first Chilean efforts at land reform, undertaken by a conservative center-right coalition in 1962–63. Subsequent sections of the book deal with the more extensive reform efforts of the Christian Democratic government, between 1964 and 1970. In keeping with the other objectives of the study, however, each section and each chapter also deal, from somewhat different perspectives, with the analytical questions posed earlier. Chapters 3 through 6 examine the manner in which the strategies and behavior of interested social groups were affected by the need to operate within an urban environment and the manner in which their choices were shaped by the representative institutions of the left, center, and right. Chapter 7 discusses the impact of urban groups on the question of land reform, particularly as they enter into the struggle for governmental funds and attention in the period after the land reform legislation had already been passed. In the concluding chapter, an attempt is made to draw together the various analytical themes considered throughout the book, and to compare the Chilean experience more explicitly with other cases of land reform found in Latin America.

Part 1 The Sociopolitical Background: Pressures for Change and Initial Responses, 1950–1964

Chapter 1 Chilean Politics and Agrarian Reform

Referring to Latin America as a whole, Charles Anderson has observed that "The normal rule of Latin American political change is that new power contenders may be added to the system, but old ones may not be eliminated." [1] In other words, Anderson argues, when traditional elites are confronted with challenges from below, they are inclined to permit new social forces to organize, to participate in politics, and to compete for a share in the resources of the state, but only on the condition that these new forces permit older interests and institutions to remain intact. This generalization graphically summarizes the nature of the social transformations which occurred in Chile during the half century before the advent of the land reform issue in the 1950s. Between about 1920 and 1940, after two previous decades of violent confrontations, emerging middle sectors and mining workers wrested control of the Chilean government away from the landed aristocracy, established a welfare system, and inaugurated an effort at industrialization. As Anderson suggests, however, these new urban groups did not challenge the older elite's control over rural property and over peasants.

In effect, two separate, although highly interrelated, worlds emerged out of this process of change. The nonagricultural sector of Chilean society, which for the sake of brevity is referred to as the urban world, was the site of national politics. Within this world, Chileans looked to the government and its agents for the maintenance of order and the dispensing of services and other resources. Here also was the arena within which the struggle for national office occurred. The other, rural, world was essentially one of private power. Here the landlord, rather than the government, was the final authority, and it was to him, rather than to the state, that the rural worker owed his loyalty. To be sure, many interconnections existed between the two worlds. The landowner himself lived in both of them. He occasionally called on the state to reinforce his control over peasants, and he actively intervened in the formation of government economic policies that indirectly affected the whole of the rural population. Moreover, those peasants who migrated to the cities frequently brought with them the habits of submissiveness and the parochial orientations that characterized life in the countryside. In terms of defining the scope of national politics, however, the urban-rural distinction was an important one. Until the 1950s, when peasants actually began to enter the voting booths in large numbers, the line between town and countryside was generally accepted as the border which defined the limits of political competition. Until the 1960s, when Chilean governments actually started to redistribute rural property, this line defined the limits of the state's direct authority as well.

This chapter places the land reform issue within the setting of these two worlds. The first section describes the nature of the society and political institutions which emerged within the urban boundaries. A discussion of the "rural world" and an examination of the land reform problem follows. The final section of the chapter treats more extensively the analytical issues raised in the Introduction.

Urban Society and the Chilean Political System

The Patterns of Social Organization and Cleavage:
Power Elite or Power Fragmentation?

The changes brought about by urbanization in Latin America have not followed patterns established in other parts of the world. During the 1950s, when American scholars first turned their attention to Latin American urbanization, they looked to the European experience as a model and expected the cities to be the locus for the emergence of new, reform-oriented middle classes and of dynamic new systems of economic production.[2] Since then, these views have been strongly and in many ways decisively rebutted.[3] The Latin American city was, it was pointed out, largely a preindustrial phenomenon, having emerged during the late nineteenth and early twentieth centuries as a commercial center for traditional mining and agricultural enterprises. Although a subsequent period of industrialization in the second quarter of the twentieth century did lead to the emergence of new groups and institutions, these were in many cases grafted onto the old order. They did not, as the scholars had expected, promote a confrontation between tradition and modernity. At present, there is growing agreement among scholars as to what has *not* occurred. But there is much less agreement about the best way to conceptualize and describe the newer patterns of social organization and cleavage which have emerged with the growth of cities.

One viewpoint is that the urban power structure is an extension of the rural, "two-class" social order.[4] Claudio Veliz points out, for example, that at the upper levels of urban society, the holders of industrial and commercial wealth intermarried with the older, landed aristocracy and acquired land themselves, while the members of a much larger middle sector aspired to similar status and imitated as much as possible the habits and consumption patterns of the older elite.[5] As in the countryside, the argument runs, the capacity to control the actions of others rested in the hands of a small oligarchy — the holders of landed, commercial, and industrial wealth. These, in alliance with their middle sector supporters, dominated the society as a whole. Other writers, though not denying the existence of vast inequalities in status and income, have qualified or rejected the power elite notion, stressing instead the profound divisions among the established urban groups. Charles Anderson, for example, speaks of a perpetual struggle among many small cliques of power contenders, each with its own special means of influencing the state.[6] Robert Scott uses similar terms, writing not of one but of many elite groups: "All of the elites," he states, "are in mortal competition with each other. In the face of particularly strong pressure from below, varied interests found in the establishment may close ranks for a time, and the challengers may react with a temporary coalition, but cooperation soon will come to an end. Each of the elites is seeking to maximize its political power and to protect the perquisites of power — material benefits, social and political status, and a sense of being able to control one's own destiny." [7]

The power elite notion, which has been treated with considerable skepticism by political scientists in the United States, cannot be lightly dismissed in respect to Chile. The Chilean upper class, urban as well as rural, *is* undoubtedly the most cohesive and the best organized of the various social strata. Until the 1960s it was able to function as a veto group within Chilean politics, helping to prevent such issues as land reform from surfacing in political debate. Furthermore, although the upper class was finally forced to share power with a variety of middle sector and labor groups, the inflationary costs of the welfare reforms and bureaucratization which laid the basis for this accommodation were borne largely by the marginal sectors in the countryside and in the urban slums.[8] In this important respect it *is* possible to speak of the structure of Chilean society in terms of a broad division between an established minority stratum and a larger, disestablished majority.

In many other respects, however, the power elite concept obscures as much as it illuminates. For a number of reasons we would, with Anderson and Scott, emphasize instead the extreme fragmentation of power that exists within the Chilean urban arena.

First, the concept of a ruling oligarchy badly blurs the wide differences in background among those individuals who had by mid-century come to comprise the established minority stratum. The process of urbanization and political change has in Chile been marked by a tendency to incorporate into the urban power structure an ever-widening number of occupational groupings, patronage cliques, and regional interests. Each of these has sought to build into that structure special legal privileges which would protect it from the competition of those above and below. This characteristic was reflected, for example, in the evolution of the social security system. By the end of the 1950s, this system had mushroomed from two basic white- and blue-collar funds, established in 1925, to forty-one separate fiscal and administrative units, each of which reflected the particular demands and the special strength of strategically located white- and blue-collar groups.[9] Similar patterns of struggle and influence can be inferred from the crazy quilt of special tax exemptions, duty-free territories, multiple exchange rates, and special subsidies that evolved from the 1920s to the present.

Most of these changes were, of course, instituted without cost to the traditional upper class. Nevertheless, they introduced into the urban political system new power resources not subject to the control of the traditional aristocracy. The military organizations, state corporations, and the sprawling government bureaucracies, whether conservative or not, tended to act in their own interests rather than in those of the upper class.

More important, the range of established urban power group-ings, by the 1940s, included not only the politically conservative upper and middle strata, but also a variety of organized groups drawn from the mining and factory proletariat, from sectors of the urban service industries, and from the growing public bureauc-racy. The incorporation of such groups makes it difficult to apply a power elite model, if only because these groups could not easily be placed into either the exploiting oligarchy or into the exploited lower class. On the one hand, these white- and blue-collar workers formed the nucleus of support for Chile's Marxist and populist movements. They usually viewed their interests as opposed to those of the upper class, and they frequently employed power resources — strikes, demonstrations, and voting strength — which allowed them to compete directly with the older elite for control over government policy. On the other hand, it was also difficult to identify these workers with the larger, unorganized, lower class majority. Until the 1960s, the members of Chile's union organiza-tions never comprised more than 15 percent of the total working class and were generally located in the most productive sectors of the economy. Union workers were the major beneficiaries of the welfare reforms and their incomes were many times higher than those of the rural workers and of the casual laborers and self-employed vendors who inhabited the city slums.[10] Frequently, the unionized workers, like the upper strata, tended to act against the interests of the large, unorganized majority. "The various groups of the professions and civil servants," notes Osvaldo Sunkel, "followed . . . a policy of protection and improvement by limiting entry and obtaining increasing social benefits for each specific group." [11] Similarly, blue-collar unions devoted "most of their energies to creating barriers limiting access to work in [the] high productivity sectors." [12]

A final reason for adopting the Scott-Anderson model and for rejecting the power elite notion is that the latter tends to obscure the extreme tensions in the relations among the established urban groups. The process of accommodation by which such groups were incorporated into the old power structure rested on a narrow economic base. Although during the 1930s and 1940s industrialization stimulated some growth, it was limited by the small size of consumer markets, by low productivity within other economic sectors, and by high costs and inefficiency within the industrial sector itself. For most of the past fifty years, the Chilean economy has been plagued by low growth rates, by a persistent race between price and salary increases, and by a general excess of labor supply over demand at every level of the commercial and industrial structure.[13] In practice, this meant that the aspirations of each of the competing power groups could be satisfied only partially and that none could be completely secure in the gains that it had made.

Thus, in spite of the process of accommodation, a constant undercurrent of discontent continued to exist among the groups which comprised the urban "establishment." This can be seen most clearly in the white- and blue-collar sectors. In almost every major street demonstration, protest march, or riot that has occurred in Chile, bank clerks, secondary school teachers, and government bureaucrats can be found among the leaders.[14] Strong dissatisfaction can also be perceived among the other established groupings. The major industrial associations regularly complain about price controls and inadequate government credit. Various middle sector groups bemoan the high rates of taxation. Landowners operating within the urban sphere complain of governmental discrimination and of inadequate price supports. Although most of these groups have acquired the means of protecting themselves within the political process, the struggle between them is intensified by the extreme scarcity of economic resources. The quest for security is, therefore, an endless one, characterized by the achievement of limited and particularistic objectives, as well as by considerable bitterness, occasional violence, and not infrequently by strong opposition to whatever government happens to be in power.

Chilean Political Institutions

In the Latin American context, the distinctive feature of the Chilean urban order is that, in Chile, the struggles between established social groups have generally been contained within a parliamentary framework. Countries such as Brazil, Argentina, Peru, and until the late 1950s, Venezuela and Cuba, resemble what

Huntington has termed "radical praetorian" types of society —
those in which the conflicts between urban middle class groups,
existing upper class elements, and small blue-collar unions are
unmediated by specialized and commonly accepted political institutions and procedures.[15] In such societies, Huntington argues, the
vacuum left by weakly organized political parties and interest
groups is filled by social groups and institutions, each of which
employs the special power bases available to it in order to gain
a share of the available resources. Students, military men, priests,
and aristocrats, rather than congressmen, presidents, and party
leaders, are thus the most important political actors. Bribery,
street demonstrations, and coups are no less important than the
mobilization of electoral support as means of influencing the state.
Constitutional forms and procedures may exist in these societies,
but they are accepted only tentatively, and can be fairly easily
discarded or replaced when it suits the purpose of the contending
social forces.

In contrast, "civic" societies are those in which social conflicts
are mediated by relatively well-developed and specialized political
institutions. Huntington defines political development (or institutionalization) in terms of a high degree of adaptability (a demonstrated capacity to survive environmental challenges); complexity
(the presence of many functional subunits); autonomy (the
relative independence of political procedures from outside forces);
and coherence (the capacity of political decision-makers to unite
in the face of outside pressures).[16] By most of these criteria,
Chile appears relatively institutionalized. The origins of its constitutional structures extend well back into the nineteenth century,
when parliamentary forms were accepted by the then dominant
aristocratic families as a means of resolving internal conflict. The
electoral and parliamentary system became more adaptable and
complex as it extended access to the emerging urban social forces
during the twentieth century. And as these social forces gained a
place within the existing system, the various forms of direct action
they had used to gain admittance were gradually translated into
electoral and legislative currency, thus increasing the autonomy
of the system as a whole.[17] The result of this process of political
change was a record of stability matched only by Uruguay in Latin
America.[18]

Of course, the differences between political development and underdevelopment, however these terms are defined, are best thought of in terms of a continuum, rather than of a dichotomy. No political system is completely developed or underdeveloped. All political institutions involve mixtures of modern and traditional norms, and all are in some ways shaped by the societies in which they emerge. The Chilean parliamentary and electoral system was in many ways limited in its development because it emerged within a socioeconomic system which shared many of the characteristics of Latin America as a whole. As noted earlier, for example, the adaptation of the constitutional system rested on the same type of tacit agreements characteristic of most other Latin American societies — namely, that the rural masses were to be denied access to the government and that the rights of participating groups were not to be violated. This reduced the coherence of Chilean governmental institutions by restricting the capacity of their members to agree on a wide range of policy questions. Moreover, the acceptance of constitutional procedures in Chile appeared more tentative than in countries like the United States and Great Britain. During the 1920s and 1930s, street violence, paramilitary organizations, conspiracies, and coups d'etat were employed to win office and influence governmental policy, and even after that time various nonconstitutional power resources were never entirely discarded as auxiliary weapons in the political struggle.[19]

Nevertheless, once it was established that emerging groups would not challenge traditional perquisites, there was no necessary incompatibility between the ongoing struggle for resources and the maintenance of constitutional structures. Thus, in the decades between the 1920s, when these structures temporarily broke down, and the 1960s, when land reform became a major issue in Chilean politics, the trend was toward a greater autonomy for Chile's parliamentary and electoral institutions. Though not completely legitimized and accepted, these institutions had nonetheless become more widely valued and more capable of playing an independent role in shaping the expectations and behavior of the more radical elements within the system. The extent to which this was the case was well illustrated in 1952 when the caudillo Carlos Ibañez returned to the presidency of Chile after a period of over twenty years. From 1927 to 1931, Ibañez had governed Chile as a military strongman, and his subsequent election to office was widely interpreted as an expression of a popular dissatisfaction with the constitutional, multiparty system. Throughout his term of office, however, Ibañez hewed strictly to constitutional forms. Writing to his Argentine counterpart, Juan Perón, Ibañez explained that the times had changed since he had last ruled Chile in the 1920s:

The governments of the Right (1933–39) and the Radicals (1939–52) became entrenched in the organization of the country; they took possession of economic power by means of almost unbreakable connections; and as a smoke-screen for the great social and political masquerade which the country has experienced they created with incessant efforts of propaganda and false verbalism, a misguided but powerful democratic consciousness in the masses, who as a result take a dim view of a governor who had been presented to them for more than twenty years as a "hateful dictator" by a national oligarchy permanently colluded [*sic*] with the corrupt parties of the extreme left.[20]

The obverse side of this institutional development can be seen in the gradual retreat of social forces and institutions from direct participation in politics. After the formal separation of Church and State in 1925, the Catholic hierarchy gradually retreated from the political arena, although individual clergymen continued to act and to find spokesmen within the Conservative and Christian Democratic parties. Similarly, the presence of the Chilean military became less conspicuous over time. The last successful coup d'etat occurred in 1932. Between 1935 and 1940, there were six attempted military interventions. From 1941 to 1950, only two attempted coups were reported in the press. Between 1951 and 1960 — a decade of economic stagnation and growing social tensions — only one military conspiracy came to light.[21] The conflicts within urban society came to be expressed less and less through conspiracies and coups, and more and more through parliamentary cabals and cabinet turnovers.

Many of the same tendencies have characterized the evolution of the Chilean party system within this larger parliamentary framework. On the one hand, the Chilean party system lacked many of the features attributed to strong party systems. With the rural workers considered beyond the pale of legitimate competition, none of the parties, including those of the left, were in a position to acquire a large, organized mass base of support. Moreover, reflecting the fragmentation of the politicized sectors of urban society, most of the major parties were beset by internal factionalism and splintering, processes which have sometimes led to an extreme proliferation of minor party groupings within the Congress. Finally, as might be expected in a society of this sort, the party system as a whole was beset by a strong undercurrent of antiparty sentiment.

On the other hand, mixed with these elements of weakness was a marked capacity among the political parties to rebound from periodic splits, electoral losses, and antiparty movements, and to emerge from each crisis somewhat stronger than before. In the 1920s, the Chilean centrist and rightist parties were little more than loosely structured and highly personalistic cliques of parliamentary notables, while the leftist parties were comprised of the small northern labor movement, middle class intellectuals, and various factions within the military. However, after a period of repression imposed by Ibañez between 1927 and 1931, the parties began to expand their bases of support and to consolidate their organizations. Moving outward from the Congress during the 1930s and 1940s, the Radical party consolidated a network of local and regional organizations (*asembleas*), discarded anticlericalism as its major ideological concern, and definitively embraced a state welfare orientation as a means of attracting lower middle class elements into the party framework. In the same two decades, the parties of the left, the Communists and Socialists, also began to move beyond their small base of mining labor, reaching and organizing new factory workers in the urban centers of the country.

This expansion was interrupted during the early 1950s, when the quasi-authoritarian Carlos Ibañez again ascended to the presidency. Supported by an array of loosely organized splinter movements, Ibañez explicitly portrayed himself as an independent who could rise above multiparty politics. His victory in 1952 reflected the widespread antiparty sentiment within the Chilean electorate and left the established parties temporarily confused and disorganized. However, like many personalist leaders in Latin America,

Ibañez was unable to consolidate his base of support or to give his movement programmatic coherence. Almost as soon as he assumed office, his loosely structured coalition began to disintegrate, and the major parties entered a new period of consolidation which took them beyond the levels they had achieved in earlier decades. The trend could be seen clearly in the legislature, where the number of parties declined from nineteen in 1953, to twelve in 1954, to only eight in 1961 and 1964.[22] Between 1960 and 1969, only four major party groupings operated in the congressional arena: the Radical and Christian Democratic parties in the center, a coalition of Communists and Socialists on the left, and a bloc of Liberals and Conservatives on the right. Since the beginning of the 1950s, the major parties' collective share of the congressional electorate (divided about equally among the four major groupings), increased from 50.5 percent in 1953, to 70.7 percent in 1957, to 83.4 percent in 1961, and to 93.5 percent in 1965.[23]

The sources of this durability are not easily uncovered. As has already been suggested, Chile lacks the high level of social integration and consensus which is said to provide the underpinning for party competition in such countries as the United States, Great Britain, or Sweden. More appropriate analogies are probably to be found among the smaller European countries that Lijphart has termed consociational democracies.[24] In such democracies, separate and often antagonistic subcultures have, historically, been organized by individual parties into distinct "vertical columns," joined together only at the top by cooperation among the representative elites. Even here, the applicability of the consociational model to the Chilean situation is inexact; for in Chile one finds neither the distinct subcultures, nor the relatively high degree of party identification that provides ongoing sources of support for individual European parties. In a very general sense, however, it is possible to conceptualize Chilean multiparty politics in terms of vertical patterns somewhat similar to the systems described by Lijphart. At least three major characteristics of the Chilean system as a whole have allowed each of the Chilean parties to send down strong roots among the conflicting groups of urban society and, through cooperation among the various party leaders, to link these groups into the constitutional order.

antry, and to resist the pressures of a landed group that was a major power in both the city and the countryside.

The Rural Subsystem and the Problem of Land Reform

In the city a variety of governmental and party organizations played a major role in expressing and regulating social conflict. In the countryside the *latifundia,* or haciendas as they were sometimes called, were the major instruments of social control. Although these estates had long been linked to the outside world through the sale of agricultural commodities, and although the landowners themselves usually lived in the cities at least part of the time, the internal structure of power within the latifundia was self-contained, highly authoritarian, and removed from the struggles and conflicts that characterized urban life. At the bottom of this structure the rural workers (*inquilinos*) lived and worked on the estates and depended on the patron for housing, for medical attention, for food, and for the small plot of ground necessary for subsistence. At the apex the landed patron and the members of his immediate family controlled the interchange between the workers and the outside world and set the rules for life and death within the estate itself. The relation between patron and worker was defined by total authority on the one side and total dependence and obedience on the other.

Although this form of social organization was common in Latin America, there is much to suggest that the Chilean system of large estates was especially noteworthy for its inclusiveness and durability. This distinctiveness was emphasized by McBride in the 1930s. "Chilean agriculture," he commented, "is still based mainly on the hacienda . . . the rural population is made up chiefly of hacienda dwellers, neither small farms nor agricultural villages constituting, as in most parts of the world, the characteristic units of country life." [26] More recent comparative data suggest similar conclusions about the special importance that the latifundia still play in Chilean rural life. In Russett's attempt to rank countries according to the degree of land tenure inequality, Chile, along with pre-revolutionary Bolivia, ranked highest of the twenty Latin American nations in land concentration.[27] In 1955, according to another study, large estates covered over 79 percent of Chile's agricultural land surface. This percentage was the highest among the six countries for which data were available.[28]

The reasons for the importance of the hacienda in Chile probably lie in its initial pattern of settlement. In other parts of Spanish America, where the invading conquistadores encountered large, sedentary, and highly organized Indian populations, they employed a system of labor grants (the *encomienda*) to impress the Indians into service. Although in many cases these grants served as the bases for large private estates, encomiendas were often employed for purposes other than an appropriation of the land itself. Sometimes Indians were used for mining or for service in the cities. In other numerous instances, tributes were exacted from Indian communities which were otherwise left alone. Thus, alongside the estate system, there also emerged other types of rural structures — the vestiges of the Indian communities, villages of small and middle proprietors, part-time laborers, and sharecroppers. In quite a few places, in fact, the estate system did not expand until the nineteenth century, when the growth of the international commodity market induced landowners to enlarge and consolidate their holdings.

But in the Central Valley regions of Chile — the area originally settled — the conquistadores encountered a different situation. There, in contrast to the Inca and Aztec areas of Latin America, the Spanish found only a sparsely populated area inhabited by nomadic or less sedentary agricultural tribes not easily impressed into service. In this situation the encomienda was not particularly useful if the recipient could not control land for grazing cattle or, later, for raising wheat. In a relatively short time, therefore, the encomiendas were either transformed directly into large landholdings, or they were abandoned. More and more during the course of the sixteenth and seventeenth centuries colonial authorities turned to direct land grants to reward their followers; and although not all of these grants were extensive in size, the more aggressive recipients were generally able to expand their holdings without restraint, while smallholders, the remaining Indians, and soldiers were gradually homogenized and transformed into a landless peasant class. Thus, by the end of the colonial period, Chile was principally a country of large private estates.[29]

Changes in this picture did begin to occur gradually in the 1860s, after the abolition of Chile's primogeniture laws, and more rapidly during the twentieth century, as Chile's southern regions were settled. By the middle of this century, the *minifundia,* or small subsistence plots, had become an important type of landholding.[30] For the most part, however, this did not change the all-encompassing importance of the latifundia in Central Chile, as the proliferation of minifundia occurred principally in the newly developed regions of the south, where the system of large estates had not been as firmly established. In the southern agricultural provinces in 1955, almost half (47.8 percent) of the economically active rural population consisted of proprietors. But in Chile's central regions, the most populous area of the country, only 18.6 percent of the active population consisted of proprietors, while more than four-fifths of the peasants remained landless.[31]

The contrasts between these developments and those in other Latin American countries are important for understanding the considerable stability of Chile's rural social structure. In other areas, as already noted, the consolidation of landholdings frequently occurred in the nineteenth century. Although Church properties were often the targets of this consolidation, much of it took place at the expense of Indian communities and smallholders, often after bitter legal or even armed local struggles. In countries such as Mexico, Guatemala, and Bolivia, this struggle left a heritage of bitterness which sometimes catapulted peasant and Indian groups into politics. In other words, in these countries, the emergence of haciendas was not the product of a remote past, but the result of a more recent predatory expansion that was often within the living memory of rural society.

Moreover, in other parts of Latin America and in some parts of southern Europe, the large estates and subsistence plots constituted parts of the same economic axis, with peasant owners dividing their time between work on their own land and employment on neighboring estates. This arrangement increased status conflicts and tensions and thus contained the potential for eruption into political battles. But in Chile the growing class of subsistence proprietors was essentially removed form the orbit of the large estates. Geographically remote from Central Chile, smallholders posed a relatively small challenge to the estate system that persisted in that area. There, it seems, the hacienda structure had acquired a certain timelessness and, with it, a profound internalization of the norms of the master-and-man relationship.

These features of the rural subsystem were the major basis for the landowners' veto power within the larger Chilean society, for they permitted the landowners to deal relatively easily with the local challenges to the land tenure structure that first emerged during the 1920s and 1930s. In 1919, McBride reports, attempts were made by leftist organizers to unionize inquilinos and to federate these peasant groups with mining organizations established in nearby regions. Again, in the 1930s, the left was reported to have had some success in organizing peasants within the Central Valley region, which led to a "number of uprisings among tenants, accompanied by violence in several cases." [32] For the most part, however, such attempts were premature. At that stage the latifundia remained, in McBride's words, "one big family," difficult to penetrate from the outside and still compactly knit together from within.[33] Far from their base of strength within the city, with limited physical access to the estates, and with peasants themselves often indifferent or hostile to their efforts, union organizers from outside the estate faced a difficult, if not an impossible situation.[34] Subject to expulsion, blacklisting, and possible starvation, individual peasant malcontents were clearly even more vulnerable to repression.

The landowners' tendency to organize themselves into parties and pressure groups, their capacity to develop strong political ties with upper middle class sectors of Chilean society, and their willingness to acquiesce in the limited welfare demands of salaried and blue-collar strata reinforced their power at the national level and virtually assured the preservation of their rural prerogatives during the years between 1920 and 1950. Attempts to alter the rural status quo through governmental action were certain to meet "with the determined and well organized power of the entire . . . landed group, which is highly skilled in political action . . . Their influence permeate[d] all major political blocs." [35] Moreover, as urban groups gradually won some benefits within the system during the 1930s and 1940s, they tended to lose much of their initial incentive to align with peasant forces. Thus, by an agreement which was sometimes tacit and sometimes explicit, centrist and leftist groups abandoned efforts to shake the rural authority structure. Strict literacy requirements, which disenfranchised the peasantry, were not challenged by the center-left governments. Under pressure from the powerful National Society of Agriculture and from traditionalist sectors of the Radical party, the Popular Front coalition in 1941 itself issued an executive order prohibiting the formation of peasant unions and withdrawing legal recognition from those few unions that had already been established. Throughout the decade of center-left government and well into the 1950s the countryside was literally sealed off from the direct influence of the state and was considered outside the bounds of legitimate party competition.

Nevertheless, during the second quarter of the twentieth century, forces were at work which, by mid-century, produced the conditions necessary for a major challenge to the land tenure system. The progressive breakdown of the ties between landowners and rural workers, a process which was only in its early stages when labor and middle groups first demanded recognition, finally surfaced during the 1950s, at last producing significant signs of peasant unrest. At the same time, the inability of the latifundia system to satisfy the consumption needs of the cities produced a second form of challenge from outside the rural society. These challenges are described below.

The Peasant Challenge

The politicization of the Chilean peasantry can be related to a variety of forces which, in varying mixtures and to varying degrees, operated both in Chile and in other parts of Latin America. One set of forces, apparently at work throughout the continent, tended, in spite of the political and social rigidities of the agricultural subsystem, to break down the peasant's isolation and to expose him to the influences of the outside world. Starting about the end of World War I and accelerating rapidly throughout the following decades, the growth of provincial towns, the development of more complex marketing systems, and the spread of transistor radios into rural areas contributed to the weakening of traditional bonds. In addition, the lot of the peasant tended to deteriorate markedly in the decades between 1930 and 1950; and though it is impossible to gauge fully the extent of the strain which this deterioration placed on the rural social system, the likelihood is that it was the source of much of the political change which occurred in the countryside during the subsequent decades. Three factors appeared to underlie this general decline.

One source of strain resulted from the intermingling of the old and new aristocracy, a process which attenuated the family traditions and loyalties that had historically cemented relations between landowner and worker in the Central Valley regions. Traditionally, landed property tended to stay within the hands of a single family, and both the paternalism of the owner and the loyalty of the inquilino were values transmitted from father to son through a succession of generations. The individual who would someday be the patron had, as McBride put it, played with the worker "as a child, caroused as a young man, and worked in a real community of interest through later years. Before his own generation, there had existed the same relationship between his father and theirs." [36] Already by the 1880s, of course, new owners, enriched by new mining wealth and encouraged by increasing land values, had begun to move into the Central Valley. Again, during the depression of 1907, many old aristocratic families were forced to sell their land. The transformation of members of the new upper middle class into landowners, however, appeared to reach its height in the decades following World War I.

Between 1925 and 1960 over 60 percent of Central Valley properties changed hands, primarily as the result of the acquisition of land by newly rich urban dwellers.[37] Because land was purchased as a symbol of prestige and often as a hedge against inflation, the new owners were frequently uninterested in making radical transformations in traditional modes of production. It is probable, however, that these purchases did tend to dilute the paternalism and the community of interest between worker and patron that McBride had described as characteristic of the traditional fundo community. Although no hard data are available to confirm the point, several writers agree that absentee ownership was fostered and increased during this period, and "that land acquisition by new urban middle sectors resulted in deteriorating conditions for agrarian labor." [38] McBride himself noted that in the early thirties landowners, both old and new, appeared increasingly inclined to leave the administration of the estates entirely to renters or administrators, and he warned that "it is almost impossible for any one to replace the patron in the traditional Master-and-Man relationship. With the increased movement of hacendados to the cities, the inquilinos have been left without the patriarchal authority that has largely helped to keep Chilean labor in its place." [39]

About the same time that clientage bonds began to be loosened by these tendencies, a second set of pressures tended to squeeze peasants from another direction. In the effort to encourage growth within the industrial sector and to provide the bases for new welfare measures, the governments of the late 1930s and 1940s adopted pricing, subsidy, and foreign exchange policies which consistently discriminated against agriculture and which encouraged a flight of investment funds and resources into industry and construction.[40] While urban groups were acquiring land for prestige and real estate purposes, older landowners were diverting agricultural profits into new industrial and commercial enterprises, further constricting the increases in agricultural production.

Landowners of course complained bitterly about this discrimination, and these complaints, discussed in Chapter 2, figured prominently in their arguments against land reform. Yet it is likely that the contraction of income within the rural sector affected peasants far more than landlords, and that rural workers, rather than aristocrats, bore the main burden of capital investment within the cities. Mamalakis and Reynolds, who have provided strong documentation for this proposition, point out that "unskilled agricultural workers, who suffered a close to 20 percent decline in real wages between 1940 and 1952 [were] the principal victims of sectoral clashes. Salaried employees and proprietors of unincorporated enterprises in agriculture [were] able to move against the tide and experienced an increase in real earnings of more than 50 percent during the same period." [41]

The third development with a corrosive effect on the rural social system was the enlargement of a class of free laborers (*afuerinos*), who resided in villages rather than on the latifundia, and who contracted their labor by the day to one or to several landowners. In some areas of the country (the winegrowing regions of Talca, for example), efforts to commercialize production during the 1940s promoted the development of this class. In other areas the sheer growth of population forced the sons of inquilinos off the latifundia and into the neighboring hamlets and towns. In any case, the emergence of this class was rapid, especially within the Central Valley region. In the 1930s McBride estimated that inquilinos outnumbered the afuerino stratum by about two to one.[42] By 1955 afuerinos slightly outnumbered inquilinos. Whereas the former constituted about 34 percent of the active rural population, the latter comprised only 30 percent, the remaining segment being composed for the most part of small proprietors. In the Central Valley provinces, the percentage of afuerinos reached an even higher total — over 41 percent of the active rural population.[43]

The implications of the increased number of afuerinos for the stability of the rural social order were clear. Living in the villages, sometimes traveling from region to region in search of employment, and often working for several employers on a casual basis, the afuerino was at once subjected to a far wider variety of influences than the inquilino and, at the same time, was far less likely to enjoy the traditional paternalism of the large landowner. Existing at the edge of traditional society, the free laborer was inevitably an unsettling influence, characterized as "drunken, vicious, lazy, and undependable and of provoking many difficulties in the relation between the inquilino and the farm owners." [44] By 1960 this type of worker had, understandably, become one of the principal bases of voting support for the Chilean Marxist parties.[45]

The results of these developments began to be felt in the mid-1950s, when reforms of voter registration and of balloting procedures permitted the expression of rural discontent within the political sphere. In Aconcagua, O'Higgins, Colchagua, Curico, Talca, and Maule, the most rural of the Central Valley provinces, the electorate expanded from 8 percent of the population in 1949 to 28 percent in 1965, as the newly enfranchised peasants moved into the voting booths. The result was a steady decline of rightist voting strength in these areas (from 54 percent in 1949, to 35 percent in 1961, to 17 percent in 1965) and a steady increase in the number of Marxist voters.[46] In fact, these Central Valley provinces — forbidden to Marxist politicians during the 1940s — nearly provided the Marxist presidential candidate, Salvadore Allende, with a national victory in the presidential elections of 1958. Running again in 1964 against the Christian Democratic candidate, Allende polled an absolute majority (52 percent) of the male voters within these provinces, even though he lost the national election by a wide margin.[47]

As these figures suggest, the tightly knit latifundia structure was at last becoming unraveled. The extent and nature of this unraveling were, of course, not yet fully clear. It is possible that the historic evolution of the latifundia in Chile and the settlement of tenure disputes early in Chilean history continued to put a considerable damper on rural radicalism. What was also clear, however, was that the landowner could no longer expect to remain unchallenged in his monopoly of land and power. To an important extent the emergence of land reform as an issue in Chilean politics during the 1950s corresponded to the growth of peasant pressure on the rural social structure as a whole.

Urban Unrest, Intellectuals, and Agrarian Reform

About the same time that the rural subsystem was being challenged from within by the peasants, its viability was also being called into question by developments within the urban sector of Chilean society. The major condition which led to this challenge was a severe contraction of economic growth, coupled with a sharp acceleration of inflationary pressures. Between 1950 and 1960 the annual increase in per capita GNP averaged only 0.3 percent, as compared to 1.5 percent in the preceding decade.[48] The average annual rate of inflation, on the other hand, doubled during these two decades, from 18 percent during the 1940s to 36 percent in the 1950s.[49] The results of a survey of Santiago residents, reported by Federico Gil, indicated the increasing sense of uneasiness caused by these pressures. "The majority," states Gil, "felt their standard of living had dropped, and 44 percent stated that their economic status in 1957 was inferior to that of five years before. Only one-fourth of the informants thought that their economic position had improved. It is interesting to note that the 'economic' problem seemingly affects virtually all social categories." [50] In the view of many economists, these problems could be traced in part to the obstacles that the inefficient agricultural sector had begun to place in the way of further economic development.

Of course, the agrarian social structure was neither the sole cause of the economic slowdown nor the primary target of urban unrest. Discontent among city dwellers often tended to be expressed in votes for antiparty candidates, in opposition to austerity programs, and in protest demonstrations and occasional rioting, rather than in concrete demands for structural change. Moreover, the economic contraction which had led to this protest was attributable to many bottlenecks and inefficiencies, which — along with agriculture — included discrimination against the export sector, the emergence of an oligopolistic industrial structure, a costly social security system, and a highly regressive tax structure.

That the inefficiency of the agricultural sector was *one* of the causes of the overall economic difficulties was, however, a fact that few could dispute. During the mid-1940s, as the size of cities increased, Chile was transformed from a net exporter of agricultural commodities into a net importer, and the country was faced with a foreign exchange crisis of increasing magnitude and intensity. Between 1949 and 1963 the value of net food imports into Chile grew from 23.9 million dollars to 141.7 million, with obvious repercussions within the economy as a whole.[51] Although few city dwellers appeared directly concerned with the agricultural problem in their day-to-day political activities, this problem clearly underlay much of the insecurity which they experienced. In the course of the 1950s the links between lagging agricultural production and urban malaise came to be articulated by widening circles of the intellectual community.

The first major statement of the economic aspects of the Chilean agrarian problem was undertaken by a committee of European economists who in 1953 conducted a study of the agricultural situation under the joint auspices of the United Nations and the Chilean government. The findings of the committee revealed an extreme irrationality in the employment of land and labor resources. Vast expanses of land, the commission pointed out, had been left uncultivated. Up to one-half the arable land surface was devoted to natural pastures. Crop yields per acre on cultivated lands were far below potential yields. Wheat and cattle, the customary products of the Chilean latifundia, continued to be the major farm outputs, in spite of considerable prospects for the more efficient production of poultry, industrial crops, sugar beets, beans, and potatoes. As for the remedies for these inefficiencies, the committee was cautious and moderate. Its recommendations tended to stress more technical aid, credit, better price incentives, and more efficient marketing arrangements for existing landowners. The commission also indicated, however, that at least part of the problem of low productivity was built into the nature of existing rural social relations:

> More skilled labor is required at present to handle crops, livestock, soil, and machinery. The traditional inquilino does not have that skill, has little incentive to acquire it, and even more important, the brightest elements in the younger generation see a better future in industry or in urban life. The method of payment for inquilinos, mostly in kind . . . , favors the wasteful use of labor and discourages the introduction of equipment. It tends to keep labor productively low even if modern equipment is used . . . *Any scheme for improvements of agriculture, therefore, must recognize the limitations imposed by the agrarian structure.*[52]

During the subsequent decade, as the economic situation deteriorated still further and as the inflationary spiral reached unprecedented heights, criticisms of the agrarian social order mounted in intensity, usually expanding and elaborating on many of the basic themes set forth in the U.N. committee's initial report. In particular, the committee's warning about the "limitations imposed by the agrarian structure" served as the basis of criticism for a growing number of Chilean "structural" economists who argued that these limitations were the principal cause of low agricultural productivity, that this in turn was a principal cause of inflationary pressures besetting the city, and that massive land reform was thus a precondition of further growth and of monetary stability within Chilean society.[53]

Summarized briefly, the main points of the structural argument were as follows. First, low agricultural productivity pushed up the price of food for consumers in the city. Because expenditures for food constituted a large portion of most consumer budgets, food price increases led to demands for higher wages, which in turn set off price increases in the nonagricultural sectors of the economy. Second, the basic cause of inefficiency in agriculture was the land tenure structure, which concentrated wealth in the hands of aristocrats not inclined to be concerned with management or productive investment and which left the landless inquilino without the means or incentives to make improvements. Third, efforts to end inflation through "orthodox" austerity measures (reduction of government expenditures, controls on wage demands, higher taxation, and so forth) would never accomplish their objectives because they did not strike at the structural root of the problem. Fourth, the problem of growth and stability could only be solved by a government willing to take landed property away from the unproductive aristocrats and to redistribute this property to a potentially more enterprising class of peasants.

This chain of reasoning was subject to rebuttal at a number of critical points. The assertion, for example, that agricultural price increases stimulated price increases in the larger society rested on shaky empirical foundations. In six of the twelve years between 1949 and 1960, agricultural prices were equal to or below the price levels for industrial products.[54] Although it must also be added that the years in which agricultural prices exceeded industrial price levels were in fact the years of maximum inflation in Chile, the causal connection between the two phenomena must be regarded as far from proven. The same must be said about the assertion that a consumption-oriented aristocracy was the principal cause of low agricultural production. The granting of subsidies to competing foreign imports, the imposition of price controls on domestic products, poor farm-to-market networks, and the monopoly positions of middlemen were alternative (although not necessarily mutually exclusive) explanations of the same phenomenon. Finally, even granting that aristocrats had retarded agricultural production and that this in turn had retarded the overall growth of the economy, it was by no means clear that large-scale land redistribution was the most efficient way of correcting this problem. The precise relationship and the possible tensions between increasing agricultural productivity and distributing parcels of land to peasants were questions that were not generally treated in detail by the structural economists.

Whatever its strengths and weaknesses, however, the structural argument spread rapidly into broader circles of the Chilean intelligentsia. Aside from the argument's intrinsic merit, it was probably attractive for a number of additional reasons. For one thing, it offered a coherent "Chilean" alternative to austerity proposals espoused by and associated with such conservative international lending agencies as the International Monetary Fund and the World Bank. It also focused conveniently upon the traditional oligarchy as the principal cause of Chile's economic problems. Third, the structural case lent considerable respectability to the idea that social reform was essential to, rather than incompatible with, the objective of economic growth. Finally, although it was possible to quarrel with various aspects of the structuralist argument, its proponents had throughout the 1950s supported their overall conclusions about the inherent inefficiencies of the rural social structure with an impressive, if still inconclusive, body of data.[55] Even after discounting for the ideological biases that underlay many of these studies, they did add up to a persuasive case for the proposition that some sort of reform of the agrarian structure was an important prerequisite for growth and that such revision was relevant, in a general way, to the alleviation of urban discontent.

By the late 1950s, therefore, student leaders, the heads of various professional associations, the progressive wing of the Catholic hierarchy, and many writers, journalists, and economists had adopted structuralist notions in one form or another. Collectively these intellectuals constituted a powerful source of pressure. They were, for one thing, the most articulate sectors of the society, with ready access to the mass media, with a command of the technical skills necessary to bolster their arguments, and with a broad, receptive audience within the inter-American community. Moreover, the fact that the intellectuals were frequently associated with one or another of the major parties — most notably the Christian Democrats and the Marxist parties — tended to amplify their ideas by carrying them more or less directly into the field of competitive politics. Finally, the concurrence of foreign experts and scholars working within the many international organizations centered in Santiago added even greater weight to the opinions of native intellectuals. Whether or not this circle was right in its diagnosis of agricultural inefficiencies and whether or not it was correct in the cures proposed for these inefficiencies, this group of intellectuals was a force which projected the issue of land reform inextricably into the urban political arena.

The Politics of Land Reform: Some Preliminary Remarks

Land reform is a process in which a government acquires land from one set of proprietors and redistributes it to another, usually to peasants. The process may, of course, be accompanied by a variety of complementary measures. Moreover, its scope may be massive or limited in terms of the amount of land distributed at any one time; its pace may be rapid or gradual, occurring within a relatively few years, or drawn out over several decades; and the process itself may involve varying mixtures of violence and compromise. Because there can be such a wide variation in the nature of a land reform process, it would seem wise to abandon attempts to expand definitions beyond this commonly accepted core meaning and to turn instead to two other related sets of questions about reform: (a) what are the conditions which lead governments to undertake land redistribution and what are the forces which shape the scope, pace, and peacefulness of the process? and (b) what is the effect of this process on the intended beneficiaries of the reform and on the system which undertakes it?

Although the two sets of questions are clearly intertwined, intuitively it seems obvious that the second is the more important and the least understood. Although reforms are generally felt to be related in some way to the accommodation of peasant masses, political stability, and the like, in fact relatively little is known about what types of reforms will lead to what types of results. Conceivably, a land redistribution program can appease peasant masses and remove them from the political sphere or it can be used by a regime to mobilize rural supporters against actual or potential opponents. Conceivably, a land reform can stabilize an established political system, serve as a basis for a new political framework, or accomplish neither of these results. Until it is clear which of these results pertain in a given country and how they relate to a given reform, it is impossible to gauge the full significance of the reform itself.

This question is difficult enough to answer in countries where the reform process has already ended, but it is unfortunately virtually impossible to answer in countries where governments have been unable or unwilling to undertake a reform effort, or where, as in Chile, this reform effort is only newly under way. In this sort of situation, therefore, it would seem more useful to fall back to a primary emphasis on the first set of questions, to treat reform as a "dependent variable," and to inquire into the conditions and interactions which presumably will determine the possibility and extent of governmental actions. In the pages that follow, attention will be given to three broad factors which shape this action: (a) the strategies and objectives of the political leaders and special publics who are directly involved in the reform; (b) the effects of the urban environment on the struggle between these groups; and (c) the role of representative institutions in organizing and mediating the resulting process of change.

Leadership Strategies: Reform as a Coalition-Building Effort

In considering the strategic options open to reformist elites, the assertion that power is fragmented, rather than concentrated in the hands of a single, dominant oligarchy, is of fundamental importance. If society is not divided into two camps of "haves" and "have-nots," for example, then reforms are not likely to emerge simply as the result of a contest between popular and conservative forces. As Robert Scott has pointed out, "The pressing political problem is not so much to counteract a power elite by encouraging pluralism but to find ways to unite the many elites and their followers and to harness their political activities for constructive national integration." [56]

In a context of fragmented power, however, efforts to promote a broad national consensus on developmental objectives are likely to involve the reformer in as many difficulties as a dependence on a two-sided confrontation. Leaving aside the fact that programs like land reform are bound to invite bitter opposition from at least some segments of Chilean society, the suspicion and bitter competition among the remainder of this society render such a consensus virtually impossible. Mancur Olson underscores the difficulty still further. Olson points out that even in situations where there is a common interest in achieving a given objective, there is bound to be disagreement on who should pay the costs of achieving it. If the benefit in question is one that can be enjoyed by all individuals within a given group, moreover, Olson argues that the most rational course for each individual is to shift the burdens onto others.[57] Without coercion directed against some groups, nonrational ideological appeals directed toward others, and the extension of special benefits to still other elements, efforts to promote collective action are likely to fail, whether these actions are designed to increase agricultural productivity or to accomplish other, less explosive, developmental objectives.

If reform is to come, therefore, the process of building support is likely to fall somewhere between the polar extremes of direct and immediate resolution of conflict through confrontation and the equally miraculous formation of a national agreement. The leadership strategies with the highest potential payoff are likely to be directed toward coalition-building efforts, which can weld groups with different and conflicting interests together in support of a specific government or specific governmental measures. In Chile, with its division into many competing power groups and a large number of poweiless marginals, two strategic approaches appear to offer the greatest possibilities of success. One approach, usually espoused by Chilean leftist elements, is actively to promote a polarization of social forces, aligning the newly politicized marginal elements and at least some segments of the established power groupings — organized workers and salaried employees — against propertied social sectors. Although workers' and peasants' interests may compete on many points, both might conceivably be joined together by a government that distributes special benefits and patronage to both. If these measures are accompanied by efforts to organize and control this disparate following, the remaining established elements within the society would conceivably be placed in a position where they would no longer be able to mount an effective opposition to land reform.

An alternative strategy — actually adopted by the leading members of the Chilean Christian Democratic party — is the reformmongering approach, discussed extensively by A. O. Hirschman and Charles Anderson.[58] Reformmongering stresses the need to draw support from moderate elements of both the left and the right. Although this does not preclude the organization of new power groups from among the marginals, greater emphasis is placed on the task of neutralizing or pacifying old ones. Some groups might be brought into the coalition by the argument that reform is the alternative to revolution; others might be neutralized by the argument that they would escape the burdens of reform; while the support of still others could conceivably be won through side-payments or extraneous loyalties which induce them to ignore their specific objections to agrarian reform.

In actual practice, of course, no rigid distinction can be drawn between these two approaches. It is at least logically possible for a government to waver back and forth between one or the other, or to combine elements of both. Nevertheless, the fact that a leadership group leans toward one approach clearly has important consequences for the prospects of rural change. The polarization approach, for example, automatically focuses the bargaining process on a limited subset of the population, leaving other groups outside the pale of accommodation. Reformmongering, on the other hand, is predicated on the possibility of accommodation throughout the society as a whole, and it makes the reformer wary of cutting ties with any single group within the population. Second, the major risk of the polarization strategy is that such a process will end in a coup d'etat, rather than revolution. Reformmongering, by contrast, risks dissipating the energies of the reformer in a fruitless juggling act. The payoffs of a polarization strategy, finally, are likely to involve a relatively massive restructuring of rural society, while the reformmonger's need to appeal to a much broader range of interests is likely to make the results of that approach more limited and incremental, at least over the short run. The choices confronting prospective reformers, therefore, are difficult ones, which in many ways define the level of conflict and the possibilities of accommodation that exist within the system as a whole.

Once a reform coalition is formed, opposition elements have similar sets of choices to make. Confronted with the challenge of a reformmonger, who has patched together a supporting coalition, both leftist and rightist elements must make decisions about where to rally support and how to frame their opposition. For the leftists, the choice is between supporting the coalition and cooperating in the reform effort, or challenging the coalition from below with mobilization efforts of their own. For rightist groups, the choice may be one of moderating their opposition in order to appeal to groups inside the dominant coalition, or of rallying neutrals to their side, in the hope of splitting the coalition apart. The fragmentation of Chilean society forces opposition elements, like the reformers themselves, into a quest for allies and support, which can block the process of reform or turn it to the oppositions' advantage.

To understand the process of reform in Chilean society, then, it is necessary to understand the interplay between all of these strategies. The prospects of governmental action and the *types* of governmental action will turn on the manner in which the political elites, the landowners, intellectuals, and other interested elements perceive their options and define their interests. Because these assumptions may vary over time, and because they are defined by many groups, the battlelines involved in the reform process may never be clearly drawn. Conflict may escalate or subside; the reform coalition may splinter or recompose itself with new elements; competing coalitions may emerge and disappear as the different groups within the society maneuver for position.

Urbanization and Land Reform

The term "urbanization," as used here, refers not only to the growth of big cities and the development of modern institutions, but to the emergence of a wide variety of groups with divergent life styles, values, and interests. Whether these groups are classified as modern or traditional and whether they live in small towns or large urban centers, they share in common the fact that they do not live directly from agricultural production and that their status is not derived directly from their relationship to the land. In this sense the emergence of urban groups and the expansion of an urban environment would seem to be of obvious importance for understanding the prospects of rural change. Actually, however, there is considerable debate over this proposition.

One group of writers tends to discount any positive relationship between urbanization and land reform prospects by emphasizing the social, economic, and political ties that have emerged between the traditional landowning sector and high status groups within the cities. Though these writers are often the same ones who adopt the oligarchical view of Chilean society, it is not necessary to accept this premise in order to appreciate the strength of their argument about land reform prospects. Even if the urban and rural upper classes do not constitute a power elite, their interconnections are still sufficiently strong to present a formidable challenge to any change-oriented government.[59] Another view, implicit in the reformmongering studies of Hirschman and Anderson, is that urbanization has enhanced the prospect of reform because it has increased the number of groups and interests to which reformmongers can turn for support in promoting rural change.[60] It expands the area of maneuver required by a government interested in altering the rural status quo.

Although both of these theses can be applied to *parts* of the Chilean reform process, neither by itself takes into account the full range of potential for, and obstacles to, the implementation of land reform. Both underestimate the fact that the growth of urban society carries with it a new structure of incentives and a new logic of its own, which is not directly associated with the conventional conflicts between left and right. The decline of agricultural property as the major basis of wealth and status, for example, probably helps to decrease the explosiveness of the land reform issue. At the same time, however, the rural-to-urban transition also tends to increase the range of competing claims and demands from groups who perceive little salience between their own day-to-day interests and rural reform. Widespread urban disaffection increases the prospects that a reformist coalition might be carried into office, but the numerical decline of the peasantry decreases the political importance of the groups which are the direct beneficiaries of rural change. Under different circumstances, in short, the existence of a large and powerful urban population can have either a positive or a negative impact on the prospects for reform. As the politics of the Chilean land reform unfolded, several types of problems and influences appeared, associated roughly with three overlapping, but distinct, phases of the reform.

The pressures for change, 1950–1964. During these years, the crystallization of peasant unrest in the countryside, a broad, diffuse protest within the cities, and a more explicit articulation of the land problem by intellectuals combined to popularize the idea of land reform. Before the first reform laws were passed in 1962–63, debate over the reform issue tended to take on a two-sided quality, which ranged popular forces, both urban and rural, against landed defenders of the status quo, obscuring the conflicts among both the opponents and proponents of rural change.

The rural breakthrough, 1964–1967. In 1964 a reformist Christian Democratic government, which had promised to create 100,-000 new proprietors within five years, was elected to office with the widespread backing of the discontented and fearful urban middle sectors. The effort of this government during the next three years placed the struggle over the land on a new plateau. By 1967 a workable land reform law had been formulated and passed through the Chilean Congress, peasants had been organized into large labor unions, and — for the first time in Chilean history — a Chilean government had begun to expropriate and redistribute private agricultural property. During this period the relations between the social and political elites with interest in affecting agrarian policy tended to oscillate between conflict and accommodation, as each group attempted to formulate or reformulate strategies designed to win allies and to neutralize enemies within the urban sector.

The emergence of the urban-rural cleavage, 1968–1970. With the establishment of a legal framework for reform and with the initiation of a genuine process of expropriations and resettlement, the conflict over reform reached still a third plateau, in which the government attempted to extract from the urban sector the resources necessary for implementing the reform. This attempt altered the major lines of cleavage over the reform issue. Whereas in the first two periods opposition to reform came principally from landed groups with a direct interest in preserving the rural status quo, new resistance now began to emerge among powerful urban elements which were indifferent to rural change but which were disinclined to pay the costs of this change. Whereas before 1968 the existence of many powerful city groups was more or less positively related to the prospects for reform, after 1968 their role was more clearly negative, and broad urban protest that had once been directed against conservative governments now began to be directed against the reformist Christian Democratic government itself.

The Sociopolitical Background

Representative Institutions: The Vertical Brokerage System

The operation of Chile's representative institutions within this shifting context is the final factor to be considered in examining the process of reform. Earlier we had described these institutions in terms of Huntington's four criteria of adaptability, complexity, coherence, and autonomy. Chile's relatively high ranking on most of these dimensions indicates, in effect, that analytically its political organizations must be treated as variables separate from the other forces operating in Chilean society, and not as mere epiphenomena. The major contrast is with the "praetorian" societies of Latin America which, *whether democratic or authoritarian in form,* remain vulnerable to the destructive interplay of competing social forces. In Chile, political institutions "make a difference." The currency of the electoral and parliamentary arena predominates over other power resources, as a means of gaining office and influencing policy. Political parties and interest groups (rather than the Church, the army, or the mob) actually play an important role in articulating and aggregating interests and in selecting leaders.

We also emphasized in the preceding pages that no political system, however institutionalized, operates with total independence from its social environment. This is especially true of representative organizations which, like Chile's parties, emerge within a parliamentary context. In some modernizing areas without parliamentary or constitutional traditions, the political party has become the primary instrument for mobilization and change, as well as the major source of legitimacy within the political system. The "party of solidarity," to use Apter's phrase, attempts to remake the society in its own image, and in this sense may be considered an independent variable in the modernization process.[61] This is not the case with intermediate organizations operating within a constitutional arena. The job of representative institutions is to represent. They respond to, as well as modify, demands formulated elsewhere in the system. They reflect, as well as moderate, the conflicts within the larger society. As organized links between government and society, representative institutions can best be viewed as intervening variables; they give expression to the interests of existing social forces, and they dull the edges of conflict which accompany modernization and change.

The vertical structuring of the Chilean representative system around left, right, and center sectors was in part a product of the antagonisms between the clusters of organized and unorganized interests within the urban sphere; but the stability of the system was maintained by the political elites at the top of each sector, each of which had a strong interest in maintaining political order. As peasants became politicized and as the government turned its attention toward rural reform, the result was what we shall term a "vertical brokerage" process, in which these elites simultaneously articulated contending positions on land reform and filtered out the claims of their more disruptive constituents. The profound division within the multiparty system placed important limits on the brokerage process, which could not produce a genuine consensus on the issue of land reform; but the capacity of the political elites to interpose themselves between the government and "their" social supporters helped to avert confrontations between the contending sectors, placing restraints on conflict and facilitating the reformmongering efforts of the governmental leaders.

At the same time, as representatives of the major groupings within the urban subsystem, the Chilean parties and interest groups also responded to the pressures and anxieties emerging from that quarter. Thus, the nature and effectiveness of their vertical brokerage role tended to change as each party faced the incentives and imperatives associated with the three periods described above.

In the period between 1950 and 1964, when urban and rural interests in land reform appeared to converge, the entire party system shifted to the left on the question of land reform, responding to what was perceived as a national desire for change. This perception affected not only leftist and centrist sectors, which began to espouse reform and to organize peasants during that period, but also the rightist parties, which acted to moderate the response of landowning groups toward these pressures for change.

A similar mixture of moderation and reform could be discerned during the rural breakthrough. Although the initiative came from a centrist regime which was opposed by forces to the right and the left, the breakthrough must be considered the result of a system-wide effort involving cooperation and accommodation as well as conflict among the competing political groups. Organizations all along the political spectrum tended to interpose themselves between the reform government and radical special publics, muting antagonisms and making possible in the Congress and in the countryside an activity which many had thought impossible only a few years before.

The propensity of the different sectors to reach last-minute compromises and to avert confrontations continued during the third period, as urban and peasant interests began to diverge. The apparent need for a choice between agrarian reform efforts and ongoing urban programs was resolved by inflationary settlements which permitted, at least in the short run, the continuation of both. Unlike the accommodations which underlay the rural breakthrough, however, these inflationary settlements raised serious questions about the long-run capability of the system to deal with the agrarian problem. They reflected and foreshadowed growing disaffection in the cities, new and more radical opportunities for the opposition parties, and an increasing loss of urban support for the reform government itself. Though the rural breakthrough indicated that the system was capable of overriding the veto power of established landed groups, the post-1968 period posed an even more serious challenge. It implied a need for the system to break loose from its urban moorings and to impose sacrifices on its largest and most important sources of direct social support.

Chapter 2 The Alessandri Reform, 1962–63: A Redefinition of Rightist Interests

It was during Jorge Alessandri's presidency (1958–1964) that land reform first moved from the level of abstract theoretical debate to the more immediate arena of congressional action and legislative decision. In 1962 a coalition of Radicals, Liberals, and Conservatives passed a land reform law that permitted the expropriation of certain categories of agricultural lands. The following year the coalition passed a constitutional reform allowing the state to pay for abandoned and inefficient agricultural properties in bonds, rather than in cash. Since the intiative was sponsored by representatives of the most conservative segments of Chilean society, the reforms of that period were limited in scope and had little direct impact on the land tenure structure itself. Nevertheless, in several respects they marked an important turning point in the history of the land reform question in Chile. First, the legislation provided an important link between the highly conservative Alessandri regime and the left-of-center Christian Democratic government which succeeded it in 1964. Even more important, the support of these measures by rightist groups was an admission on their part that land reform was within the legitimate sphere of state activity, and it thus marked the beginning of a more flexible orientation toward the prospect of rural change.

This chapter will focus primarily on the "internal" debate within rightist circles which led to this change in orientation. Of special importance was the brokerage activity undertaken by leaders of the two rightist parties, the Liberals (Partido Liberal, PL), and the Conservatives (Partido Conservador Unido, PCU). In the Congress these leaders adopted a defensive posture toward the forces of change, accepting with great reluctance the mild reform initiative of their coalition partner, the Radical party. Within the more narrow world of upper class interest groups, social clubs, and aristocratic families, however, Liberal and Conservative leaders acted as the instigators of a more moderate stance toward reform. They persuaded larger sectors of the landed class to accept concessions that had once been considered nonnegotiable. And they encouraged the idea that bargaining and compromise, rather than rigid resistance, formed the best strategy for the defense of conservative interests. The first two sections of the chapter deal with the external pressures on the rightist parties to moderate their opposition to land reform, and the internal, structural features of these parties which led them to accept land reform legislation. Next, the internal debate which accompanied this acceptance is examined, first within the parties themselves, and then between the party leaders and their constituents. The final portion of the chapter evaluates the Alessandri legislation in terms of its significance for the later, more serious, efforts of the Christian Democratic regime.

External Pressures for Moderation

Prior to 1962, landowners reacted with uncompromising hostility to actual and potential challenges to the estate system. The social basis of this reaction lay in the strength of the traditional ties, between the peasants and patrons and between the rural elite and conservative urban elements. Legally and ideologically, however, the landlords fortified their position with constitutional bulwarks which virtually prohibited the redistribution of rural property. According to the 1925 Constitution, private property could not be expropriated without an immediate cash payment by the government to the owner. Deferred payment (that is, payment in bonds), which most observers felt was financially necessary for land redistribution, was forbidden. The rightists considered such guarantees the sine qua non of private property, and few rival groups operating within the constitutional framework felt free to challenge them.

When the structuralists began to criticize the agricultural sector during the 1950s, the landowners adduced socioeconomic arguments to supplement their legal-ideological rationale for the preservation of the rural status quo. Rightist leaders vigorously denied, for example, the reliability of census data indicating a high degree of land concentration. They responded to structural arguments which linked low agricultural production to land concentration by developing counterarguments which attributed the economic dif-

ficulties to price controls, low agricultural credit, and poor marketing conditions. Whereas most structuralists called for some form
of land redistribution, leaders of the rightist parties and of the National Society of Agriculture called for more government subsidies, higher tariffs on imported foodstuffs, and greater security
for existing investments in agricultural property. To be sure, these
prescriptions were not made by rightist spokesmen alone. A variety
of economists who did not share the ulterior motives of the rightists
made similar recommendations.[1] In the hands of the landed elite,
however, antistructural arguments were transformed into a closed
defense of the existing system, with a separate vision of the rural
reality, an alternate body of data to those employed by the structuralists, and a categorical rejection of structuralist proposals for
rural change. As the influential conservative newspaper, *El Mercurio,* stated in a 1957 editorial, "The land tenure system does
not need any reform whatsoever. What is lacking is a methodical
plan of agrological reform . . . that might improve the application of technical procedures so that the countryside might produce
more." [2]

Liberal and Conservative politicians were instrumental in moderating these points of view. But they did not do so willingly. On
the contrary, modifications in their positions were reluctant responses to pressure from the international environment, from the
opposition challenge to the center-right coalition, and from the
centrist elements within the governing coalition itself. From the
perspective of rightist party leaders (although not from the perspectives of all of their followers), these pressures seemed to leave
no alternative to a more flexible stance.

International pressures. Between 1959 and 1961 a number of
changes in the international political sphere had important impact
in Chile. The Cuban revolution galvanized the Chilean left, increasing its interests in land reform and in peasants as a source of
political support. For other sectors, the revolution indicated that
social concessions might be needed to preserve the more basic elements of the status quo. The Alliance for Progress constituted a
second source of pressure, for it signified United States endorsement of the idea of land reform, and it held out the incentive of
massive economic aid if such reforms were effected. This incentive
appeared especially important to the conservative Alessandri,

whose receptiveness to land reform legislation increased markedly after he signed the Punta del Este Charter. Finally, a change in the orientation of the Catholic Church provided a spur to a more moderate posture on the part of landowners. In the course of the preceding decade a series of papal pronouncements had given impetus and respectability to the idea of social reform. These pronouncements had special echoes in Chile, where there already existed an important colony of progressive foreign Jesuits and, within the domestic Church hierarchy, a strong tendency toward social Christianism.

Although these factors served to change the general political climate within Chile, their importance can easily be overestimated. In almost all parts of Latin America they induced most segments of the society to pay lip service to agrarian reform. Land reform legislation was, however, slow in coming, and most land reform laws that were passed failed to embody the basic constitutional concessions and expropriations provisions deemed necessary for reform. More concrete results in Chile resulted from factors distinctive to its political system, which created specific political interests favoring an agrarian reform law and gave a certain immediacy to the notion that some sort of adjustment was necessary.

The opposition challenge. The desire of the majority coalition's leaders to retain their position as the governing bloc was the most important of these factors. While the combined electoral strength of the Radicals, Liberals, and Conservatives had temporarily given them a solid majority, all three sectors had been on the defensive for at least a generation, and all had reason to fear the challenge of the opposition parties. Between 1940 and 1961, the rightist bloc had seen its share of the electorate decline from an average of 36 percent during the 1940s to 27.2 percent during the 1950s.[3] To be sure, these averages concealed some wide swings in strength, one of which — in 1958 — permitted the right to control the executive mansion. This was, however, the first time a rightist president had been in office in twenty years. The Radicals seemed in a somewhat stronger position. With the exception of 1953, when all major parties suffered severe setbacks, their share of the congressional electorate had held steadily at around 20 percent of the vote. In spite of this, however, they had not won a presidential election since 1946, and their share of the presidential vote had after 1952 declined markedly, from 20 percent in the 1952 election, to 16 percent in 1958.[4]

The vulnerability of the center-right majority was increased still further by the surge in strength of reform-oriented parties, all of which had adopted land reform as a central plank in their platforms. The Marxist coalition had only barely missed winning a plurality in the presidential elections of 1958, and after that time a leftist presidential victory was widely acknowledged as a real and immediate possibility. The growth of the relatively new Christian Democratic party was even more spectacular. From an insignificant electoral base in the early part of the 1950s, this party had run third in the 1958 elections, with 20 percent of the vote.[5] By 1961 it had become the second largest single party in Chile, second only to the Radicals themselves in congressional strength. The growth of these parties in both urban and rural areas encouraged the idea that land reform had become a popular issue, and it was taken by many leaders within the governing coalition as a signal that future victories would depend on their willingness to meet the competition with reform measures of their own.

Intracoalition pressures. All leaders of the majority coalition perceived these signals. Their response varied, however, with the class background and composition of the governing parties. The leaders of the predominantly middle class Radical party (the Partido Radical, PR) were, for example, far more willing than rightist leaders to adopt the rhetoric of land reform. Within the coalition itself, it was the PR which served as the initiating force.

This did not necessarily mean that the vast and heterogeneous Radical party had become firmly convinced of the need for rural change. On the contrary, most sectors of the party, from the members of the far left wing to the conservative leaders then in power, had concentrated previously on other matters — state ownership of industry, education, and social welfare for urban white-collar workers. They had exhibited little interest in changes either in the rural social structure or in the peasants themselves.

Moreover, the majority within the Radical Executive Committee could aptly be characterized as the most conservative representative of the "accommodated" bourgeois class. Members of this majority had been granted entry into respectable upper class circles; they had gained a significant measure of wealth and prestige; and they were deeply suspicious of change and disorder. Under their direction the party had given its general support in Congress to the Alessandri administration, and it had begun negotiations with Liberal and Conservative leaders for an electoral alliance that could confront the Marxists and the Christian Democrats in the 1964 presidential elections. For a number of reasons, however, the Radical leaders were far more disposed than the right to press for congressional action on land reform.

In the first place, the Radical party as a whole was far more dependent on elected office for influence and social advancement than were upper class rightists. In the 1940s all sectors of the party used political office as the preeminent route of social mobility. Even though many leaders had made it into the upper reaches of society, the bulk of the party membership continued to depend directly or indirectly on the government for patronage, jobs, subsidies, and favors. The premium the Radicals placed on elected office had, in the past, frequently provided them with a strong incentive to engage in wide swings in electoral alignments and had encouraged a great flexibility in adopting those slogans, rhetoric, and appeal that appeared necessary to remain in power. Since the perquisites of office had sharply diminished since the PR's loss of the presidency in 1952, it might well be imagined that party leaders had become more disposed than ever before to follow the dictates of political expediency by espousing an apparently popular program like land reform.

Internal party politics might have been an additional incentive. Far more than the rightist politicians, the Radical leaders ruled over a heterogeneous and decentralized collectivity, which embraced a wide spectrum of policy preferences and political strategies. One wing of the party — which was to come to power after 1964 — urged alliance with the Marxists. A large, flexible core of congressmen, who were less strongly committed to either the left or the right, had strong reservations about the political wisdom of an alliance with the Liberals and Conservatives. Because of the decentralized structure of the Radical party and of the tenuous hold that any set of Radical leaders had on top party offices, the viewpoints of these opposing factions had, at least marginally, to be taken into account. Though there was little evidence that these sectors were strongly committed to land reform, the executive committee leaders may well have felt that by pressing for this kind of "progressive" measure, they could make a center-right coalition more palatable.

Finally, the primarily urban-based Radicals perceived few economic or ideological risks in taking up the cry for a balanced, orderly program of rural change. Even the most conservative Radical leaders were often veterans of Popular Front days, when the party had led a battle for state control over major industries and for government planning; consequently most did not share as deeply as did the right the strong, unconditional commitment to private property. Moreover, while many Radicals were deeply concerned with the maintenance of the status quo, only a few had the same direct interests in *rural* property as did the rightists. Only 11 percent of the Radical congressional delegation elected in 1961, for example, owned rural property. This was less than one-fifth of the percentages for the Liberals and Conservatives.[6] In short, the Radical leaders had far more to gain and far less to lose than the right by pressing for agrarian reform.

In spite of their basic conservatism, therefore, the leaders of the PR were inclined to keep pace rhetorically with their competitors to the left. In 1959 a group of Radical congressmen generally associated with the party's right wing introduced a bill calling for tax sanctions against inefficient or abandoned rural property. At the time, these proposals were probably designed more for public consumption than for congressional action, and they were quietly dropped when leaders of the National Society of Agriculture voiced objections to the Alessandri government. In the next few years, however, the term agrarian reform began to appear more and more frequently in the rhetoric of the Radical congressional delegation. By April 1961 some sort of agrarian legislation appeared to figure seriously in the Radicals' presidential plans. A Radical national convention which met during that month upgraded the 1959 proposals by calling for the direct expropriation of rural property, with compensation to be paid in thirty-year bonds. Even earlier the Radical leaders of the party's executive committee had begun to hint that their leadership in a center-right coalition would be conditioned by the right's willingness to accept some kind of reform legislation.

The immediate catalyst which led to the right's acceptance of the

Radical proposals was the outcome of the congressional elections of March 1961. This election was marked by gains in congressional strength for the Communists and Socialists and an even greater advance by the Christian Democrats. Taken together, the major opposition parties increased their representation in the Chamber of Deputies from thirty-seven to fifty-one seats. All but one of these seats, moreover, came at the expense of the Liberals and Conservatives, who dropped from the fifty-eight representatives elected in 1957 to only forty-five in 1961.[7]

This strengthened the position of the Radical party in maneuvering for influence within the coalition. Before the March elections, the Radicals had rounded out the Alessandri majority only on an informal basis. And though they had moved toward an electoral coalition with the right, negotiations for such a coalition had not yet been concluded. After March 1961, rightist leaders felt a special urgency in consolidating the coalition by inviting the Radicals into the Alessandri cabinet and by formalizing the establishment of a center-right electoral bloc. The Radicals, on the other hand, grew even stronger in their insistence that any such arrangements be conditional on the passage of reform legislation.

Their bargaining positions weakened, many PL and PCU leaders felt that they had little choice but to accept the Radicals' conditions. After a few months of sparring, the Radicals entered the cabinet in August 1961. Immediately thereafter, tripartite commissions composed of representatives of the three governing parties were formed to work out the details of the reform legislation. Controversy and bargaining between the Radicals and their rightist allies continued within these commissions and within the Congress itself. At several points, when the right appeared to waver on the question of accepting provisions for expropriations and for payment in bonds, Radical leaders threatened to withdraw from the cabinet. Meanwhile, Liberal and Conservative representatives were quite successful in whittling down many of the initial Radical proposals. By this time, however, the right's acceptance of the legislative measures depended less on the Radicals than on the capacity of Liberal and Conservative leaders themselves to head off opposition from their own landed constituency. This task was accomplished during 1961, while the details of the legislation were being hammered out in the tripartite commissions. With the resolution of the debate within the rightist circles, congressional acceptance was a foregone conclusion. The agrarian reform bill (Law 15020) was passed by the coalition in 1962. The constitutional amendment permitting deferred payments for land was accepted in 1963.

The Liberals and Conservatives: Internal Pressures toward Renovation

The Liberal and Conservative parties which had finally acquiesced in these measures were both outgrowths of nineteenth century aristocratic factions. In the language of Marx, both reflected the interest and outlook of the landed upper class. Sixty-four percent of the Liberals and 43 percent of the Conservatives elected to Congress in 1961 were landowners and members of the National Society of Agriculture; all of the rest bore names which were associated with the old aristocracy.[8] Although these two parties sometimes differed on marginal questions, the major rivalries between them had long been settled. Both acted as a solid bloc in defense of the rural status quo.

If we can believe much of the general literature on Latin America, it might seem somewhat surprising that men of this sort were inclined to bend before electoral and congressional pressures on questions concerning land reform. "Aristocrats" need not do so, it is said, because their power depends on the direct use of personal contacts, wealth, and prestige — all of which can be used to offset or nullify the results of elections.[9] Moreover, they are inclined to cling stubbornly and blindly to the ownership of land and their control over peasants as the major base of their social status.

To some degree, these characteristics were shared by Chilean rightists. But in thirty years of participation within the multiparty system, Liberal and Conservative leaders had acquired other power resources and other interests as well. By 1961 each party had become something more than the expression of decisions arrived at elsewhere, and party leaders had acquired loyalties of their own that tended to distinguish them in some measure from the social groups out of which they had emerged. They were career politicians as well as landowners. This distinction, of course, by no means obliterated the party leaders' deep concern with preserving their own economic privileges or those of their families; but it does much to explain the relative flexibility with which the right responded to the incentives of the larger political system and with which it defended conservative interests after 1961.

One factor which distinguished the Chilean right from analogous aggregates of landowners elsewhere in the continent was the urban basis of its electoral support. When landowners elsewhere in Latin America do enter into electoral politics, their voting base not infrequently rests on their economic controls over land and their personal ties to the peasantry. For example, Celso Furtado has noted the existence in pre-1964 Brazil of a congressional and electoral system which strongly overrepresented the predominantly rural states "where the landowning oligarchy is most firmly entrenched." [10] This, he argues, permitted the Brazilian right to maintain a stranglehold on the legislature, in spite of leftward trends within the urban electorate. In Chile, although representation is also skewed toward the more rural provinces, an important and less frequently noted aspect of the right's electoral base was its capacity to maintain strength in the cities as well. In 1961, for example, 45 percent of the right's electoral support came from the urban provinces of Santiago and Valparaiso.[11] Rightist voting percentages in these urban provinces (34.1 percent and 27.5 percent) exceeded by substantial margins the percentages attained by the competing sectors.[12] Fifteen rightist deputies (constituting about one-third of the right's congressional delegation) were elected from these areas. By contrast, the Radicals had elected only nine representatives from these areas, while the Marxist coalition and the Christian Democrats had each won only eight seats.[13]

It should be emphasized that the right's appeal to city voters by no means rested on its willingness to be "progressive" in policy orientation. On the contrary, much of the urban support came from the wealthier, conservative city dwellers, whose numerical importance was increased by the small size of the electorate. Fixed personal loyalties between employers and workers, and the desire of migrants newly arrived in Santiago for paternalistic protection, were probably also important bases for rightist voting strength within the cities. Nevertheless, it is also likely that the votes of city dwellers, subject to a variety of cross-pressures, were far less certain than the automatic support that rightists could command in rural Chile. In the relatively competitive urban environment, Liberal and Conservative politicians could not remain entirely insensitive to possible shifts in sentiment and loyalties; for this reason a strain of populism, and an emphasis on welfare and social security, were not infrequently blended into the more traditional appeals made by the right. It is not surprising, therefore, that in the 1950s these rightist politicians tended to view with some concern the gains made by the reformist Christian Democratic party among city workers and middle class Catholics.

The entry of the right into competitive electoral politics also had some important effects at the elite level of the parties. Like their rivals of the left and center, rightist politicians had made some effort to strengthen their ranks by recruiting university students and other urban professional people. In the 1930s, for example, the Conservative party had gone so far as to incorporate the reformist Falange movement — later to become the Christian Democratic party — and to grant its young leaders cabinet-level positions. Though this alliance soon proved unsatisfactory to both sides, the two rightist parties continued to enjoy some success in attracting students, writers, and academicians into their leadership ranks; by the late 1950s, both the Liberals and Conservatives had built small, fluid, but not entirely insignificant, youth, labor, and technical divisions into the party structures. In 1961 these groups were instrumental in promoting a movement for ideological renovation within the rightist bloc.

An even more important and enduring aspect of rightist party organization was the establishment of certain patterns of advancement through which all sectors of the party elite had to pass before reaching the top levels of leadership. By the ascriptive standards of the nineteenth and early twentieth century, one was born into positions of political leadership. Seats in Congress were purchased or inherited by aristocrats, much as they would join a social club. Increasingly, however, it had become necessary for rising politicians to precede membership in Congress with apprenticeships as local leaders, as workers in the youth movement, or as functionaries within the party or the government. In 1961 only 13 percent of Conservative congressmen and only 12 percent of the Liberals went into congressional positions without first serving in one of these lesser posts.[14] This contrasted sharply with the experience of the right's 1941 congressional delegation. Twenty years before the passage of the first reform law, 47 percent of the Conservatives and 46 percent of the Liberals had had no previous party apprenticeship before becoming deputies or senators.[15] Thus, though social status remained an essential prerequisite for holding high party office, it had by 1961 apparently become increasingly difficult for landowners or industrialists to advance politically by virtue of their family connections or wealth alone. It would be an exaggeration, of course, to characterize these leaders as professional politicians. They did not, after all, earn their livings in politics, and they did not usually spend all of their time in political activity. Yet clearly these rightist leaders were something more than amateurs. The term "career" politicians will be used to describe them, with the understanding that although their party role overlapped other social roles, they nonetheless had an identity and skill special to the art of political maneuver.

These patterns of recruitment and organization tended to channel and restrict the more traditional bases of power at the disposal of the upper class. Considerable influence could, of course, still be wielded directly through social connections and wealth, and the leaders of the rightist parties had by no means abandoned the economic interests and social values of their upper class family and friends. But party structures and orientations, the need to maneuver within the congressional framework, and the importance of gaining support within the broader urban electoral arena provided a measure of autonomy for these political leaders and influenced the way in which they interpreted their options and interests within the system. In the early 1960s, these internal factors encouraged a more moderate rightist orientation toward the problem of reform.

Student and professional sectors constituted one source of pressure. For the most part, these newer recruits were from upper class families, and many owned land. Usually, however, they were also practicing lawyers, trained academics, architects, or engineers who considered themselves far more modern than the older "aristocratic" elements. They provided the backbone of a "renovationist" tendency within both rightist parties. Politically, these sectors argued that the right's retention of urban electoral support would ultimately depend on its willingness to face up to the problems of urban and rural structural change. Ideologically, they emphasized the importance of making operational the humanitarian and progressive strains within Liberalism or Christianity, "in order to combat egoistic and reactionary sectors as well as Communism." [16] And, like the Christian Democrats, they were often inclined to criticize older party leaders for having converted the party ideologies into apologies for the status quo. At times, these criticisms could be vigorous indeed. One local committee of the Conservative party, for example, argued publicly that

the present material forms of the economic and social order are [unsustainable] and contrary to the national interest. The PCU is not an efficient tool for giving Chile a social Christian order, nor is it in a position to battle Marxism for the allegiance of the young, the workers, employees, technicians, or intellectuals . . . [17]

These views were undoubtedly in the minority through most of the 1950s. However, the near victory of the Marxists in 1958 and the losses in the 1961 congressional elections produced a growing feeling that only a more flexible and progressive orientation would arrest the right's demise as a major political force. For brief periods following the March elections, the Liberal and Conservative executive councils therefore turned to leaders associated with these renovationist tendencies. In the early spring of 1961, a factional struggle for the presidency of the PCU arose between "reformists," headed by Hector Correa, and the more conservative wing of the party, led by Luís Valdés. In what was considered a rather surprising upset, Correa defeated Valdés in a vote of the party's general council, and served as the PCU president from April to November 1961. A political leader of similar views, Mariano Puga, acted as president of the Liberal party during 1962–63.

As subsequent events were to indicate, the changes in leadership were short-lived and incomplete. The effects of Puga's tenure in office proved a disappointment to many of his more advanced Liberal backers, while Correa was ousted in a power play only months after his election. Nevertheless, the election of these new officers did reflect the importance that many rightist leaders had begun to place on a new, more progressive posture. As the electorate moved to the left, most of the rightist political elite, including those who were being challenged by the renovationists, were inclined to move along with this trend. Even the backers of Luís Valdés — Correa's more traditionalist rival within the PCU — promised a greater "awareness of the social reality" so that the party might "gradually increase the progressive support [it] has found in the urban and labor sectors, where the worker has once again opened his eyes." [18] A more centrist orientation was also urged by Francisco Bulnes, the man who was to replace Correa as the party's president. Looking back on the pressures that necessitated such an adjustment, he pointed out that

From one side, the [Marxist coalition] . . . was advancing daily in its positions, carrying off the electorate . . . especially in the rural areas. From the other side of the picture, *the Christian Democrats were not winning votes from the extreme left . . . but were carrying off our own sympathizers and even some of our militants* (my italics).[19]

Although the pragmatic inclination to deal with these challenges by confronting competing parties on their own terms, as well as the more idealistic considerations of many renovationists, served to push the Liberals and Conservatives toward a more reformist rhetoric, this did not mean that either party readily accepted the specific Radical proposals for land reform. The temporary ascendency of the renovating groups within the parties did not preclude bitter struggles over whether to accept the Radical legislation. The losses of 1961 and the need to respond to the competition of reform-minded opposition did, however, serve to make the right more receptive to the general idea of reform, and to set the stage for their eventual support of the land reform measures that were passed in 1962 and 1963.

Intraparty Debate: The Question of Deferred Payment

Among the many complex questions specifically related to the land reform issue, the one which stirred the greatest controversy among rightist groups was whether to accept Radical proposals for a constitutional amendment that would permit deferred cash compensation for the expropriation of abandoned or inefficiently cultivated rural property. In its original form, the Radical initiative allowed the state to compensate the owners of such properties over a thirty-year period with an immediate cash payment of only 10 percent of the total indemnity. The rightist reaction to this proposal can be divided roughly into two stages. The first was the maneuvering and the final decision to accept deferred payments within the rightist parties themselves. These intraparty struggles extended through the summer and fall of 1961. The second stage was the debate between the rightist party leaders and their broader landed constituency. This debate began well before the party decisions were officially made, but it erupted into public controversy only after November 1961. It reached a critical turning point in a vote taken within the National Society of Agriculture in January 1962. It subsided more or less completely when the amendment was sent to Congress in the same year.

At the intraparty level of debate, the conflict was most severe within the Conservative party. Under the leadership of Hector Correa, the new president of the PCU, the Conservatives had begun to negotiate with the other official parties in the tripartite committee. Hoping to gain a relatively free hand in the negotiations, Correa had apparently given an informal personal commitment that the party would accept the Radical proposals. His efforts were frustrated, however, when the opposition within the PCU unexpectedly forced a negative vote within the ruling junta, a move which provoked Correa to go on an extended leave of absence from his active duties. A special party committee was appointed to study the constitutional question, but it was packed with men thought to be basically out of sympathy with the Radical amendment. Active leadership of the party was, meanwhile, assumed by Francisco Bulnes and Sergio Diez, who were considered more responsive to the viewpoints of the traditional party groups.

The maneuver that defeated Correa did not, however, mean a defeat for the deferred payments amendment. The men who replaced the ousted president tended to be more conservative in their policy orientations, but they were still skilled politicians who were sensitive to many of the pressures that had led to Correa's election in the first place. Like Correa, the new president of the PCU, Francisco Bulnes, placed great importance on the need to move toward the center in order to retain the support of the urban sectors.

An additional problem faced by Bulnes was to conciliate those party members who had supported Correa and who now reacted bitterly to his ejection from the presidency. One such group, the provincial committee from Aconcagua, resigned en masse. In Valparaiso another group of Conservatives decided to remain within the party, but they reiterated their "firm purpose . . . that the party promote and support the agrarian and tax reforms . . . that can permit the establishment of an authentic social order based in the Christian concepts that inspire the action and doctrine of the Conservative party." [20] Finally, the new president was strongly convinced that coalition with the Radicals (who had made the original reform proposals) was essential to prevent the victory of the Marxists and a possible dissolution of the Conservative party. Several years later, in a report to the party, he stated: "We were losing faith in our destiny and in our raison d'etre. Many conservatives already thought that the party could never again exercise any influence on the national destiny, and the weakest were, as in Aconcagua, already beginning to abandon a ship that they believed condemned to sink. The only way out of this problem was to form a combination with the PR." [21]

For these reasons, Bulnes played an important role in persuading the party to accept the deferred payments amendments. Within the special committee, he and his collaborators emphasized the urgency of coalition with the Radicals, and the importance that the latter placed on the land reform legislation. Swayed by these arguments, the committee voted to accept the principle of deferred payments, although it hedged by suggesting that the period of payment be only five years. Bulnes was later to urge that the time period be extended to ten years, and the party, at the insistence of the Radicals, finally accepted a term of fifteen years.

A parallel process of self-criticism and decision had meanwhile also gone on within the Liberal party; and although neither the leadership shake-up nor the internal dissension was quite so great as among the Conservatives, the PL was not without its difficulties. By the time the executive council voted to approve the amendment, three of its most prominent members had resigned in protest. The major pressure for reform was led by the youth organization, and especially by its president, José Garrido, who was later to head the governmental planning agency for agriculture. The trade union section of the party also argued that "the working class should be made to realize that the Liberals are not a bulwark of the economic right" and that "impulse must be given to the agrarian reform on the basis of projects already studied by the technical committee of the party." [22] Finally, the man who was president of the party during 1961, Ladislao Errázuriz, had decided to give his backing to the project. Although definitely a man of traditional orientations, he was convinced for many of the same reasons used by Bulnes that deferred payments were essential. Under his leadership there was never any real danger that the PL would refuse to accept such a step.

The Deferred Payments Debate: The Parties versus the Landowners

With the decision by the Liberals and Conservatives in the fall of 1961 to accept the Radical proposals, the debate shifted to a broader form of discussion between the rightist politicians and their upper class constituents. The most important upper class interest groups to which the rightist parties were answerable were the National Society of Agriculture (Sociedad Nacional de Agricultture, SNA) and the Society for Factory Development (Sociedad de Fomento Fabril, SFF). The former represented and was dominated by the large landowners of Chile's Central Valley. Formed in 1837, the Society had an aristocratic membership which considerably overlapped with that of the rightist parties themselves. Thirty-two percent of the SNA council membership in 1961 had at one time sat in the Congress, and 12 percent were currently on the party executive juntas.[23] The leadership of the SFF, on the other hand, tended to be separate from both the Liberals and Conservatives and from the SNA. Only one out of the thirty SFF councillors had ever sat in the Congress, but several were supporters of Jorge Alessandri. The top officers of the SFF — the president, vice president, and secretary general — all owned land. The biographies of all but three of the remaining council members, however, showed no involvement in the direct ownership or management of agricultural property.[24]

Also of major national significance were two other large agricultural groups: the Consortium of Agricultural Societies of the South (CAS), and the Agricultural Associations of the North. As their names implied, these groups represented smaller, regional farmers, who were in many ways the rivals of the "aristocrats" within the

SNA and resentful of their political connections with the Liberals and Conservatives. Formed in the late 1930s, these groups at first supported the Radicals. Later on, however, many shifted their support further right, to the authoritarian, antiparty movements led by Carlos Ibañez and Jorge Prat. Finally, a number of locally based associations and six major producers' associations (grouping the producers of single products, such as wheat, rice, sugar beets, and seeds), completed the interest group structure. Although loosely aligned with the SNA, these associations generally criticized the SNA leadership for not having pressed more energetically for higher prices and more government investment in agriculture. Between 1959 and 1962, the heads of several producers' associations united to form the Agricultural Federation (FEDAGRI) as a national rival of the SNA. This grouping of regional associations, along with the CAS, formed the most active centers of opposition to the new constitutional measures.

Significantly, the SFF (the industrial society) tended to remain on the sidelines. Interviews with SFF leaders conducted in 1965 and 1966 indicated that privately they opposed the Radical amendment as a threat to private property. At the same time, however, the desire to avoid embarrassing their former colleague, Alessandri, along with a recognition that the amendment was directed primarily at the landed groups, prompted the SFF leaders to avoid public intervention.[25] Finally, in spite of their strong ties to the rightist parties, the leaders of the SNA themselves remained deeply divided on the issue. In view of the Society's prestige as the oldest and largest pressure group organization, the undecided SNA council became the major battleground of the proponents and opponents of deferred payments.

The shift, late in 1961, from the parties to the pressure groups as the main arena of debate was also marked by a shift in the categories of debate. Whereas intraparty discussions tended to focus on electoral and congressional considerations, the arguments now tended to revolve more directly around the defense of the landed interests themselves. Arguments in favor of the amendment were based on three major points: the amendment was essential to the preservation of the constitutional system; it could be of advantage to the interests of the landed sector; and the limited nature of the amendment ensured that no real damage could be done.

These themes were raised, for example, by Liberal Deputy Domingo Godoy, who argued that the expropriation of abandoned lands could help to raise agricultural production and to create a new rural middle class with a vested interest in avoiding massive social overturns: "If through the agrarian reform, we can give access to the land for the most efficient peasants . . . we will have eliminated the criticism that the farmers are not duly exploiting the land. These new proprietors . . . will constitute a middle class of peasants that is indispensable to assure a greater social stability." [26]

Echoes of these ideas were found within the SNA itself. Allied with the Liberals and Conservatives on the SNA council was a younger group of agronomists and technicians who manned the Society's extension service, its monthly journal, and its technical staff. After the election of the Christian Democrats, these agronomists and technicians assumed the general leadership of the Society, and their position on land reform began to diverge from that of the parties. During the Alessandri period, however, they urged support of the party leaders. In a memorandum they presented to the council, special emphasis was placed on the idea that the rural property structure could no longer be defended indiscriminately. Land tenure changes could be legitimately based on a distinction between efficient and inefficient landowners, as an essential concession to preserve stability. "Nothing will be gained," the memorandum stressed, "With a fierce defense of all proprietors without exception, since this would show . . . a refusal to reform juridical institutions in an evolutionary way. Dikes will be created that ultimately will be swept away by prejudice for the entire social structure." [27]

The memorandum also pointed out that the reform could be of great advantage to efficient proprietors. Limited and moderate use of deferred payments might be better than progressive taxation, since the latter would put a broader and potentially dangerous tool in the hands of any government determined to revise the property structure. In any case, concluded the memorandum, the passage of the amendment would bring increased foreign aid which could be channeled into agricultural credit, the building of rural infrastructure, and the importation of farm capital.[28]

At the same time, the limited nature of the amendment was also stressed. Only badly cultivated or abandoned properties could be paid for in bonds. The average farmer could count on cash payment for any expropriation. The amount of payments would be readjusted to compensate for inflation, and any default on payments would require an end to further expropriations. The bonds could be used to cancel any debts that the landowner might have with the government. Finally, expropriated farmers would be able to appeal to the regular courts to protect their interests. The memorandum emphasized that this last provision would be one of the most important protections: "One of the dangers that is seen in the reform is that it would permit a *massive* agrarian reform. This cannot be produced because the recourse to the Tribunals of Justice . . . will impede a massive agrarian reform by the very limitations of the proceedings." [29]

As might be expected, the opposition to the reform tended to equate the amendment with the destruction of private property and the basic elements of equity and justice.[30] Beneath these charges, however, lay a shrewd analysis of the risks of such a concession to agricultural interests. The current threat to the status quo, it was argued, by no means justified such an important concession of principle as deferred payment. Other tools, such as fines, might serve as a sanction for whatever inefficiency existed. The CAS, for example, argued: "The aspiration to expropriate a few abandoned or badly cultivated lands does not in itself justify a constitutional reform. If these lands must be sanctioned, the entire country can support the resources necessary for it, as beneficiary of the social peace that [this move] is intended to obtain." [31] The limited provisions of the current amendment, moreover, would simply raise expectations without supplying mechanisms adequate to satisfy them: "The people have instinct. It is not easy to fool them. They will think, and with reason, that what can be conviction in the Left is simple, occasional demagogy in the Conservatives and Liberals. They will continue following their leaders, and with much more reason after seeing them triumph, destroying the bastion of private property." [32] Modest though the specific provisions of the amendment were, acceptance of the reform would unleash a dynamic that would ultimately be far more dangerous to all proprietors than a refusal to do anything at all: ". . . it can be maintained tomorrow that it is as legitimate for a payment made in fif-

teen days to be made in fifteen or one hundred and fifty years . . .
The amendment presently projected will not permit the realization
of what is intended, [and] a way will be sought to prolong the
terms as much as might be desired, now without the need of breaking any solid principle." [33]

Answers were provided by men like Fernando Coloma, a vice
president of the PCU, who held that "a government that had such
purposes . . . could simply dispense with this [constitutional] 'for-
mality' . . ." [34] But to some extent, this reply missed the point of
the criticism. From the perspective of 1961, a Radical victory
seemed likely. The combined percentage for the PL, PCU, and PR
had risen from 47.2 percent in the 1958 presidential elections to
53.2 percent in the 1961 congressional elections, despite a loss of
votes for the two rightist parties. On the other hand, in 1958
Allende had won 28.9 percent of the vote, but the Marxist in 1961
obtained only 22.9 percent.[35] The opponents of reform were concerned not about the action of a future Marxist government, but
about the effects of the refom on a future Radical administration.
Thus FEDAGRI predicted: "All the prudence that can be applied
will be exploded by public pressure, sustained by the fact that the
government has requested and obtained the legal arms for deferred
payment. As limited as the range of the constitutional reform might
be, it creates a precedent that will make its amplification necessary." [36]

There were dangers, of course, that rejection of the constitutional amendment would break up the center-right coalition or
cause it to lose the election. These possibilities were not lost on
the opponents of the reform, but they argued privately that these
were risks worth taking. In the first place, the Radical leadership
was anxious to regain control of the presidency and might well have
continued the coalition without the constitutional reform. Moreover, present concessions by the Liberals and Conservatives would
not stop the Radicals from imposing further concessions as the
price of remaining in the future government coalition, and it
seemed pointless to cede a solid legal obstacle in advance of the
elections. If a Marxist or Christian Democratic victory was coming
in 1964, limited concessions were not likely to be effective in stop-
ping it. In short, the opponents argued that only if the proponents
had accurately calculated the nature of the crisis — neither too

early nor too late — would their position be truly protecting agrarian interests.

A month after both parties had agreed to support the amendment, the broader debate reached a turning point within the SNA council, where a vote on the issue ended in a tie. Although the council's action could hardly be considered a rousing confirmation of the parties' position, its failure to reject the proposal meant, in effect, a victory for its proponents. For one thing, the vote marked an important juncture in the public actions and attitudes of the Society; for the organization's officers, who were generally sympathetic to the parties' position, were now free to encourage a further softening of the SNA's general stand on reform. Moreover, the tie prevented the Society from siding officially with the FEDAGRI and the CAS, a move that might well have caused the bill to be withdrawn from congressional consideration. After the crisis had passed within the SNA, at least some of the groups that had originally opposed the reform became silent. Others explicitly reversed their positions.[37] Although sporadic public debate continued throughout 1962, the back of the opposition was broken. FEDAGRI was disbanded and most objections ceased after the passage of the reform measure in 1963.

The Alessandri Laws: A Redefinition of Rightist Interests, and a Link of Continuity

The final legislative products that emerged from this process — Law 15020 and the constitutional amendment — were subject to strong criticisms from reform-minded Chilean and foreign experts. These criticisms were based on the general argument that the legislation was filled with obstacles to the smooth and efficient realization of massive reform in the countryside. The conservatism of the constitutional amendment, which gave the state only fifteen years to pay out bonds, put a severe financial limitation on the state's ability to move rapidly in acquiring land. Moreover, in limiting expropriable land payable in bonds to abandoned and inefficient properties, the state was restricted from touching average land that might be needed for redistribution. More important, the definition of abandoned and inefficient properties was so vague that endless court proceedings would be necessary to determine if specific lands actually fell within this category. And while special courts were established to expedite these disputes, possible appeal to the regular courts ensured further juridical snarls that could slow or stop expropriations proceedings.

Whatever the shortcomings of the law itself, it was evident by the end of the Alessandri administration that no group within the governing coalition had the will or energy necessary to administer the reform. During the congressional debates, officials of the administration had expressed their hope of establishing about 5,000 proprietors per year and estimated the cost of such a program at about 77 million escudos. In fact, however, only about one-tenth of this sum was actually allotted to the appropriate administrative agencies; from November 1962, when the reform law was passed, until the Alessandri regime left office in September 1964, only 1,200 new proprietors were actually settled on land.[38] Also clear was the fact that the regime had no taste for utilizing the expropriations clauses in the law. Land was acquired by transferring state-owned properties to the reform agencies and through the outright purchase of private lands — often at terms quite advantageous to the original owners. The expropriation process remained a dead letter throughout the Alessandri period.

The Alessandri reforms were thus weak when judged in terms of the needs of the Chilean countryside. Viewed from the perspective of the previous position of the Chilean right and of the contemporary position of comparable groups in other Latin American countries, however, the judgment must be different. Law 15020 was, after all, written with the support of conservative classes at a time when most Latin American governments had not even begun to consider the problem seriously. In those countries where reform bills were written, they were usually passed against the opposition, rather than with the support of rightist groups. A full two years after the basic Chilean decision had been made on deferred payments, for example, the National Agrarian Society of Peru argued that ". . . the reform must be founded on the constitution and juridical norms, eliminating payment in bonds for expropriated lands and suppressing the diverse confiscatory means of the bill." [39]

After 1963 the Chilean rightist parties and the SNA restricted their concern to efficient landowners, leaving others to the sanction of expropriation and payments by bond. Although rightists continued to challenge the economic justifications given for agrarian reform, they had recognized that putting abandoned lands into cultivation could in fact help to increase agricultural production. And though they still emphasized the tensions between the economic and social objectives of a land reform program, they had admitted the possibility that, with proper safeguards for efficient owners, the two objectives were not mutually exclusive. Finally, the admission that special reform legislation was necessary and legitimate represented perhaps the most important change in the viewpoint of the right. One Socialist senator did not exaggerate too much when he stated in the senate: "If the [issue of land reform] had been raised five years ago, there is no room for the slightest doubt that [the right] would not be debating in such a hurry. Those same sectors would have been here with no less than heated bayonets, disposed to stop the dispatch of a law that even accepted the principle, the idea that it is necessary to make an agrarian reform." [40]

In any event, criticisms of the essential weakness of the Alessandri legislation may be somewhat overdrawn, because the shortcomings of the law itself are often confused with the apparent unwillingness of the Alessandri government to administer the law. The Alessandri legislation had little impact on the countryside at least in part because it was designed to gain the support of groups other than the peasants. Even for the Radicals, who had initiated the legislation, a change in the land tenure structure or the appeasement of groups with strong ideological commitments to such changes were apparently secondary purposes. Although both the Radicals and the right had looked with anxiety at the left's gains among the peasants, the internal debate within the Liberal and Conservative parties indicated that they had undertaken the legislation for purposes of urban consumption. For most of the elements of the Democratic Front coalition, the reforms were designed to counter the inroads being made by the Christian Democrats among the "progressive" sectors of the urban middle class. For Alessandri, the reform was viewed as a device to elicit funds from the United States. Thus, the political value of the expropriations provisions was symbolic, rather than operational.

The Christian Democratic government which succeeded the Alessandri regime in 1964 responded, however, to a different constituency. It was strongly influenced by radical intellectuals, and it saw in the peasants a major potential source of political support. In the hands of this government, the Alessandri legislation *did* provide the basis for at least the beginning of a land redistribution program. Under the terms of the old law, the two most important institutions in charge of the Christian Democratic land reform — the Corporation for Agrarian Reform (Corporación para la Reforma Agraria, CORA) and the Institute for Agricultural Development (Instituto de Desarrollo Agropecuaria, INDAP) — had been granted legal powers to expropriate, to buy and sell land, to extend credit, and to administer acquired properties. Under the Frei regime, these organizations were, without additional legislation, able to take the leadership in drawing up the Christian Democratic bill, in administering its interim program, and in rallying and organizing the peasants in support of a more extensive reform.

Finally, while awaiting the passage of its own law, the Frei regime was able to use the "abandoned and inefficient" clauses of the Alessandri legislation to expropriate over 479 fundos, and to make land available to over 8,051 rural families.[41] Although the new government still lacked the legislation that could force the owner to accept payment in bonds without a long court struggle, the threat of a new law with much tougher terms induced many owners to settle out of court on terms favorable to the government. Additional legislation that would have streamlined the procedures of Law 15020 could probably have, in the early stages of the Frei administration, passed the Congress without much difficulty. But this possibility was never publicly considered by the Christian Democratic government, even as a temporary measure, since it preferred to wait until the much stronger terms of its own law would allow it to act with greater efficiency and economy.

The Rightist Parties: The Bases of the Brokerage Role

Two aspects of the debate within upper class circles appear especially important in understanding the brokerage role of the rightist parties. One was the difference in viewpoints, loyalties, and interests between members of the upper class who were party politicians and those who were not. The second was the responsiveness of the politicians to the cues and incentives of the electoral and congressional system — especially to apparent changes in the outlook of the urban electorate and to shifts in the balance of power within the Congress. Both of these characteristics of rightist behavior require some additional comments in order to understand the more complex role played by landowning groups during the Christian Democratic period.

The distinctions between rightist party politicians and ordinary landowners had long been noted within rightist circles themselves. The party politicians have always been subject to charges of politicking by those of their peers who work outside the established party framework, and many politicians of the right in turn readily admit that they are not only farmers and industrialists. As one Conservative leader put it some years after the passage of the Alessandri legislation, "We had to take into account the political and electoral problems as well as the technical ones." [42] Participation within the constitutional and multiparty framework had led therefore to a differentiation of roles within the Chilean upper class. The career politicians on the right had developed new, constitutional bases of power that supplemented older, more traditional resources of influence. Far more than their fellow members of the upper strata, the politicians had an interest in expanding these constitutional power bases and in preserving the framework in which these bases of power had developed. Unlike the independent rightists, the status and power of the career politicians were jeopardized not only by threats from the left, but by extraconstitutional pressures from the right.

It should not be surprising that, during the Alessandri period, these differences should have led the politicians to play a strong moderating role in the land reform debate. (For some quantitative evidence about the relative moderation of rightist party leaders, see the Appendix at the end of the chapter.) Party leaders had much more to gain than independent landowners or industrialists from their support of the constitutional and agrarian reforms. These extremely modest measures were, after all, a small price to pay for the prospect of continued membership in a governing coalition and for defusing the growing electoral threat from the opposition parties. Throughout the Christian Democratic period, as well, the rightist party leaders continued to be somewhat more moderate than many of their landed constituents in meeting the far more serious challenge posed by the new regime. Their long experience in working within the congressional framework appeared to incline rightist leaders to tailor their demands to the new alignment of political forces that emerged after 1964, to bargain for what they could get within that alignment, and to stop short of actions and positions that might have thrown the system into total stalemate.

Yet skilled politicians can do more than make passive adjustments to the "givens" of an existing political situation. They may also attempt actively to change the situation itself, so that it might become more favorable to their own interests and to the interests of the groups they represent. In the period from 1958 to 1964, the rightists attempted to adjust to the growing urban strength of the Christian Democrats by moderating their own position. In the post-1964 period, the emphasis of the right shifted. Its electoral strategy was based on an attempt to reverse the leftward trend within the middle class segments of the electorate by capitalizing on the anxieties and uncertainties involved in the process of change and by offering a return to stability, order, and hierarchy.

In part this shift was due to the far more sweeping ambitions and objectives of the new Christian Democratic government. Although the laws supported by the right during the Alessandri administration were among the most limited in Latin America, the legislation proposed by the Christian Democrats was among the most radical. The shift was, however, due in part to other factors.

One countervailing restraint on the moderation of the right was built into the nature of the electorate itself. Historically, the Liberals and Conservatives found most of their urban support among propertied, Catholic, upper middle class city dwellers who collectively formed a substantial minority of the big-city voters. Liberals and Conservatives could, in 1961, hope to add to this nucleus of support by competing with the Christian Democrats for the votes of more moderate or progressive sectors of the middle class, but this strategy had diminishing returns.[43] Gains that might be won by bidding for progressive votes would at some point be outweighed by losses suffered within the more conservative sectors of the city, which had voted for the right precisely because this sector represented tradition and order. These constraints were not widely recognized by rightist politicians before 1964, but they became quite important after the defeat of the Democratic Front and the election of the Christian Democrats. Even during the earlier period, however, at least some rightist politicians warned of the electoral risks involved in moving toward the center. "What party," asked one, "can be considered more rightist than the Conservatives? Let us be careful that [in moving toward the center] there is not a vacuum created, since if there were one, there would always be a conservative party on the right. Besides, if we move to the center, I fear that it will be a very weak center, with very few members." [44]

In the context of the early 1960s, neither the extent nor the nature of urban discontent were fully understood by the actors within the system. Reformist parties espoused structural change and received urban votes; but their advocacy of land reform was probably only marginally related to their electoral victories in the cities. The reform laws supported by the right, therefore, had little political impact among the groups at which they were aimed. A severe and surprising defeat for the Democratic Front in a 1964 by-election convinced the members of the coalition that their alliance was no longer electorally viable. To prevent a Marxist victory, the Liberals and Conservatives threw their support to their rivals, the Christian Democrats; but soon afterward, they moved into a position of bitter opposition. When the Christian Democrats appeared to be serious about carrying their reform plans forward, the right shifted from the "progressive" posture it had adopted before 1964 to an attempt to mobilize an explicitly anti-reformist urban electoral base.

The strategic reliance on city voters which encouraged the right's brokerage role in one period thus tended to discourage it in the next. The politicians' propensity to emphasize the importance of bargaining and compromise with their congressional adversaries continued during the Frei period to add a stabilizing note to the reform process, but party politicians nonetheless drew closer to their more extreme, independent critics. When the parties thought they could arrest the decline in their political strength by forming part of a winning coalition, they were willing to moderate their economic positions on agrarian reform in order to pick up support from reform-minded groups. As these chances decreased and they moved toward an "out" position, they began to emphasize differences and obscure points of agreement with the party in power.

Although the right's shifting strategies were to alter its role in the reform process, the concessions that it had already made could not be easily undone. The Liberals and Conservatives had helped place a workable, if quite modest law, "on the books." In so doing they had promoted the idea that land tenure changes need not be intolerable and that the subject was a legitimate topic for political debate. More important, the action of the right during the Alessandri period may well have facilitated "splitting the difference" once the Christian Democrats came to power. The landowning groups could criticize much harsher terms of expropriation, for example, but they could no longer object to the principle of expropriation itself. Bargaining would have existed, no doubt, even if there had been no previous legislation. By bringing the landowners' position closer to the center of the debate, however, the politicians enabled more moderate rightist groups to make additional concessions with less fear of recrimination from their own supporters for "selling out."

Appendix: Rightist Party Experience and the Deferred Payments Debate

The debate over deferred payments offers the opportunity to present some supplementary evidence in support of the general proposition that party experience has tended to produce a more flexible stance on the issue of land reform; for in the debate, rightist leaders divided unambiguously for or against a specific measure deemed essential to changes in the land tenure structure. In order to determine if there was a relationship between party experience and position on land reform, political and economic backgrounds were compiled for thirty-four of the forty SNA councillors who had voted on the deferred payments amendment. To supplement these data, a second set of biographies was compiled for an additional thirty individuals who figured prominently in arguments for or against the amendment. Within each group, a

The Sociopolitical Background

majority of the individuals who had served political apprenticeships (local leaders, youth leaders, or party functionaries) approved the amendment, while a majority of those without such
experience was opposed. Similarly, a majority of the men then (in
1961–1963) serving as congressmen or as members of the rightist
executive juntas were in favor of deferred payments, while ma-

Table 1. Vote on constitutional reform by SNA councillors, by political
background

Position on reform	Experience as apprentices in rightist parties		Councillors serving on party executive juntas		Councillors serving in Congress	
	Yes	No	Yes	No	Yes	No
For	11	4	4	11	3	12
Against	6	13	0	19	0	19
Total	17	17	4	30	3	31

Source: Diccionario Biográfico de Chile, 1962–1964.

jorities of the other individuals within each group were opposed.
The numerical distributions for the two groups are shown below
in Table 1 and Table 2.

The composite total for both groups of individuals is shown
below in Table 3. The overall pattern of the table seems rather

Table 2. Position on constitutional reform of other leaders in the debate,
by political background

Position on reform	Experience as apprentices in rightist parties		Leaders serving on party executive juntas		Leaders serving in Congress	
	Yes	No	Yes	No	Yes	No
For	15	0	8	7	5	10
Against	5	10	4	11	4	11
From Table 1	17	17	4	30	3	31
Total	37	27	16	48	12	52

Source: Diccionario Biográfico de Chile, 1962–1964.

Table 3. Political backgrounds of leaders in the deferred payments debate (in percent)

Position on reform	Experience as apprentices in rightist parties		Leaders serving on party executive juntas, 1961–1963		Leaders serving in Congress, 1961–1963	
	Yes (N = 37)	No (N = 27)	Yes (N = 16)	No (N = 48)	Yes (N = 12)	No (N = 52)
For deferred payment	70.2	14.8	75.0	37.5	66.7	42.3
Against deferred payment	29.7	85.1	25.0	62.5	33.3	57.6
Total	99.9	99.9	100.0	100.0	100.0	99.9
	($p > .005$)		($p > .01$)		($p > .25$)	

Source: Diccionario Biográfico de Chile, 1962–1964.

clearly to support the proposition that activities within the parties and the Congress had a moderating impact in the debate over land reform. Although the relationship between congressional membership and a positive vote on deferred payments is not statisti-

Table 4. Position on deferred payments, by economic categories and political apprenticeship (in percent)[a]

Position on reform	Agriculturalist		"Mixed" (Commercial-Agricultural)		Commercial-Industrial	
	Appren-ticeship (N = 20)	None (N = 10)	Appren-ticeship (N = 8)	None (N = 11)	Appren-ticeship (N = 4)	None (N = 5)
For deferred payments	60	20	75	10	75	–
Against deferred payments	40	80	25	90	25	100
Total	100	100	100	100	100	100
	($p > .05$)		($p > .01$)		($p > .25$)	

Source: Diccionario Biográfico de Chile, 1962–1964.
[a] Total N = 58. Biographies on six of the sixty-four individuals in Table 3 were unclear as to economic background.

cally significant, this appears to be due to the small size of the total sample.

Unfortunately the small size of the total sample makes it impossible to ascertain with any confidence whether the relationship between political party activity and support for deferred payments persists when economic backgrounds are controlled. Conceivably, the relationships in Table 3 reflect different economic interests and social backgrounds. However, the limited evidence which is at our disposal suggests that this is not the case. In Table 4 the apprenticeship variable, which divided the sample most evenly, is examined for individuals with similar economic backgrounds. Again, the low chi square values appear to be due to the small size of the sample, for the relationship noted above appears to remain quite strong. Of the agriculturalists without economic ties to other sectors, eight out of the ten men without political apprenticeships opposed the reform. Of the men with both agricultural and commercial interests, ten of the eleven nonapprentices were also opposed. Finally, all five of the nonapprentices in the commercial or industrial sector were in opposition.

Part 2 The Christian Democratic Initiative: Setting the Terms of Debate, 1964–1967

Chapter 3 The Christian Democratic Factional Struggle and Agrarian Reform, 1964–1967

Eduardo Frei, the man who succeeded Alessandri, had promised the voters a "revolution in liberty." The absolute majority he gained in the 1964 elections was the first won by a presidential candidate in Chile's modern history. The congressional victory of the Christian Democratic party (Partido Demócrata Cristiano, PDC) in March 1965 was equally unprecedented. Until 1957 the movement had never won over 3 percent of the popular vote. By 1965 the party had gained 42 percent of the vote, a majority control of the Chamber of Deputies, and almost one-third of the members of the Senate. In light of the fact that the Marxist parties had captured most of the rest of the votes, the election results were not unreasonably viewed as an overwhelming popular mandate for change.

The *kind* of change desired was, of course, another question entirely. Both major presidential candidates had set forth a detailed list of proposals, which included such measures as agrarian reform, control of the financial and export sectors, and mobilization of the marginal population. But it was likely that a diffuse dissatisfaction, rather than a popular endorsement of these proposals, constituted the driving force behind the Christian Democratic victory. Among the many themes mixed within the PDC appeal were anti-Communism and reformism, authoritarianism and constitutionalism, Catholicism and secularism — something, in short, for everyone.

By the elections of 1964 and 1965, Christian Democratic strength had thus spread from the urban middle sectors to virtually all levels of Chilean society. New voters in the urban slums, peasants, women of all social classes, significant proportions of organized labor, all lined up behind the party banner. At the elite level, there was comparable heterogeneity. The party had originally been founded by a small band of upper and middle class Catholic intellectuals, but by 1964 its leadership included landowners and industrialists, employees, and blue-collar work-

Table 5. Social backgrounds of party deputies (in percent)

Party affiliation	Land	Commerce	Independent professionals[1]	Functionaries[2]	Empleados[3]	Blue-collar workers	Total
Liberal[a]	64.0	56.0	12.0	8.0	–	–	25
Conservative[a]	42.8	42.8	28.5	4.7	–	–	21
Radical[a]	11.1	22.2	44.4	37.0	7.4	–	27
PDC[b]	18.4	10.5	52.6	1.3	23.6	2.6	76
Socialist[b]	–	7.6	15.3	23.0	23.0	30.7	13
Communist[b]	–	–	38.8	5.5	38.8	22.2	18

Source: *Diccionario Biográfico de Chile*, 1962–1964; 1964–1966.
[a] Deputies for 1961–1965.
[b] Deputies for 1965–1969.
[1] Practicing lawyers, university professors, journalists, doctors, etc.
[2] Employees of the national government.
[3] White-collar workers. The category includes primary and secondary teachers.

ers. As Table 5 indicates, the social composition of the Christian Democratic congressional delegation was far more varied than that of any of the other major parties. Within the party elite, there were spokesmen for almost every ideological and policy position that could be found in Chile. This chapter will examine the way the factional struggle engendered by this heterogeneity affected the launching of the Christian Democratic land reform between 1964 and 1967.

The importance of this factional struggle was quickly grasped by opposition politicians within Chile's multiparty system, and interestingly enough, both the rightists and the Marxists reached similar conclusions about its impact on land reform. Members of the conservative opposition charged that the relatively moderate position on land reform taken by President Frei's followers had been superseded by the views of extreme elements within the Christian Democracy. Left-wingers had, they argued, captured the reform movement, impelling the party to abandon previously held orientations toward gradual change and to move off in more radical and dangerous directions.[1] Marxist observers concurred, although of course they evaluated the phenomenon somewhat differently. "Progressive" Christian Democratic forces, argued the

Marxists, had at least temporarily gained the upper hand in the drafting of the land reform legislation. They warned, however, that internal contradictions within the Christian Democratic co-alition would ultimately threaten this left-wing control. For the Marxists, the rise of a multi-class Christian Democracy meant simply that old wine had been poured into a new bottle: ideo-logical struggles that had hitherto raged between the separate parties of a multiparty system would now take place within the framework of the Christian Democracy itself. The radicalism that admittedly characterized the initial PDC approach to agrarian re-form was thus bound to be counteracted sooner or later by reac-tionary elements within the party.

On at least one point made by opposition politicians there can be little dispute. The sweeping objectives of the new reform pro-gram (100,000 new proprietors in five years), the broad pro-visions of the new bill, and the high priority given to the process of land division after 1964 departed considerably from the past positions of Frei and other top party leaders. During the 1950s, Frei had rarely mentioned land reform in his writings and speeches.[2] And even after 1960, when the agrarian problems had become a central issue of political debate, the idea of massive ex-propriations had not been stressed. The emphasis had instead been placed on a more limited and gradual process of change, which would simultaneously increase the number of family farms, safe-guard the investments of efficient agriculturalists, and involve col-laboration as well as conflict with existing large landowners.[3]

Attribution of the changes in this moderate approach solely to internal left-wing pressures seems, however, somewhat question-able. Electoral and international factors affected the reform stances of politicians all along the ideological spectrum, and during the 1960s the Marxists and the right, as well as the Christian Demo-crats, all moved farther to the left on land reform. Moreover, the presidential and congressional elections of 1964 and 1965 ac-centuated these pressures. For the first time in Chilean political history, both of the major presidential candidates — Frei and Salvador Allende, the candidate of the Marxist coalition, the Popular Action front (*Frente de Acción Popular,* or FRAP) — identified themselves with aspirations for structural change. An accelerated increase in peasant voting and crushing defeats for the parties of the traditional right made some sort of effort at land reform a good probability.

Even taking these considerations into account, however, the evolution of the Christian Democratic agrarian reform was in important ways shaped by the factional struggle within the party. But the relationship between the land reform program and this factional struggle was far more complex than the opposition politicians had indicated. The major impetus for the reform did come from the party left wing, and the pressure from this element probably gave the program a radical thrust and a position of importance that it might not otherwise have had within the general policy of the government. Nevertheless, control by the party radicals was by no means as complete as the right had charged. At the same time, the internal struggle over the program was by no means as extensive as had been indicated by the left. On the contrary, the division between the party "extremists" and "moderates" over the question of land reform was far more narrow than it was on any other issue. In many respects, therefore, land reform served as an important bond of unity between groups that clashed over almost everything else. This process of cleavage and compromise within the governing party helped to set the terms of debate and the possibility of action for the system as a whole.

The Pattern of Factional Struggle

The coherence of the Christian Democratic party resulted largely from the extraordinary solidarity of a core of leaders — the president himself, key cabinet ministers of the Frei administration, and most of the party's executive officers — who had previously participated in the founding of the National Falangist party, the forerunner of the Christian Democracy. Whereas the Christian Democracy was a relatively new party, founded in 1957, the individuals comprising the Falangist core could trace their association back to the late 1920s. This group of leaders had, while classmates at the Catholic University of Chile during that period, begun to discuss the possibilities of a "third road to development" — one that would reflect "social christian ideals" and that would avoid the egoism of "liberal capitalism" and the repressiveness of "Soviet Communism." Although the precise nature of this third road was never clearly elaborated, it served as the impetus for the Falangists' entrance into politics, first (from 1932 to 1938) as a semiautonomous youth auxiliary of the Conservative party, and then (from 1938 to 1957) as a small, independent party of protest. As students and as politicians, the Falangists were articulate critics of existing social inequities, who over time gained a reputation for being above ordinary partisanship and for being unwilling to sacrifice principle for political gain.

Paradoxically, the vagaries of the multiparty system also provided the Falangists with a considerable degree of practical political experience. Between 1932 and 1938 they were able to acquire cabinet posts and congressional seats through their affiliation with the Conservatives. In subsequent years the Falange continued to be represented in the legislature and in a few cabinet coalitions, in spite of the small size of its popular vote. By the time of his election to the presidency, Frei himself had been a senator since 1949 and twice a cabinet minister. In important respects, therefore, the Falange had enjoyed the best of two worlds. In thirty years of protest against the system, its leaders had developed a "remarkable community of interest and purpose." [4] Thirty years of activity *within* the system had, on the other hand, tempered this community of interest by imposing on the Falangists the need to make decisions and the capacity to survive them. By the time of the 1964 elections, these men were thus well equipped to survive the responsibilities of office.

As a major political force, however, the Christian Democratic movement comprised a far broader range of groups than the Falangists themselves. As the Falange (renamed the Christian Democratic party in 1957) gained electoral support, splinter groups from the Conservative party, segments of the declining Ibáñez movement, political independents, and university students moved into the Christian Democratic fold, in the process laying the basis for the bitter factional struggles which erupted after the party took office in 1964. After 1964, the party divided into two main factional groupings. One of these — an "officialist" wing — tended to espouse a relatively moderate line of action and to support the policies of the Frei administration. The other constituted a strong left wing, which tended to challenge Frei's authority within the party.

The officialist wing of the party consisted of most of the Falangists themselves and of the splinter group politicians and political independents who had entered the party during the 1950s. Often large landowners or industrialists, these splinter group politicians and independents had apparently been attracted to the PDC by the more conservative, anti-Marxist aspects of the Falangist appeal, although in some cases political opportunism undoubtedly played a role. Whatever the factors that led to their entrance into the Christian Democracy, they joined most of the Falangists as strong backers of the Frei government, and several were included within the cabinet itself. Although some of the newer recruits to the party appeared to take policy positions to the right of the president, most agreed in principle with the idea of moderate and orderly reforms of Chile's major social and economic institutions — the general policy line of the Frei administration. These reforms might include some redistribution of income and power through wage and tax policies, expanded educational opportunities, and a greater freedom for union activities. At the same time, however, an aggravation of the class struggle was to be avoided. Most officialists advocated close cooperation with the private sector, and most gave high priority to measures which would control inflation and increase capital investment. On the other hand, officialists seemed willing to leave to others the task of organizing peasants and urban workers, and most actively opposed the nationalization of foreign-owned industries.[5]

The left-wing challenge to this approach came for the most part from the young intellectuals and professionals who had been recruited into the Christian Democratic youth movement during the 1950s and 1960s. Although some left-wing leaders came from a slightly more middle class segment of the party than did the officialists, the differences between the two factions appeared to be a function of age rather than class.[6] Most officialists (both the Falangists and the newer recruits to the Christian Democrats) were between fifty and sixty years old during Frei's term of office and had entered politics in the period between the two World Wars. The major left-wing leaders were in 1964 often only thirty or thirty-five years of age, and their political views tended to reflect the new tensions, values, and aspirations of the post–World War II period. Unlike most officialists, for example, the Christian Democratic left-wingers identified Chile's future development with that of the third world, rather than with Western Europe. Socialist Cuba, rather than Christian Democratic Europe, was an object of admiration, if not of imitation. And whereas the officialists often emphasized the division between Christian Democratic and Marxist forces, many of the leftists strongly advocated a Christian Democratic–Marxist alliance that might consolidate the political victories won by the "progressive forces" in the 1964 and 1965 elections. Finally, for most leftists, a redistribution of power rather than economic development along "neocapitalist" lines deserved the greatest attention of the new administration. As one major party document, aptly titled the "Non-Capitalist Road to Development," argued:

We desire an economic growth which removes us from, instead of committing us to, capitalistic criteria. We want progress, but we also want the great effort of the people to benefit the majority and not to consolidate the power of a few economic groups . . . The Christian Democratic party thus rejects as contrary to its principles the alternative of converting itself into the "party of Chilean development," without other specifications. It seeks, on the contrary, to orient economic development toward the construction of a new society of workers: harmonious, democratic, and popular.[7]

These differences should not, however, be exaggerated. The lines of factional struggle were far more complex and fluid than this brief summary would suggest, and it is important to stress the point that many factors worked toward unity, as well as toward division within the party. The most important of these — the solidarity of the Falangists themselves — has already been mentioned. In spite of tactical and policy differences, most Falangists tended to keep internal conflicts from leaking to the public or to the other members of the party leadership.[8] This capacity to remain unified in the face of opposition, combined with the Falangists' prestige as the founders of the Christian Democratic movement, greatly increased their support from all segments of the Christian Democracy. Most of the left-wingers themselves had, moreover, begun their political careers as Christian Democrats, and their loyalties and interest were closely bound to the success of the party and its leaders. Many in fact owed their advancement within the party to the patronage and protection of the older leaders. Thus, until the very end of the Frei administration, both the officialist and left-wing factions were disposed to resolve their differences through compromise, and both managed to prevent policy disagreements from turning into schism. With only rare exceptions, intraparty battles tended to be fought in party councils and, at times, in the press, rather than in the Congress or in the electoral arena.

Nevertheless, in many ways, the Christian Democratic leftists behaved, as it were, like a party-within-a-party. Many openly acknowledged the label of party "rebels," ascribed to them by the press. For a time they published their own journal, which was often more critical of the administration than the opposition parties themselves. Like the competing groups outside the Christian Democracy, the left-wingers tried to block or alter the initiatives of the government. Also like the outside opposition, they proposed alternative leadership and alternative policies to the ones offered by the regime itself. Eventually, many left-wingers split away from the party late in 1969 in order to support the Marxist candidate in the 1970 presidential elections.

The Factional Struggle and Agrarian Reform

When placed within this framework of growing factional strife, the flow of influence which produced the Christian Democratic land reform bill appears like a countercurrent moving against the general trend. For in the case of the land reform, many of the usual patterns of intraparty conflict were reversed and a quite different set of power configurations emerged. Although most government programs were initiated by the officialist wing of the Christian Democracy and sometimes invited the support of outside landed and business groups, the major inspiration and the wellspring of support for the land reform came from young intellectuals associated with the party left wing and from the Marxist parties. In most instances it was the officialists who occupied key governmental posts, while the left wing functioned as an opposition group, without the power to alter the basically moderate direction of the Christian Democratic administration. On the issue of land reform, however, party leftists played a major role in the organization of the administrative apparatus and in the writing of the reform law, while the officialist wing constituted at least a potential nucleus of opposition.

Just how and why this curious reversal occurred is not entirely clear. Some of the leftists — especially those associated with the Economic Commission for Latin America, the Food and Agricultural Organization of the United Nations, and with the universities — could lay claim to a special competence in the field of land reform, and this experience may have made them appear the logical leaders of a reform program. Undoubtedly, however, the astute Falangists also perceived the advantage to be derived from giving their militant young colleagues a stake in the administration. In any case, by 1964 it was clear that the age, the outlook, and the sources of support for the men who were to administer the program differed considerably from those who were entrusted with the other concerns of the Frei regime. The law that they were to propose was to be quite different from the moderation of government proposals in other areas.

Typical of the larger circle of intellectuals who played a role in the land reform program were the men chosen as the new heads of CORA and INDAP, Rafael Moreno and Jacques Chonchol. In contrast to the older leaders who dominated the cabinet, both Chonchol and Moreno represented the new generation of leaders who had begun to challenge the Frei administration. Whereas the median age of the twelve cabinet ministers was forty-nine, Moreno was only twenty-six years of age in 1964, and Choncol thirty-eight. Moreno was a close personal friend of Frei. But as a former leader of the PDC youth movement and as an energetic new administrator of a glamorous program, he was closely linked to the left-wing critics of the regime. The ties were even clearer in Chonchol's case. Also beginning in the Christian Democratic youth movement, Chonchol during the 1950s had become associated with various United Nations organizations. As a representative of the Food and Agriculture Organization (FAO), he had spent two years in Cuba (1962–63), aiding the Castro government in the planning and drafting of its land reform law. Although he was not formally a Marxist, Chonchol's radicalism and his experience in Cuba made him a dramatic figure within the Christian Democratic and Marxist left and something of a bête noire to the rightist opposition.

The differences between Chonchol and the officialist wing of the PDC over the specific question of land reform are difficult to document, since the officialists did not consistently set forth the type of land reform they desired. In his monographs and articles on the subject, however, Chonchol clearly set forth ideas and assumptions that departed abruptly from the general positions of the government leaders, which advocated orderly reforms in which income redistribution would be kept within the limits of economic development and upper class groups would benefit as well as sacrifice. In contrast, Chonchol stressed the importance of a "massive, rapid, and drastic" alteration of the land tenure structure — a phrase later incorporated into the party platform.[9] For Chonchol, inflexible resistance, rather than partial cooperation, was the anticipated response of the landed class, and a certain amount of disruption was to be accepted as an inevitable by-product of social change. Social and economic disorder was to be minimized by telescoping the reform into as short a period as possible, rather than by moderating and extending the process: "A change like agrarian reform . . . tends to create, while it is being executed, instability, insecurity, and anxiety. This is inevitable. Thus, the logical thing to do is to try to supersede this lapse of instability as rapidly as possible." [10]

Many of these premises were reflected in the provisions of the new constitutional reform of property rights and the new land reform legislation presented to the Congress in 1965 and passed in 1967. Both eliminated the guarantees that landed proprietors had previously enjoyed, and both provided the state with a virtual carte blanche in the acquisition and distribution of land.

As the basis for the land reform, the new constitutional amendment swept away all of the obstacles left by the Alessandri amendment. The earlier reform had limited the types of property to be paid for in bonds and had carefully defined the conditions of payment and the jurisdiction of the courts. The new amendment left all substantive decisions about expropriations and payments to ordinary legislation and to the administration. The only constitutional limitations were matters of form and procedure: expropriations were to be only for reasons of public utility, they were to be authorized by law, and the owner of the property was to receive an indemnity.

In the land reform bill itself, the size of a property, rather than its state of cultivation, was to be the most important reason for expropriation, and compensation for efficient as well as inefficient holdings was to be made partly in bonds. Although abandoned or inefficient lands could still be totally expropriated, under the new law even a "normally" efficient owner would be legally entitled to reserve an area of land equivalent to the value of only eighty "basic" hectares in Santiago province. Also subject to expropriation were lands in zones declared by the president to be "areas of agrarian reform," all lands held by corporations rather than individuals, and any of the separate parcels owned by persons whose total property exceeded the limit of eighty hectares. In deference to the officialists' position that private entrepreneurship should be given special treatment and protection, exceptionally efficient owners were to be allowed a reserve of 320 basic hectares, instead of only eighty. But the standards of efficiency were vaguely defined, and the efficient owner was, like the others, to be compensated in bonds for land that was expropriated.

The terms of payment and the procedures for expropriation also indicated that redistribution of land rather than the promotion of productive private investment was to be given major emphasis by the new leaders. The owners of properties expropriated for reasons of size would be compensated with a 10 percent cash payment and bonds redeemable over a twenty-five-year period. All other expropriated proprietors (for example, those who had not cultivated their properties) would be given an initial cash payment of from 1 to 5 percent of the value of their property and bonds that would be redeemable over a thirty-year period. Also, all owners were to be paid at the assessed value rather than the commercial price of their properties, a provision which reduced drastically the total compensation. And, in contrast to the old deferred payment plan, the owner would not be fully compensated for the deterioration that inflation might in the future cause in the value of the bonds. Instead, the amount of readjustment was to vary inversely with the size of the property. In the procedures prescribed for acquisition of land, CORA was entitled to take immediate possession of property without waiting for an affirmative court decision, and it had the authority to decide which section of an expropriated property could be reserved for the owner. To expedite the resolution of any legal conflicts, special local and appellate courts were established, and no appeal to the regular court system was allowed.

Finally, the provisions for the disposition as well as the acquisition of the land also reflected the assumptions of the left wing, rather than the officialist approach. Frei and his older lieutenants had often spoken of the need to create an entrepreneurial class of small and medium peasants. Many of the leftist leaders had on the other hand argued that if drops in production were to be minimized during a massive land redistribution process, the state would have to take a major role in the management of property. Accordingly, the new bill provided for a legal transition period, to run from the time a property was expropriated until the peasants were granted new titles of ownership. During the *asentamiento,* as this period was called, the land was to be managed jointly by local CORA administrators and committees elected by the peasants themselves. Although normally this period was to last only two years, it could be extended indefinitely at CORA's discretion; when the period did end, the peasants themselves would have the option of requesting collective as well as individual parcels. Whichever they chose, CORA was to retain considerable jurisdiction over the rights of transfer, withdrawal from cooperatives and collectives, and the credit and marketing procedures to be employed.

For reasons to be discussed presently, the appointments of Chonchol and Moreno were not actively opposed by the Christian Democratic moderates, and most officialists were inclined to accept passively the law they proposed. But the most active and vocal support came from groups generally opposed to the Frei regime. At the congressional level, the Marxists gave strong backing to the constitutional and land reform measures. The Communist Secretary General urged the Marxist forces to "leave aside all sectarian positions which tend to consider the Christian Democracy or governmental agencies such as CORA and INDAP as enemies number one. If we are to be objective, such entities, as well as the Christian Democratic peasant organizations, are working . . . against the landowners." [11] Socialist politicians were somewhat more reserved in their public support of the reform initiative. Like their Communist allies, however, they voted in favor of the reform bill; and the Socialist newspaper, like that of the Communist party, was quick to defend CORA and INDAP against the attacks to which they were subjected from the right.

Even stronger support came from the opposition groups *inside* the party — the left-wing congressmen, youth leaders, and the staffs of the technical commissions — for it soon became evident that the land reform program was one of the few governmental initiatives around which these groups could actively rally. The ideological inroads in the generally moderate policy of the administration made by the land reform program were noted and approved by most of the left-wing leaders. "The bill," remarked one left-wing congressman, "went somewhat further than the President really wanted to go." [12] Another noted that "the reform of the land tenure structure was the most important in giving a beginning to the new stage of government, because it finds the party united, and because it signifies a political, economic, and social fact of real revolutionary transcendence." [13]

In short, the party left-wingers viewed the land reform law as the one truly "revolutionary" aspect of the "revolution in liberty." Between 1964 and 1969, this fact in turn may well have encouraged them to remain within the party framework; for the radicalism of the agrarian initiative made it easier for the party left-wingers to accept other, more moderate, measures of the regime. This seemed to be the case, for example, in the passage of Frei's copper reform law, a measure deemed critically important by the moderate sectors of the party. The copper reforms authorized the Chilean government to purchase stock in the American-owned copper mines and permitted tax concessions in return for additional American investment. Initially the measure had been bitterly opposed by the party leftists who, like the Marxists, preferred outright nationalization. The leftists' expectation of a radical agrarian reform law, however, tended to encourage acquiescence in the copper reforms. This was made clear at a party caucus in 1965, a time in which both measures were pending before the legislature. As one commentator described it, "The [leftists] announced their full accord with the revolutionary clauses of the [agrarian reform] bill, and Jerez [a leading left-wing congressman] argued that if they had maintained strict discipline on the copper agreements . . . it was because they now wanted the timid ones in the party, the vacillators, and those who prescribed a 'reform with sugar' now to maintain the same [disciplined] attitude." [14]

The organization of the land reform administration, no less than the elaboration of the land reform bill itself, also tended to mute the conflict between the Frei regime and its internal opposition, for the appointments of Moreno and Chonchol as the heads of CORA and INDAP countered what was otherwise a general exclusion of party leftists from important policy-making positions within the government. Under the aegis of the two young reform administrators, groups otherwise consigned to a role of criticism were given something to do. University students were dispatched into the countryside to assist in promoting the education and organization of the peasants. Economists, sociologists, and agrarian experts were hired to prepare reports on the progress of the asentamientos already established under the Alessandri law. Youthful left-wing congressmen were permitted to act as the legislative floor managers for the land reform bill.

Of course the incorporation of the leftists into these positions cut in two directions. If it tended to give the radicals a stake in the administration, it also increased their leverage in a vitally important program. Early in the Frei regime it became clear that the firing or resignation of Chonchol or Moreno would have serious repercussions in broad sectors of the party elite. On at least one occasion, Chonchol and Moreno used threats of resignation as important weapons in a struggle over the financing of the reform.[15] On other occasions, pressures from CORA and INDAP leaders, PDC left-wing congressmen, and the FRAP forced the officialist leaders to withdraw tactical and marginal concessions they had offered to the landowners.

At the same time, the co-optation of radicals into the ranks of the administration also tended to restrict the kind of leadership they could supply for the party left wing. In spite of Chonchol's clear sympathies with the Christian Democratic "rebels," his public statements of criticism against the Frei administration were rare and guarded. When in 1967 a group of party leftists began to publish an opposition journal, Chonchol made some initial contributions. His collaboration was withdrawn, however, after he had to choose between remaining as head of INDAP or continuing these activities. Yet left-wing leaders at both the congressional and the administrative level apparently recognized the value and the importance of continued influence within CORA and INDAP. As one left-wing congressman pointedly remarked during a private interview: "Although most of the people in the government belong to a different current in the party, not all of them do. Those in charge of the agrarian reform are a very different story. Here the tecnicos are doing a fine job." [16]

The Officialist Wing and Agrarian Reform

During the legislative phase of the land reform, open dissent from the other side of the PDC — the officialists — did not materialize. One important reason for this, no doubt, was a broad consensus about the desirability of some sort of land reform effort. This consensus underlay any disagreements that may have existed as to the specific scope or objectives of the reform. Important as the differences between Chonchol and the officialists were, they did not carry with them the inevitability of open conflict. A related reason for the absence of an officialist opposition was that many of the more conservative party members were convinced that the radical provisions of the land reform bill would not be fully applied in practice. Throughout the passage of the reform legislation, Frei and other members of the Cabinet insisted that efficient proprietors would not be penalized by the reform; and they implied that in practice, the actual scope of expropriations would not go as far as the law permitted.

Nevertheless, many within the officialist wing were privately disturbed at the direction taken by the administration on this issue and at the scope of the law itself. Considering the upper class origins of many officialists, their economic and social ties to outside landowners and industrialists, and their relatively moderate political outlooks, at least some adverse internal reaction was to be expected. Rightist politicians and interest group leaders estimated that from twenty-five to forty Christian Democratic deputies as well as several cabinet ministers and the president himself all partially sympathized with their criticisms of the bill.[17] Interviews with seven Christian Democratic deputies who were owners of land tended to support the right's assertions. Although the extent of their reaction varied from mild concern to strong opposition, all of the seven deputies were in some measure reserved about the radicalism of the Christian Democratic proposals. "Those who mention 100,000 new proprietors," stated one PDC deputy, "have their heads in the clouds. Only the most capable peasants should be chosen as proprietors." [18] Another put it even more bluntly: "There are many [Christian Democrats] who are quite concerned about the reform bill, but they are not listened to. Their motives are suspect, and they are afraid to open their mouths for fear of being called reactionary." [19]

Even accepting as an initial premise the idea that an internal consensus on the desirability of land reform helped to reduce the conflict over the details of the proposals, it is thus important to insist that the *potential* for a broad internal opposition existed. Since voting discipline was maintained and almost none of the private reservations spilled over into public controversy, it is necessary to inquire further into the restraints that held the officialist dissidents in line. What prevented the crystallization of a Christian Democratic right-wing opposition? How did the muted debates over the specifics of the legislative proposals influence the final shape of the law?

Understanding the personal role of the president himself is central in these questions. In spite of the departures from his earlier positions on the land reform bill, Frei threw the weight of his considerable prestige behind the measure. The extent to which this support stemmed from a genuine acceptance of the radicals' viewpoints and the extent to which it stemmed from a preoccupation with mitigating the effects of the factional struggle cannot of course be known with certainty. According to leaders of the right, the president often hinted that his discretion had been limited by the pressures of the left wing. In public, however, Frei kept his own counsel. Although he often asserted his willingness to remain open to "constructive suggestions" from the right, he also made it clear that he would not waver in his commitment to the basic provisions of the bill.

The president's stance severely restricted the reaction of party moderates and conservatives. It is probably fair to say that his prestige was enough to counterbalance any inclinations to oppose the project that might have existed within the officialist sector. This prestige was reinforced by the special ties of dependence that linked many officialist politicians to the leadership of Frei. Whereas the Christian Democratic leftists had entered politics at a time when radicalism appeared to offer a good electoral payoff, most officialists had little hope of an electoral future outside the framework of the PDC. The non-Falangist sector of the officialist wing in particular had been recruited into politics from declining political splinter groups or as political independents without electoral power bases. Their current offices often stemmed from their personal allegiance to Frei, and their hope for reelection rested on their continuing capacity to identify with the old Falange.

Moreover, in contrast to the left-wingers, many of the party rightists were unable to find independent power bases within the party itself. The leftists' direct recruitment into the Christian Democracy, their activity within the party assemblies, technical commissions, and youth movements, permitted them to gain internal party support that did not depend entirely on their acceptance by the top party and government leadership. On the other hand, as former conservatives, Ibañistas, or independents, many members of the officialist wing held their positions at the sufferance of the Falangist leadership, most of which supported Frei. Several cabinet ministers, who were identified with the officialist sectors of the Christian Democracy, were not even formal members of the party, and their power rested almost entirely on the confidence of the president. With dwindling electoral support outside the Christian Democracy and with little chance for building an organizational base within the party, dissident officialists had little hope of mounting an independent right-wing challenge to Frei's endorsement of the land reform program.

Although dissident Christian Democratic officialists were still permitted some room for maneuver, their action could not parallel that of the left-wing opposition. Although the party leftists could challenge Frei's authority within the party, enter into direct opposition to basic governmental policies, and offer alternative groups of leaders, the objections of the party conservatives were restricted to the marginal aspects of the land reform bill. Like the party leftists, party conservatives could cooperate with outside opposition groups, but it was a cooperation on a far more limited scale than that which occurred on the left. The broad, immoderate strains of rightist opposition were emphatically rejected by otherwise sympathetic PDC deputies. This rejection was strikingly illustrated in an incident recounted by one of these deputies in a private interview:

Just after the [congressional] election, I was invited to the house of a friend of mine. As it turned out, there were twenty-six people there who wanted me to sign a public manifesto protesting the expropriation of rural corporations. I have nothing against corporations, I head one myself. But as a deputy, I just cannot be involved in this sort of thing and I turned them down flat. In their houses, as friends, I will talk with them and try to convince them, but in no other role.[20]

The framework within which the dissidents could operate still provided them, however, with the opportunity for some influence over the details of the reform legislation. While strongly endorsing the measure, Frei had also insisted that the party should remain open to dialogue with and suggestions from the right. Throughout the debate over the merits of the project, the president himself conferred frequently with representatives of the National Society of Agriculture, the Liberals, and the Conservatives. His major lieutenant, Bernardo Leighton (then the Minister of Interior) met privately with conservative groups almost immediately after the reform bill was published, assuring them that they could expect to achieve at least some modifications in the bill.[21] Complementing and reinforcing the government's efforts to maintain some ties with the landowners was an equally strong determination to prevent nonagricultural sectors from entering into the reform controversy. Left-wing attempts to initiate bills providing for the control of financial monopolies, for example, were either vetoed by the president or allowed to languish in the Congress. "What we cannot permit," argued PDC president Patricio Aylwin, "is that those who have nothing to do with [agrarian reform] become confused and compromised in defense of the interests of [the landed elite]: The small . . . and medium progressive farmers, the industrialists and the merchants . . . , the urban proprietors who are scornfully fooled when it is said to them that afterward, their houses will be taken away." [22]

In short, though the top government and party leaders were publicly committed to imposing sacrifices on the upper class, they also admitted the legitimacy and possibility of upper class participation and survival in the process of reform. In this context the PDC conservatives could afford to make limited responses to the appeals of the outside opposition.

All of the deputies interviewed reported that they had acted on behalf of some of the amendments that had been proposed, either by rightist politicians or by leaders of the SNA. Alterations in the system of payments for expropriations, slight modifications in the amounts of land to be reserved by expropriated owners, and the introduction of somewhat greater equity into the expropriations proceedings — all originally suggested by the SNA — were pushed and eventually passed through the combined efforts of cabinet leaders and the officialist deputies. Similarly, a small number of highly efficient wine-producing corporations in central Chile were exempted from expropriation. On a somewhat broader level, some of the deputies interviewed used personal contacts with cabinet leaders to modify the tone of debate between the government and the outside right. One committee chairman recounted a meeting with the president in which he successfully urged the injection of a note of conciliation into a speech that Frei was about to make in the provinces:

Before his trip, I went in to see him and said, "If you really mean what you have said in the past, why don't you tell the people that you intend to leave ninety percent of the property untouched and that you are not going to give land to all the peasants." When he made his trip, these were the very points he stressed in his speech. [23]

Restricted though this type of activity was in the context of the larger purposes of the land reform measure, it may still have had considerable importance, not only in terms of the final details of the bill itself, but also in keeping open the lines of communication during the bargaining process which accompanied the bill's passage through the Congress. Some of the amendments pushed by the party conservatives were accepted by the PDC left and emerged as sections of the final law; some were not. But aside from the small agricultural sectors which may have been aided or penalized by the success or failure of these amendments, efforts within the Christian Democracy on behalf of landed groups provided an important inducement for the latter to moderate their opposition.

Left-Wing Effects on Land Reform

In view of the left wing's control of key administrative positions and its apparent ascendancy in the legislative phase of the reform, the relatively gradual pace of the actual land redistribution process (summarized in Table 6) appears somewhat surprising. The totals presented in the table are, of course, quite respectable, especially considering that until 1967 the Christian Democrats had had to work under the limitations of the Alessandri law. Yet it does not belittle the significance of the PDC effort to suggest that, even after 1967, the scope of the reform resembled the rather moderate orientation of the officialists far more than it did the rapid, massive, and drastic strictures of Chonchol. And this in turn raises the question of whether left-wing pressure, however important it was in the drafting of the law, had any real impact on the results of the reform itself.

It is difficult to give any clear answers to this question for a number of reasons. For one thing, the influence of a group is most

Table 6. Chilean land redistribution, 1965–1969

Year	Farms expropriated	Total area (thousands of hectares)	Number of families settled
1965	99	286.8	2,061
1966	265	145.6	2,109
1967	217	354.8	4,218
1968	223	725.2	5,644
1969	314	1,078.2	6,404
Total	1,118	2,590.6	20,436

Source: Economic Commission for Latin America, *Economic Survey of Latin America, 1969* (New York: United Nations Publication, 1970), pp. 154 and 157.

evident when its will has prevailed over the conflicting wills of other groups. In view of the rather muted disagreements within the Christian Democracy over the issue of land reform, and considering the general consensus that some sort of land reform was desirable, there is no clear answer to what might have happened to the law or to its administration if left-wing pressure had been absent. Moreover, in the discussion of the impact of intraparty factionalism on land reform, the larger constraints that the environment placed on the reform process have temporarily been ignored. It is difficult to judge the extent to which the relatively moderate pace of expropriation was due to the balance of power *between* the two wings of the Christian Democracy and the extent to which it was due to forces which neither faction could control. Yet in order to place the radical young reform administrators and the law they elaborated in some perspective, some speculations may be ventured.

Perhaps the most important general constraint faced by the entire party was the problem of scarce resources. A rough estimate of the investment costs of the land reform can be obtained by looking at the total budget expenditures of CORA and INDAP between 1965 and 1967. In that period the two agencies spent a combined total (in 1967 escudos) of 794,802,000 escudos.[24] Calculating roughly eight escudos to the dollar, the total expenditures of the two agencies came to almost 100 million dollars — approximately $12,500 for each of the families affected by the reform. Some of these expenditures, it is true, went for purposes other than the acquisition and redistribution of land. Credit to small proprietors, unionization expenses, and extension aid were also areas of activity for the two agencies. Also, these figures do not take into account possible returns on investment through increases in production or through repayment by peasants. Even so, it is clear that the reform program placed an important financial burden on the Christian Democratic government. Even with massive doses of foreign aid, the establishment of 100,000 new proprietors would have involved an enormous, if not impossible, reallocation of resources in a country where the per capita income was less than $400 and where the supply of foreign exchange depended heavily upon the fluctuating price of copper. This was a problem which no Christian Democrat, whether moderate or radical, could afford to ignore. But the need to find funds for the reform program was a political as well as an economic problem. Financing involved judgments about the priorities that should be established among given programs and about the social groups that should contribute to and benefit from these programs. In this sense the overarching problem of funding related back to the balance between the two Christian Democratic factions and in particular to the assumptions of the officialist sector of the administration.

During the presidential campaign and afterward, Frei had claimed that his reform of the American copper companies would provide the financing necessary for the land reform. Through tax reductions to the American copper companies the PDC government had hoped to win their agreement to double their production by 1970 and in the long run to increase fiscal revenues. Although not openly stated, the agreement with private American companies was probably also expected to incline the American government more favorably toward the prospect of giving aid to programs of structural change. Without becoming involved in the details of the Frei proposal, however, it should be noted that the economics of the argument were highly debatable. The copper program involved investment as well as returns, and it was probable that the expenses of the tax reductions, coupled with the government's commitment to purchase stock in the American companies, would not have been balanced by increased production until sometime toward the end of Frei's presidential term. The argument could, in fact, be made that between 1964 and 1970, the period when the bulk of the land reform was to be carried out, the agrarian reform and the copper program would have competed for funds. In any case, however, the opposition from both the FRAP and the PDC left wing delayed the initiation of the agreements until 1967.

With or without support from the United States, and with or without a copper agreement, it was probable that the rural "revolution" promised initially by the Christian Democrats could not have taken place without equally far-reaching urban changes. The establishment of 100,000 new proprietors would have required an effort to squeeze funds from nonagricultural economic sectors and the need to establish broad political controls over a disaffected urban population. Whatever the political feasibility of such a move, it was clearly foreclosed by the determination of the Frei administration to build onto, rather than destroy, urban social institutions and to operate within the framework of constitutional norms.

Table 7 gives a picture of the relation of agricultural invest-

Table 7. Total government investment by budget sectors, 1964 and 1967 (in thousands of escudos of 1967)

Budget sectors	1964	1967	Percent increase (1964–1967)
Agriculture[a]	224	415	85.2
Housing	487	810	66.3
Industry	99	252	183.0
Energy and fuel supply	338	486	43.5
Education	96	230	140.3
Mining	94	216	130.4
Transportation	621	665	7.0
Defense	22	58	162.7
Miscellaneous	31	57	81.5
Health	90	113	26.3
Loans	154	162	5.1
Urban	127	274	114.9
Total[b]	2,375	3,742	57.9

Source: Exposición sobre el Estado de la Hacienda Pública Presentada por el Ministerio de Hacienda don Sergio Molina Silva a la Comisión Mixta de Presupuestos el Noviembre de 1961. Dirección de Presupuesto, Folleto No. 112, Noviembre de 1967, p. 71.

[a] The percent of total budget for agriculture was 9.4 in 1964 and 11.1 in 1967.

[b] Entries in columns have been rounded to nearest whole number and do not add exactly to figures given for total expenditure.

ment to total government investment. Although resources were transferred from the private to the public sector, it is clear from the figures that a massive diversion of funds into agriculture did not take place. Agricultural expenditures rose at a rate comparable to that of other sectors of the budget, and their percentage in the total budget increased only slightly.

In spite of the right's occasional charges that the PDC radicals had "captured" the land reform, the truth may well have been the other way around. The need to work within the general policy orientation of the Frei administration required the Christian Democratic left wing to accept a more gradualist approach to land reform. By 1967, earlier promises to create 20,000 new proprietors annually had quietly been scaled down to the more realistic objective of sustaining a steady rhythm of expropriations, and of settling about 5,000 families per year. Though some of the CORA and INDAP personnel were inclined pragmatically to accept these reductions, many others, including Chonchol himself, were severely disappointed by the constraints placed on their efforts. Thus, late in 1968 Chonchol resigned from his post in INDAP, and in the summer of 1969 he led a number of dissident Christian Democratic left-wingers out of the party itself.

However, although the Christian Democratic left-wingers proved unable to expand drastically the scope of the reform, they probably were instrumental in ensuring that available resources and legal powers would be pushed to their outer limits. Within the restrictions established by overall government policy, the leaders of CORA and INDAP could from 1964 to 1968 act with considerable energy and flexibility. Their impact was felt in the reorganization of the reform agencies themselves, in the way funds were utilized in the countryside, and in the growing capacity of CORA and INDAP to make their influence felt in the larger decision-making process.

Under Chonchol and Moreno, the functions of CORA and INDAP extended far beyond what had originally been envisioned by the Alessandri administration. During Alessandri's term, the personnel of the two agencies had been concentrated in Santiago. Under Chonchol and Moreno, a network of regional offices penetrated into the countryside itself, paralleling the more conservative government bureaucracies. The local offices of CORA were charged with assessing fundos in the area, preparing the basis for expropriations, and supervising the acquisition and redivision of land once decisions to expropriate had been made. By 1967, over 90 percent of CORA's personnel operated in the field, rather than in the central city. INDAP officials sharply downgraded the institution's earlier credit and extension role in favor of a more direct effort at peasant mobilization. Government funds and facilities were devoted primarily to the organization of rural unions, producers' cooperatives, and peasant committees. By 1967, an estimated 30,000 peasants had been touched by at least one of these forms of organization. The shift to an emphasis on peasant mobilization was clearly stated by one of INDAP's young executives: "At present, INDAP has a new attitude regarding the small peasant . . . it does not function as an institution designed to give only technical aid and credit . . . On the contrary, its executives have marked out the goal of organizing the national peasantry so that it will constitute a dynamic movement, disposed to struggle for itself." [25]

The hand of the PDC left wing could also be perceived in the treatment of local landowners and in the process and location of the expropriations themselves. The aggressive use of the expropriations clauses in the Alessandri legislation has already been mentioned. Even after the passage of the more flexible Christian Democratic law, however, CORA officials were determined to avoid or cut through whatever loopholes remained in the legislation. When threatened with a series of court battles over the applicability of clauses dealing with inefficient property, Moreno in 1967 announced that all further expropriations would be based on the eighty-hectare limit. The expropriation process, moreover, hit hard at irrigated land throughout the country and tended to focus directly on Chile's Central Valley region, long considered the stronghold of the Chilean "aristocracy." Sixty-five percent of the lands distributed between 1965 and 1967 were located in the Central Valley.[26] During the five-year period between 1965 and 1969, expropriations included 41 percent of all irrigated land in the provinces of Valparaiso and Aconcagua, 32 percent in Coquimbo, 27 percent in Nuble, Bio Bio, and Malleco, and 20 percent in Santiago and Colchagua.[27]

None of this, of course, could have been accomplished without the acquiescence of Frei and of the other leading members of the cabinet. Clearly, however, the discretion over questions of expropriations, peasant organization, and land redistribution was no longer entirely in the hands of the older party leaders. INDAP and CORA had become powerful political machines that could not be excluded from the calculations of the administration. Supported by the Christian Democratic left wing, by the FRAP, and by

103

their own peasant clientele, the two agencies had acquired a considerable life of their own.

In discussing the impact of left-wing influence it is, finally, impossible to ignore the contrast between the effectiveness of the land reform program and the relatively small impact made by other programs of structural change over which the officialists retained control. One of the major changes promised by the PDC, for example, was the organization of urban slum dwellers into neighborhood groupings, which could undertake self-help projects, articulate demands, and bring pressure to bear on the political system. After the 1964 elections, an Office of Popular Promotion was established to work in this direction; but through 1967, the program had made only modest headway. The Office of Popular Promotion remained a de facto organization, without legal status, lacking in funding and in political strength within the administration. Although neighborhood councils were organized, many were controlled by the Marxists rather than the PDC; few councils exhibited the organizational coherence or the determination to act in their interests that had developed among peasant organizations in the countryside.

Of course, aside from the fact that the officialists rather than the leftists were in control of the program, there were other differences that might have accounted for its relative failure. The organization of the urban marginals lacked the drama, the attention, and the long years of debate that had accompanied the land reform. Also absent were the legal foundations that had been laid for the Christian Democratic land reform under Alessandri. But if the organization of slum dwellers did not have the political sex appeal of the land reform, neither did it have to fight the strong and bitter resistance that the land reform drew from conservative sectors. Moreover, the electoral potential of the lumpenproletariat was as important as that of the peasants, and an equally pervasive consensus existed within the Christian Democratic party about the desirability of making gains within this sector. Thus while many factors may have been important in explaining the relative failure of Promoción Popular, the differences in the factional backgrounds of the leadership certainly accounted for at least one of the reasons. Even though the beginnings of the land reform did not reach the rapid and massive dimensions that

Chonchol had proposed, left-wing pressure may well have been responsible for ensuring that land reform was sorted out of the Christian Democratic bag of promises and raised to the status of a major governmental program.

None of this is intended to reflect on the sincerity or capability of the moderate sectors of the Christian Democracy or to assert that they were not genuinely interested in promoting structural change. On the contrary, they brought with them to office a posture toward change that was unparalleled in the history of Chilean governments and that provided the conditions under which the left wing could gain influence. But moderate reformers, no matter how committed and politically astute, may well be inclined toward an attempt to impose order on a process that is inherently disorderly. The momentum of a reform can suffer from the need of the reformer to postpone or shove aside risky or antagonistic reforms in the process of balancing goals and juggling priorities, as well as from external resistance. In Chile the integration of the left wing into the governmental structure helped to make apparent that the risks of postponing land reform could be as great as those of pushing it forward. In a situation where the peasants were neither fully mobilized nor particularly violent, the party leftists helped to bring the rural problem consistently and directly to the attention of decision-makers, establishing a system of restraints and sanctions which the other government leaders found difficult to ignore. "Extremism" was thus useful, even in the execution of moderate and gradual reform.

Intraparty Bargaining and External Competition

A final issue to be raised in this discussion of intraparty politics concerns the manner in which the process of cleavage and compromise within the governing party related to the larger battles which the party as a whole faced in the legislative arena. Left-right ideological disputes tended, of course, to occur outside as well as inside the party; and conflicting Christian Democratic factions often collaborated actively with, and were in turn supported by, groups in competition with the PDC as a whole. But granting that the Christian Democracy was far from monolithic, this did not mean — as the left had asserted — that the party was simply a new

105

bottle into which the old wine of conflict had been poured. The PDC factional struggle and intraparty bargaining differed in important ways from similar processes occurring in the larger political system.

The "system-wide" pattern of conflict and bargaining in which the Christian Democrats were engaged — the alignment of forces that the Christian Democrats faced in the Congress — is shown in Table 8. The PDC's absolute majority in the Chamber of Deputies

Table 8. Composition of the Chilean Congress, 1961 and 1965, by party[a]

Party	Chamber		Senate	
	1961	1965	1961	1965
PCU-PL	45	9	13	7
PR	39	20	13	10
PDC	23	82	4	13
PS-PC	28	33	11	13

Source: Federico Gil, *The Political System of Chile* (Boston: Houghton Mifflin Company, 1966), pp. 228 and 309.
[a] There were 146 seats in the Chamber of Deputies and 45 seats in the Senate.

gave the party an important advantage in the legislative process; but because only one-half of the Senate seats were subject to renewal in each election, the Frei regime was still faced with the critical task of finding outside support in the upper chamber. To achieve a general majority on any legislative proposal, the PDC was forced to rely on the FRAP or upon the Radical party, which had responded to its electoral defeats of 1964–65 by moving into alliance with the left. The necessity of a qualified two-thirds majority for determining the details of a legislative proposal [28] also made the right an important potential ally of the PDC; for though the Liberals and Conservative senators could not supply a majority vote, they were able to provide the one-third total necessary to override the votes of the FRAP-PR bloc.

During the first two-and-one-half years of its administration the painstaking effort to steer its agrarian reform and copper proposals through the senatorial labyrinth proved to be the major preoccupation of the Christian Democratic government. For majority support on the land reform proposals the government successfully turned to the FRAP and the Radicals. Finding the needed votes for the copper legislation proved much more complex and difficult. A general majority in the senate was gained with the temporary and reluctant vote of the Radical party. Almost immediately after this victory had been achieved, however, the Radicals reversed their position. Attempting to distinguish themselves from the PDC and to make up for their pre-1964 alliance with the right, the PR, along with the Marxists, voted to eliminate all of the important details of the legislation. The eventual inclusion of these details in the copper law, therefore, depended almost entirely on the votes of the right, which had bitterly opposed the land reform proposals.

Some of the details of this difficult bargaining process will be treated more extensively in subsequent chapters. For the time being, it should be noted that both bills were eventually passed in the same basic form they had entered the Congress. In the long course of this passage, the government showed considerable skill in shifting its basis of support from left to right, while the latter groups, in turn, displayed an interesting disposition to avoid any collusion that might have frustrated this attempt. In spite of the flexibility of the "extremist" parties, however, their general opposition to at least one of the major aspects of the governmental program provided the PDC with a bitter and difficult challenge. The right voted for the copper legislation only after a prolonged effort to gain at least limited concessions on land reform.[29] The FRAP was somewhat less anxious or able to use its promise of support on the land reform as leverage for use on other issues.[30] But persistent opposition to the copper proposals provoked a bitter confrontation with the Christian Democrats that extended far beyond the halls of Congress. At least partially as an attempt to frustrate the PDC's copper initiatives, the left organized two long strikes within the mines themselves. The first of these ended only when the government jailed two of the copper union leaders; the second was terminated after troops dispatched by the government shot and killed nine miners.

These conflicts had echoes within the Christian Democracy itself, but they were far more limited inside the party. Cooperation between Christian Democratic moderates and outside opponents of the land reform legislation was restricted to the marginal details of the law. Although cooperation between the Christian Democratic left wing and the FRAP was far more extensive, this too had important limits. For example, while the PDC left-wingers opposed the copper program within intraparty debates, in the Congress they cast their votes in favor of the measure. In tests of action that extended beyond the congressional arena, moreover, most of the Christian Democratic radicals, until 1969, also chose to close ranks with the government. This was illustrated in 1966 by the events following the shooting of the miners, when the FRAP called a twenty-four-hour protest strike and appealed to sympathetic Christian Democrats for support. Although several Christian Democratic leaders publicly condemned the government's action, neither the PDC-dominated university students nor the various Christian Democratic labor groups were willing to join in the demonstration against the Frei government. Their unwillingness to do so was probably the major factor in accounting for the failure of the general strike. Although the PDC radicals shared many of the FRAP's policy positions, and though they actively worked for a broad alignment with the left, they were nonetheless in major confrontations inclined to side with the officialists.

Some models of reformmongering elaborated by A. O. Hirschman suggest some finer distinctions between intra- and inter-party politics. External conflict and bargaining resembled what Hirschman has called "shifting alliances." [31] Congressional support from antagonistic groups was obtained by an alternation between the left and the right. The internal bargaining process resembled a logrolling arrangement.[32] Opposing party factions acquiesced to measures of which they disapproved in order to win the passage of measures which they supported. Whereas the shifting-alliance tactic could not, by definition, eliminate the potentially disruptive influence of at least one of the opposition groups, the internal quid pro quo permitted the PDC to exploit to the fullest its voting majority in the Chamber of Deputies and enabled the party to face its competitors as a reasonably coherent unit.

What accounts for this difference? Hirschman suggests that logrolling is possible only when certain types of attitudinal distributions exist among the conflicting parties. Specifically, logrolling is feasible when each of two sizable groupings strongly supports one project and only mildly opposes another. In this situation, Hirschman points out, it is relatively easy to combine the two groups into a majority which would support both measures. "Both parties gain in the process since they give up opposing a measure which they do not really care much about to obtain passage of another which is of considerable importance to them." [33] In other circumstances, however, logrolling is difficult. When, for example, the predominant groupings tend to take strong positions on a wide range of questions — when political cleavages fall along ideological, rather than issue-oriented lines — the strategy of shifting alliances unavoidably becomes the approach that promises the greatest chance of success.

These propositions are difficult to test, since they refer to intensity of feeling rather than to external behavior. Nevertheless, the persistence with which a measure is proposed or opposed, the extremism or moderation of the rhetoric used to defend a given position, and the tactics used to obtain success are usually taken as indications of intensity. If this is the case, then Hirschman's suggestions help make clear at least some of the differences between the conflict and bargaining which occurred inside and outside the PDC. It is probable, for example, that PDC officialists were not as deeply agitated as the Liberals and Conservatives about the land reform bill, which would help explain why strong counterpressures did not develop within the party. Although a number of PDC officialists were not particularly happy about the type of land reform bill proposed, they did appear to differ from most Liberals and Conservatives in their acceptance of the desirability of at least some changes in the rural social structure. For the more conservative sectors of the officialist wing, open rebellion against the passage of the reform bill was certainly not worth the risk of embarrassing or undermining the generally moderate policy of the PDC government or of defeating its plan to initiate a partial reform of the copper companies.

Differences in the intensity with which the FRAP and the PDC left wing each criticized the officialist wing, however, are much less clear-cut. Although at critical junctures the PDC left wing did support the government, it often appeared almost as vehement as the FRAP in its general opposition. The left wing voted for the copper bill, but its votes came only after repeated statements of opposition and after threats of "rebellion." Though the left wing did not join with the FRAP in the attempted general strike protesting the killing of the copper workers, a public letter signed by the leftist leaders Alberto Jerez and Julio Silva strongly condemned the government's behavior:

Never will we tolerate the reactionary trademark of viewing work conflicts and strikes as acts of subversion or as unpatriotic . . . We will never tolerate armed repression against workers, and we do not accept the characterization of workers with a better living standard as "privileged" . . . If the peasants and carbon workers earn miserable salaries, that is not the fault of the [copper strikers] but of the system of capitalist exploitation that the truly privileged groups have established in this country.[34]

If the PDC left-wingers were less militantly opposed to the Christian Democratic officialist program than were the FRAP leaders, their language and public positions did not indicate it. It is probable therefore that other factors besides presumed differences in the intensity of their opinions also accounted for the fact that the PDC leftists were induced to enter into the quid pro quo, while the FRAP politicians were not. To understand the PDC left wing's entry into the logrolling arrangement, it is also necessary to take into account structural interests and loyalties which can be presumed to underlie the intraparty conflicts and agreements on the issues themselves.

Aside from broad ideological consensus, which in many cases is highly problematical, a shared interest in winning elections and a common acknowledgment of legitimate internal centers of authority (a national assembly, an executive committee, party officers, and so forth) can be counted among the characteristics that distinguish one party from others in a relatively well-developed multiparty system. Whereas bargaining among competing parties would be regulated primarily by their relative electoral strength, intraparty bargaining is more likely to be characterized by attempts to manipulate internal decision-making centers and by efforts to acquire allies within the party framework. The different bases of strength can have important effects when policy questions emerge. Even in the instances where separate parties engage in coalitions and agree on issues, they may feel impelled to stress policy differences in order to distinguish themselves from their allies at election time.[35] In contrast, even when the factions of a single party strongly disagree on a given policy question, there would presumably be some pressure to minimize this disagreement in order to present a common front at the polls. It is only as a last resort that dissident factions actually move toward rebellion or schism. Other things being equal, interparty bargaining is impeded by the competitive relations between the bargaining agents; intraparty bargaining is facilitated by common interests which cushion the clashes between the factions.

Although these distinctions only dimly approximate all the complex realities of Chilean multiparty politics, it is nonetheless noteworthy that appeals for party discipline, the evocation of party loyalty, and pointed references to the relationship between party unity and electoral success were woven in and out of the debates that raged between the officialist and left wing over the specific issue of copper. At a party conclave called primarily to debate the government's response to the copper strikes, one radical young deputy warned that "the parties that come [to the 1970 presidential] elections united will occupy power until 1976. The PDC must keep itself in one piece." [36] Referring more generally to the relation between the government (largely in the hands of the officialists) and the party (where the left was strongest), a major party memorandum, known informally as the Chonchol Plan, explicitly stressed the importance of reaching agreement on a broad range of issues: "It is fundamental that both [government and party] have the same strategy. It is not possible for the government to adopt one and for the party to have another, *whatever it might be*. If this occurs, there will be permanent misunderstandings and difficulties, weakening the action of the party as well as of the government." [37] (my italics)

This expressed desire for discipline and unity of action could not be maintained, of course, without at least some programs which could concretely reinforce these general loyalties. But by the same token, it seems clear that the PDC left wing, unlike the FRAP, felt strong pressures to accept what it regarded as "negative" policies as the price for such positive efforts as land reform. To have refused to do so would have meant that the Christian Democratic government would accomplish nothing of any importance. Perhaps this was an acceptable risk for opposition parties, which might stand to gain from these failures; but it was presumably an unacceptable risk for the members of the opposition faction, most of whom had been directly recruited into the party and all of whom had bound up all of their past energies and much of their political futures in the electoral successes of the Christian Democracy.

The two factors offered as explanations for the intraparty logrolling process — the moderation with which policy positions were held inside the party, and the common internal party interests which offered incentives toward agreement — are not contradictory; they reinforce one another. Added together they suggest that, despite the considerable heterogeneity of the PDC elite, its unity was far less fragile than many of the opposition politicians had assumed. The PDC was much more than a simple, ad hoc coalition, and it was impossible for a single issue, no matter how important, to cause it to disintegrate. This capacity to mediate conflict, and to arrive at a quid pro quo, moreover, undoubtedly strengthened the hand of the Christian Democrats in bargaining with their outside opponents. If the possibility of appealing to various factions within the PDC offered important lines of access for opposition parties, the internal bargaining process helped to limit the patterns of cooperation across party lines. Both access and limits allowed the PDC to encourage the more moderate elements within the opposition parties and to insulate itself from the more explosive ones.

At the same time, there is implicit in our discussion of the sources of Christian Democratic unity a hint of the factors which ultimately led to schism in 1969. First, although internal disagreements were less intense than those outside the PDC, they were clearly of sufficient magnitude to require a relatively sustained effort at management or resolution. In this respect neither the single logrolling process that we have described with respect to the land reform and copper nor any other process of accommodation could be regarded as final and conclusive. The bargaining process was an ongoing one. The inability of the Falangist leaders to accommodate divergent Christian Democratic interests once the reform law was passed, and the failure to renew old bargains over land reform in the light of the development of new problems of funding thus placed a critical strain on the unity of the party elite.

Second, and perhaps more important, since the maintenance of party unity depended partially on the electoral interests shared by the divergent factions, the relations between these factions were clearly jeopardized by the prospects of severe electoral defeat. Christian Democratic voting strength did diminish considerably in the municipal elections of 1967 and in the congressional elections of 1969. Facing this situation, the PDC was at a particular disadvantage; for unlike the older, established parties, it had previously been free of the need to recover from the strains of a severe electoral setback. For most of the members of the Christian Democratic elite, the unifying expectations of electoral victories had not, until 1967, been tempered by the taste of defeat. As it became more likely in 1968 and 1969 that the Christian Democrats would not retain the presidency in 1970, therefore, tensions grew markedly within the party. Confronted with new decisions about the formation of more permanent alliances with other parties and faced with the need to reevaluate past political lines, it is not surprising that many members of the party disinterred old arguments, recriminated bitterly in the debate over proposed roads to recovery, and, on the eve of the 1970 elections, parted ways.

Chapter 4 Effects of the Christian Democratic Reform, 1964–1967: The Problem of Mobilizing Peasant Support

The most significant and far-reaching land reforms of world history have come when aspiring or established political elites sought peasant allies in support against the challenge of opposing groups.[1] Such alliances can have a high payoff for both the peasant beneficiaries of reform and for the elites undertaking it. For peasants, reform may signify the reduction of old social inequalities and a step in the direction of greater economic well-being. For the reformist elite, changes in the land tenure structure may offer the means to acquire or expand the social base of its power.

Yet the formation of an elite-peasant alliance rooted in land reform implementation can involve serious costs as well as benefits, for the reform process not only eliminates old conflicts and cleavages but generates new ones. Even after the power of traditional landed groups has been weakened, conflicts and rivalries may erupt between different sectors of the peasantry, and between these peasant sectors and the middle class reformist elite. The type of property system that is created by the reform, the selection process that determines the new owners of property, governmental decisions about the extension of credit and technical aid, all promote the emergence of new status differences in place of old ones. If a reform is to be evaluated in terms of its capacity to generate support for an elite and greater equality for peasants, therefore, the evaluation must take into account the net balance between gains and losses. A reform is successful when the reformist elite has gained more peasant support than it has lost and when new inequalities are more fluid and less unjust than the traditional ones.

Any attempt to draw up a balance of the Christian Democratic reform must be postponed until more of the results are in. Most of the data on which this chapter is based cover only the first four years of the Frei regime. It will probably be many years, or even decades, before any final accounting of the PDC reform will be possible. Nevertheless, between 1964 and 1967 the Christian Democrats *did* engage in a considerable number of expropriations, first

114

under the authority of the Alessandri legislation and then under their own reform laws; to some extent their actions set the pattern for what was to follow. An examination of the institutions created, the types of peasants selected, and the shifts in electoral support during the period between 1964 and 1967 is a step in the direction of an evaluation.

The Economic and Social Impact of the Asentamientos

Among the many new forms of organization that emerged in the countryside, the transitional settlement (asentamiento) was by far the most controversial. Under the terms of the new law (and as a de facto arrangement under the Alessandri law), any expropriated fundo was to go through an initial period in which the management of the property was to be divided between a local CORA administrator, a number of functional peasant committees, and a peasant "chief of asentamiento," to be elected by the peasants. By the end of 1967, 240 asentamientos were scattered throughout rural Chile.[2]

Theoretically the asentamiento was a transitional structure, designed to train and select peasants for independent ownership. At the end of the transitional period, the peasants were to decide, by an elaborate point system, which of the asentados were to be granted titles of ownership and what form of property — collective or individual — was to be established. These decisions promised to be difficult and explosive, and there were therefore strong incentives for the CORA to extend the life of the asentamientos as much as possible. Although the law provided that the "normal" length of the transitional phase would be two years, that period could be extended to five years at the discretion of the CORA, and perhaps even longer on a de facto basis. In practice the asentamiento — in one form or another — promised to be a rather enduring feature of the land reform process.

Within the broad strictures of the reform law, the nature of the establishment and organization of the asentamientos varied widely. Expropriations were apparently not specifically related to a broad economic plan or to patterns of party competition. The first large asentamientos were established on state-owned lands. Others (25 percent of all the asentamientos)[3] were located in rural areas adjacent to small towns or cities, where estates were perhaps more

115

accessible to decision-makers. Expropriations often followed prolonged strikes or petitioning by peasant groups, but there was no correlation between the establishment of asentamientos and existing Christian Democratic voting power. Some of the areas most extensively covered by asentamientos had, in fact, been strongholds of Marxist voting strength. Internally, an asentimiento could be composed of as few as 3 and as many as 130 families.[4] The CORA administrator might reside on the fundo or work out of a local office. The tenure of the asentamiento chief, the actual power of the peasant committees, the way the work force was organized, all varied from settlement to settlement.

Because of the ideological implications of the role played by the state in all of these organizations, and because their establishment and operation lay at the very heart of the reform process, the network of asentamientos soon became the major focal point of a debate over whether they were more or less productive than the private fundos they superseded and whether their peasant beneficiaries were better off or worse off than before.

The most systematic attempts to explore these issues were made by the Instituto para Capacitación e Investigación de la Reforma Agraria (ICIRA), a semiofficial agency under government contract to provide information on the land reform. Because of its semiofficial status, the ICIRA kept much of its research confidential, while materials that were made available to the public tended to have a bias toward the Christian Democratic effort. Nevertheless, the ICIRA staff was composed of Chilean social scientists of various political persuasions, including independents, Christian Democrats, and Marxists, as well as of foreign experts from elsewhere in Latin America and from the United States and Europe, and its analysis was generally well-balanced and useful. One study, for example, which surveyed seven major asentamientos of about 1,600 asentados, presented a particularly interesting and controversial view of the progress of the asentamientos.[5]

The most debated (and the most debatable) conclusion of the ICIRA study was the assertion that the asentamientos had increased the output of the lands on which they had been established. Although the study criticized some inefficiencies in the use of labor resources, it argued that "in the first year of the functioning of the asentamiento system we can observe a better use of the land resources, either through the incorporation of [previously unculti-vated land] into production or through the replacement of low yield crops by others with a higher economic return." [6] This more inten-sive cultivation, plus more rational systems of credit and market-ing, asserted ICIRA, had between 1964–65 and 1965–66 led to a significant increase in gross output on all of the asentamientos. During the second period, returns on capital invested in the seven asentamientos varied from 41.7 percent to 2.6 percent, with the median return being 8.2 percent.[7]

These statements were almost immediately attacked, not only by the right, but also by a variety of experts who shared ICIRA's gen-erally favorable orientation toward the asentamientos. One profes-sor at the Catholic University, Paul Aldunate, argued that ICIRA cost accounting had underestimated the expenses incurred by the CORA in training the new asentados and in paying its own per-sonnel. Using ICIRA's own data, Aldunate argued that increased remuneration for the peasants themselves had actually eaten into the capital investments of the fundos.[8] Other critics went further and questioned the Institute's data, pointing to the lack of depend-ability of the pre-1965 figures and challenging the validity of some of the cost and output results after that period.[9] Still others, prob-ably quite wisely, argued simply that an attempt to evaluate the productivity of the asentamientos was premature.[10]

In view of the highly charged political atmosphere and the fre-quent use of statistics as weapons of political debate, the last posi-tion seems the most reasonable for the purpose of the present anal-ysis. The question of economic productivity can be left aside until more extensive data, over a longer period, are available. Indeed, even then, no final answer about the economic impact of the asen-tamientos may be expected. After fifty years of Mexican land re-form, economists continue to debate the extent to which Mexican agricultural development occurred because of or in spite of the land reform. In 1967 about all that could be said of the economic results of the Chilean land reform was that the asentamientos had not led to the spectacular *drops* in production which many rightists had predicted. Overall production in the agricultural sector neither improved markedly nor declined during the period from 1965 through 1967.[11]

On the social question — whether the peasants themselves felt

117

better off or worse off than they had before — the ICIRA study seems less ambiguous. ICIRA figures, for example, show that the income levels of the asentados increased substantially, and that they were often from two to five times higher than the wages of peasants not established on asentamientos.[12] When asked by the ICIRA interviewers whether their present situation was better, the same, or worse than their earlier situation, 10 percent of the asentados responded that their present situation was worse, 12.5 percent felt that it was the same, and 77.5 percent replied that it was better than before.[13]

The apparent short-term satisfaction of the new peasant asentados cannot, of course, be divorced entirely from the question of whether agricultural output on the asentamientos will be maintained or increased. If, as some had charged, the land reform was going to cause a serious drop in production, then the material benefits enjoyed by the peasants would eventually be exhausted. This danger, however, can be seriously exaggerated. In many cases of land reform, the food shortages which followed the transfer of property were frequently caused by disrupted marketing facilities and increased peasant consumption, rather than a decline in food production per se. Thus, city dwellers and not peasants were the principal victims of such difficulties. Moreover, even in situations where peasants experienced no material advances, they were often compensated by a variety of noneconomic improvements — the existence of a "pro-peasant" government, the experience of status improvements that come with the ownership of land, and perhaps also the satisfaction of seeing the old *patrón* removed from the manor house. In countries like Bolivia and Mexico, such factors tended to transform the peasants into strong supporters of the central authorities, in spite of instances of material hardship and in spite of economic stagnation within the agricultural sector as a whole. The importance of such intangibles in winning the allegiance of the Chilean peasants cannot be ignored. While an overwhelming number of asentados felt themselves better off, most also reported that such benefits as housing, medical care, and work conditions had not markedly improved.[14] That the noneconomic factors as well as the actual wage increases were important to the peasants was quite evident in the answer of one ICIRA respondent, who commented, "I like CORA because it always protects." [15]

118

Yet the establishment and operation of the asentamientos did stimulate some serious grievances among peasants. Although the beneficiaries of land reform appeared to experience an overall sense of both material and nonmaterial improvement, at least two types of problems susceptible of being transformed into important political issues were pointed out in the ICIRA report. One set related to rivalries among the asentados themselves; another to conflict between the asentados and rural workers excluded from the asentamientos.

Rivalries among the asentados themselves flowed largely from the transitional nature of the asentamiento. Unlike other land reforms, which turned over titles to land more or less directly to the peasants, the establishment of the Chilean asentamientos involved the recipients of land in a process of training and competition designed to determine which of them would be the most capable of actual ownership. This training and selective function of the new institutions of land reform generated considerable uncertainty and anxiety among the asentados. The ICIRA report indicates that the most threatened asentados generally came from that stratum of the peasantry which had enjoyed a measure of status and prestige under the traditional latifundia system — skilled workers, foremen, and others in supervisory positions. Although many such individuals were able to assume positions of leadership within the asentamiento structure, the need to compete with peasants of lower status and the prospect of losing in this competition sometimes caused them to react adversely to the reform process. In the ICIRA interviews, most of the 10 percent who felt themselves to be worse off under the asentamientos apparently came from this stratum.[16]

In at least some measure, moreover, the anxiety involved in the possibility of being excluded from ownership probably extended to other sectors of the asentados as well. Older peasants, extremely young ones, asentados disabled by sickness, and those simply lacking in initiative clearly had reason to feel uneasy. And even if this feeling was not always manifested in the form of opposition to the asentamiento itself, it could be seen in a deferential attitude toward authorities which sometimes inhibited peasant participation in management or social decisions. "At times," states the ICIRA report, "[the asentados] show a certain fear before the asentamiento

119

chief, since they believe that in questioning any decision he might make, they will be evaluated [for ownership] in a less favorable form." [17]

These problems, admitted by those sympathetic to the asentamientos, were often pointed to by the right as evidence that the reform would fail not only economically, but that it would backfire politically and socially as well. In a few scattered but spectacular instances during 1967, rightist politicians exploited these tensions and fears to organize fundo occupations by peasants seeking to *prevent* their expropriation by CORA. As the five-year terms expire on some of the asentamientos, moreover, rather explosive conflicts inherent in the process of selection will undoubtedly come to the fore. While pressures to extend the period might be expected to come from those who fear being excluded, opposite pressures might be expected from peasants who are anxious to establish definitively their rights to individual parcels. As early as 1967, spokesmen for small subsistance farmers petitioned the government for additional land that would be granted to them directly, without the requirement that they pass through the training period.[18]

The more important source of political conflict in the land reform process may well have come from the second form of rivalry — the competition between the asentados and the peasants excluded from the asentamientos. The asentados' tenacious determination to protect themselves from outside competition was evident throughout ICIRA's otherwise favorable report. In part this determination was fostered by the overpopulation of the countryside and the economic weakness of the peasants. Even where additional labor was needed on the asentamientos, however, "the asentados prefer to contract occasional labor before opening up the right to be members of the asentamiento to other persons." [19] In general, the report added, "the attitude of the asentados is to avoid giving access to the land to those peasants who did not sign the act of constitution for the asentamiento. They fear being displaced by elements outside the property, who might take away the lands which they hope to occupy." [20] Furthermore, when outside labor was brought in to the asentamientos, the wage differentials between the asentados and the casual laborers remained considerable (see Table 9).

Table 9. Comparison of daily income of asentado and contracted labor, 1965–66, on six asentamientos (in escudos of 1965–1966)

Asentamiento	Asentado	Contracted labor
Tranquilla	15.63	8.87
Los Arcangeles	12.31	5.73
El Carillo	9.54	7.23
San Luis de Panimavida	9.46	4.49
Santa Isabel	12.72	6.56
Coipin	11.37	5.64

Source: *Evaluación preliminar de los asentamientos de la Reforma Agraria en Chile*, Organización de las Naciones Unidas para la Agricultúra y la Alimentación y el Instituto de Capacitación y Investigación en Reforma Agraria-ICIRA (Santiago de Chile, 1967), pp. 32–33.

These rivalries appeared all the more serious because they tended to overlap status differences that had already divided the peasants under the traditional system. Although it cannot be stated conclusively, the benefits of the asentamiento were apparently extended more consistently to the inquilino stratum of the rural population — those workers who had already resided on the fundos, had been furnished with houses, and whose wages had been supplemented with payment in kind, medical assistance, and other protection from the old landowner. The new Christian Democratic reform law gave express preference to peasants who "had worked in a permanent form on the [expropriated] property, for at least three of the last four years prior to the expropriation agreement . . ."[21] Excluded, for the most part, were other categories of peasants with different relations to the land: subsistence proprietors (*minifundistas*), and casual day laborers and migrant workers — the afuerinos. Comparing the class composition of workers in one hundred private fundos in O'Higgins province with that of its sample of asentados, the ICIRA report reached the conclusions given in Table 10.[22]

CORA officials defended the decision to focus on the inquilinos and specialized workers on pragmatic grounds.[23] The choice of those already living on fundos minimized the disruption of expropriation. Alternative criteria for selection would have necessitated

Table 10. Comparison of the composition of the rural work force in the asentamientos of the Central Valley and in the province of O'Higgins (in percent)

Position	O'Higgins	Asentamientos
Foremen, employees, specialized workers[a]	11.0	38.1
Inquilinos	32.5	55.0
Afuerinos[b]	48.5	7.0
Others	8.0	–
Total	100.0	100.0

Source: *Evaluación preliminar de los asentamientos de la Reforma Agraria en Chile*, Organización de las Naciones Unidas para la Agricultúra y la Alimentación y el Instituto de Capacitación y Investigacion en Reforma Agraria-ICIRA (Santiago de Chile, 1967), p. 23.

[a] Combines separate categories: *mayordomo, empleado;* and *tractorista, obreros especializados.*
[b] Combines separate categories: *afuerinos* and *voluntarios.*

not only the importation of workers from outside the fundo but also the relocation of its existing inquilinos, threatening a broad range of social and political difficulties. Thus, the officials argued, many peasant sectors excluded from the land reform would have to make use of other government programs being instituted in the countryside — unionization, the formation of rural cooperatives, and the extension of technical aid and credit. Still other peasants would have to depend on the possibility of finding employment opportunities in the cities. Neither the benefits of the land reform nor those of other government programs could be extended to all of the rural poor.

Defensible though this approach was, the criteria of selection chosen by the Christian Democrats risked creating new social rigidities. According to the agricultural census of 1955, inquilinos constituted 30.3 percent of the active rural population; proprietors of all sizes constituted 35.9 percent; and afuerinos, 33.8 percent.[24] The first of these three strata is generally acknowledged to have been least disadvantaged by the traditional social system, for at least the inquilinos had enjoyed the full paternalism of the old landlords. In short, the effect of the Christian Democratic policy was to skim off the top stratum of the old rural peasant class and to make it the principal beneficiary of the new social order. Conceivably this inquilino stratum of the rural society could come to constitute an important bulwark of social and political stability. Recipes for preserving the status quo usually include a large, prosperous peasant middle class. At the same time, the problems facing the Christian Democrats clearly went beyond the simple tasks of keeping pace with rising expectations. By using existing status relations as the basis for choosing the beneficiaries of their reform, they risked the alienation of many who were penalized by the process as well as the dissatisfaction of those who wished to speed it up.

The Asentamientos and the Municipal Elections of 1967

The first nationwide electoral test of the "revolution in liberty" came in April 1967. In the municipal elections of that year the PDC won 36 percent of the total popular vote and 32 percent of the male vote. Both figures represented a drop of about 6 points from the percentages the party had attained in each category during the congressional elections two years earlier. In spite of the fact that this drop was widely considered a significant political defeat for the new government, its meaning was unclear. At least some attrition of PDC electoral support might, after all, reasonably have been expected after more than three years in office. Moreover, local issues and local personalities played a much larger role in the election of municipal councillors than they did in the choice of congressmen or a president; in this respect also the comparatively new PDC was probably at a disadvantage in relation to the traditional parties, which had long been active at the local level. Nevertheless, an examination of the municipal voting by communes, and a comparison with the congressional elections of 1965, both show some interesting voting patterns that are relevant to our discussion of the land reform and of the asentamientos.

Table 11 summarizes the changes in the Christian Democratic electoral support between 1965 and 1967.[25] The first three columns of the table divide 246 of Chile's 271 communes according to their demographic composition (city communes, mixed communes, and rural communes). The last two columns deal with those com-

Table 11. Changes in Christian Democratic electoral support between the congressional elections of 1965 and the municipal elections of 1967

(1) Percent change 1965–1967 voting	(1) City communes[a] (N = 28)	(2) Mixed communes[b] (N = 39)	(2) Rural communes[c] (N = 179)	(3) All communes with asentamientos (N = 82)	(3) Rural communes with asentamientos (N = 55)
Losses					
−6.0	92.9	35.6	35.7	40.2	38.1
−0.1−−5.9	3.6	43.6	26.8	29.2	21.8
Gains	3.6	20.5	37.4	30.4	40.0
Total[d]	100.1	99.7	99.9	99.8	99.9
p > .001					

Source: (1) Dirección de Registro Electoral.
(2) Mattelard, Atlas Comunal de Chile.
(3) Departamento de Planificación, Corporación de la Reforma Agraria.
[a] The communes of greater Santiago, Valparaiso, and Concepción.
[b] Other communes with 0–49 percent of labor force in agriculture.
[c] Communes with 50 percent or more of labor force in agriculture.
[d] Totals may not add because numbers may be rounded.

munes in which asentamientos were established. Each column is broken down, by percentages, into those communes in which the Christian Democrats suffered "heavy losses" between 1965 and 1967 (that is, losses equal to or greater than the 6 percent decline in the party's national voting strength); those communes in which the losses were between zero and 5.9 percent; and those in which the Christian Democrats increased their electoral support.

Perhaps the most striking feature of the data is the sharp difference in the urban and rural voting. In almost all of the city communes (92.9 percent), PDC losses between 1965 and 1967 far exceeded their nationwide percentage loss of 6 percent. In rural areas (those where over 50 percent of the active population was engaged in agriculture), the communes in which the PDC gained outnumbered those in which they suffered heavy losses (that is, minus 6 percent or more). Although the PDC lost ground in all parts of the country, the primary source of defection came from urban groups — especially in the large cities — which had historically been the major basis of Christian Democratic electoral strength. Among their new peasant constituency, the Christian Democrats may reasonably be said to have held their ground.

This conclusion seems to fit a more general pattern, both on a worldwide level and elsewhere in Latin America. Huntington has argued that in most parts of the developing world, the city (and particularly the urban middle class) is the prime center of opposition and unrest. The urban dwellers' immersion in a complex environment, their concern with upward mobility, and their exposure to abstract values as well as material improvement often lead to a state of perpetual dissent, in which aspirations outrace the capacity of the government to fulfill them.[26] Although peasant demands may have revolutionary effects, the substance of these demands are, in contrast, far more specific and concrete, as befits the rural workers' limited and slowly changing rural environment.[27] They are thus more easily appeased. In Latin America, the Venezuelan Democratic Action Party (AD), Peruvian Apristas, and the Mexican Revolutionary Party (PRI) are all examples of parties which found their most durable base of support in the countryside and their most uncertain strength in the cities. In the Chilean case, the time span is too short to assert conclusively that the pattern will repeat itself for the Christian Democrats, although the data at least suggest such a possibility.

Nevertheless, some important differences in the Chilean case should also be noted. Unlike the other parties mentioned, the PDC operates in a political system in which city, and not countryside, has been the most important arena of political competition. Although by 1964 the Christian Democrats had support from all sectors of the society, their oldest and most important electoral base was furnished by the urban middle classes of Valparaiso and Santiago. In the elections of 1965, 58 percent of the total Christian Democratic vote came from these two urban provinces. This initial urban dependency was nonexistent in Venezuela, where the AD always did better in the countryside than in the towns; and it is somewhat irrelevant in Mexico, where the PRI has great strength among all sectors of the population. Thus, urban defection was likely to be far more costly to the Christian Democrats than it was to these other reform parties, whose urban support was not decisive to begin with. Whereas the other parties had only to consolidate and maintain their peasant support, the Christian Democrats had to do more if they were to survive as a governing party. They had to extend their base of rural strength in absolute terms, in order to cancel out their urban losses.

Judging from the results of the 1967 elections, the prospects of doing this did not seem bright, at least to the extent the Christian Democrats depended on the land reform to gain peasant voters. In all of the communes in which asentamientos had been established (the fourth column in Table 11), the Christian Democrats did worse than they did in rural communes as a whole. In part this may be because many asentamientos were adjacent to the towns and cities of "mixed" communes, in which the composition of the labor force was not predominantly agricultural. In such communes the electoral defection may well have come from the nonagricultural sectors of the electorate, rather than from the peasants themselves. Even when asentamientos were established in predominantly *rural* communes, however, the electoral impact of land reform did not appear great.[28] The Christian Democrats made gains in only 40 percent of the rural communes with asentamientos (see the final column of Table 11); they did almost as well (37.4 percent) in all rural communes. The defections may have come from peasant groups, such as the afuerinos, which were threatened with exclusion from the reform process, and from small subsistence proprietors, whose independence was allegedly jeopardized by the establishment of asentamientos.

Unfortunately, our communal data do not cast much light on the reaction of the second group, the small proprietors. Latifundia and minifundia are, as was noted in Chapter 1, distributed unevenly in Chile, with the former concentrated roughly in the central regions, and the latter in the south. Through 1967, the land reform had concentrated in the latifundia regions, and most small proprietors had not yet been touched by the process. In twenty-six of the fifty-five rural asentamiento communes, proprietors (of all sizes) constituted only 10 percent of the total agricultural labor force. In only ten of the communes did the percentage of proprietors exceed the national percentage of 35.9; and in six of these, the Christian Democrats made gains. If the small proprietors in these areas did move away from the PDC, therefore, their defection was offset by Christian Democratic gains in other sectors of the rural population. It is also possible that, at least in the short run, the alienation of the proprietors was exaggerated. For one thing, unlike the afuerinos, small proprietors were the beneficiaries of other aspects of PDC agricultural policy — INDAP credit and aid to cooperatives, higher commodity prices and the like — which may have softened any potential reaction to the asentamientos. The most likely interpretation, however, is that for most small proprietors — concentrated in areas not yet subject to expropriations — the full implications of asentamiento were not yet clear. Isolated and uneducated, they could hardly be expected to react positively or negatively to the details of government proposals without witnessing close at hand the concrete efforts to implement this policy.

Asentamientos *were* established in areas with large numbers of afuerinos; if this group reacted negatively to the land reform, the reaction would be expected to show up in the data. Table 12 com-

Table 12. Christian Democratic voting change, by class structure and asentamientos (in percent)

Christian Democratic voting change, 1965–1967	All rural communes (N = 179)	Communes with over 40 percent afuerinos[a]		Communes with 0–40 percent afuerinos[a]	
		With asentamientos (N = 26)	Without asentamientos (N = 30)	With asentamientos (N = 29)	Without asentamientos (N = 93)
Heavy losses	35.7	50.0	30.0	27.5	31.1
Moderate losses	26.8	19.1	40.0	27.5	27.9
Gains	37.4	30.7	30.0	44.8	41.9
Total[b]	99.9	99.8	100.0	99.8	100.9

[a] Source: III *Censo Nacional Agrícola-Ganadero*, Abril 1955.
[b] Totals may not add because numbers may be rounded.

pares Christian Democratic gains and losses in four types of rural communes: those with and without asentamientos, and those with high (40 plus percent) or low (zero to 39 percent) numbers of afuerinos. Although it is important to note that the frequency distributions in the table do not reach the 0.1 level of significance, the results of the table do go in the expected direction. The Christian Democrats suffered heavy losses in exactly one-half of the "high-afuerino communes" with asentamientos (the second column in Table 12). In contrast, they lost heavily in only 27.5 percent of the other communes with asentamientos. These data, when viewed in conjunction with the earlier discussion of the rivalry between asentados and nonasentados, suggest that the land reform had driven at least some afuerinos from the Christian Democratic fold. Apparently as asentamientos were established, afuerinos came to realize that the reform institutions were designed to exclude them from access to the land. Or, if the afuerinos *were* able to gain access to the asentamientos, it was because they had struggled against the basic direction of government policy, probably with the aid of one of the opposition parties.

These conclusions, however, should be treated with considerable caution. The low significance levels in Table 12 suggest that many other factors, besides intraclass peasant rivalries, accounted for at least some of the PDC's electoral defeats. Frustrated expectations, variations in the quality of local CORA and INDAP officials, local and personal loyalties — all undoubtedly played a role. And the uncertainty generated by the transitional nature of the asentamientos may also have worked to the detriment of the Christian Democrats. These problems, unlike those fostered by intraclass rivalries, may be susceptible to management by a governing party. For it was in the asentamiento areas with few afuerinos that the Christian Democrats made their greatest gains (see the fourth column of Table 12). But the class basis of the party's selection process and the bitter competition among the peasants themselves also suggest that a limit exists to the support that can be acquired by any one party through the land reform process. Even if a governing party does make rural gains, it is likely to be faced with a relatively permanent challenge from opposition parties that gain support among other sectors of the peasantry, as well as from the cities themselves.

Opposition Gains and Losses in the 1967 Municipal Elections

All of the major opposition political groupings made gains in their national voting percentages in the 1967 elections. The FRAP's 1967 percentage of 32.1 among male voters represented an increase of 6.3 percent; the Radicals, with 16.5 percent, advanced 2.7 percentage points; while the right — presumably the weakest among male voters — went from 12.0 to 13.3 percent, a gain of 1.3 percentage points. The relative gains and losses of the three opposition blocs in the fifty-five asentamiento communes are shown in Table 13.

Table 13. Opposition gains and losses, 1965–1967, in fifty-five rural asentamiento communes[a]

Party	Gains	Even	Losses	Average percentage gains	Gains in national percentages
FRAP	20 (6.3+)	16 (0–6.2)	19	+3.6	+6.3
Right	30 (1.3+)	5 (0–1.2)	20	+1.0	+1.3
Radical	26 (2.7+)	13 (0–2.6)	16	+4.5	+2.7

[a] Numbers in parentheses are percentages.

The picture presented in Table 13 is complex. All of the opposition blocs appeared to exceed national gains in a substantial number of individual communes, with the right doing suprisingly well. Apparently, rural disaffection caused peasant voters to move in several different directions, with no clear pattern emerging. For example, it might have been expected that the FRAP would have gained heavily in the high afuerino areas, where the Christian Democrats tended to lose the most. Nevertheless, there was no relation between the FRAP's gains and losses and the "proletarian" communes, at least during 1965–1967. Only 45 percent of the FRAP's major gains came in communes which had over 40 per-

129

cent afuerinos in the rural labor force; 50 percent of the right's gains came in the same type of commune.

It is impossible to infer from this that tenure status had no relation to the direction of the vote. Although the FRAP did not make consistently heavy *gains* among afuerinos, there was a relation between its *absolute* percentages and the percentages of afuerinos in a commune.[29] While the numbers of proprietors in the asentamiento communes were too small to indicate their relation to the right and Radical vote, it is plausible to assume these parties found their greatest support within the propertied sector of the peasantry. The continuing strength of these two traditional groupings in the southern areas of Chile, where most small proprietors are concentrated, would lend support to this proposition. Possibly, as the reform is extended throughout Chile, the PDC may be expected to lose landless workers to the FRAP and some new proprietors to the right and the PR. At least in the short run, local personalities, traditional loyalties, and local issues apparently prevailed over class in determining the movement of the peasant vote toward the opposition parties.

Matching opposition gains and losses to the Christian Democratic vote itself brings out more interesting and more surprising patterns. In Table 14, the communes in which the opposition made

Table 14. Changes in the opposition vote in selected communes, compared with changes in the Christian Democratic vote, 1965–1967[a]

	FRAP		Right		Radicals	
Changes in the PDC vote	Gains (6.3+)	Losses	Gains (1.3+)	Losses	Gains (2.7+)	Losses
Gains	7 (35)	5 (26.3)	8 (26.7)	9 (45.0)	7 (26.9)	9 (56.3)
Moderate losses (0–6.0)	5 (25)	5 (26.3)	4 (13.3)	6 (30.0)	7 (26.9)	–
Heavy losses (6.0+)	8 (40)	9 (47.4)	18 (60.0)	5 (25.0)	12 (46.1)	7 (43.7)
	20	19	30	20	26	16

[a] Numbers in parentheses are percentages.

"heavy" gains (those which equaled or exceeded their national percentages) and those in which the opposition suffered losses are grouped according to changes in the Christian Democratic vote from 1965 through 1967.

As in almost all competitive multiparty systems, Chilean rural rivalry was highly complex. The opposition parties each took votes from the other, as well as from the Christian Democrats. In a substantial number of communes where the PDC suffered only moderate losses, the opposition groups either won heavily or lost. Nevertheless, Table 14 does suggest one interesting possibility: the most competitive relationship for the Christian Democrats was apparently with the right, rather than the left. Only 26.7 percent of the right's heavy gains came in communes where the PDC also made advances; 60 percent of its heavy gains were in communes where the PDC lost heavily. Conversely, where the Christian Democrats made gains, or where they suffered only moderate losses, the right tended to lose votes. Fifteen of the twenty communes in which the right lost ground were communes of this sort. In contrast, the left's gains and losses were evenly distributed and, if anything, the FRAP and the PDC appeared to gain and lose together. Only one-quarter of the FRAP losses came in areas where the PDC advanced; almost one-half of its losses came in areas where the PDC also lost heavily.

These results, like many of the others in this chapter, must be treated with caution. Because of the short time span, the relatively small number of communes involved in the analysis, and the use of communes themselves as the units of comparison, the data must be treated as suggestive, rather than conclusive. Nevertheless, the data are important if only because they indicate what was *not* happening in the Chilean countryside from 1965 through 1967. It is clear, for example, that the Christian Democrats and the left were not the only major contenders for the votes of the peasants when the reform process was getting under way. The right and the Radicals also made gains. And although some of the apparent drift back to the traditional groupings may have been only temporary, the durability of the patronage ties between landlord and peasant as well as the complementary interests of large and small landowners are factors which should not be underestimated.

More important, the data call into question the often-stated proposition that the success of the Christian Democratic land reform would mean a defeat for the left. The fact that in many communes both sectors increased their electoral support suggests that both stood to gain from the inroads made by expropriations into the traditional relationships between landlord and peasant. To be sure, it is possible that at later stages of the reform, when traditional ties are more thoroughly eroded, the left and the PDC might begin to seek votes from the other's supporters. At least between 1965 and 1967, however, both the Christian Democrats and the left were in a position to take votes from the other parties in the multiparty system, as well as from each other. There was thus a cooperative as well as a competitive relation between the two groups.

The Peasant Unions and Agrarian Reform:
The Local Struggle

Although the role of the asentamiento has thus far been the center of attention, an understanding of the general dynamics of rural change would be incomplete without an examination of the rural unionization process which accompanied the Christian Democratic land reform. The election of the new Christian Democratic government in 1964 opened the way for a radical intensification of the sporadic organizational efforts which had begun a decade earlier. Additional impetus to the unionization process was provided by the passage in 1967 of a new labor code which lifted the oppressive restrictions of earlier laws and provided both legal status and financing for the de facto organizations that had already emerged. According to the Ministry of Labor, by the end of 1967 over 40,000 peasants had been registered in legal unions.[30] Taking into account those who had not yet completed the legalization proceedings, the total number of unionized peasants may well have reached twice that number. In what ways did these unions complement and in what ways did they collide with the land reform efforts that were also under way?

The answers to these questions are complicated by the obvious consideration that not all of the new peasant unions were oriented toward the Christian Democracy. The Federation of Peasants and Indians (the FCI), formally founded in 1961, was affiliated with the FRAP-dominated Central Confederation of Workers (the CUT). The Communists and Socialists increased their efforts after the 1964 election, spurred on by the challenge of the PDC. The unions oriented toward the Christian Democracy, moreover, were divided among themselves. One sector of the PDC union movement grew out of a variety of small union organizations formed in the 1950s under the protection of liberal segments of the local and international Catholic hierarchy. Later on, considerable financial and technical aid came to these groups from public and private American sources, including the U.S. Central Intelligence Agency and the Agency for International Development. After 1964, the largest of these "Christian" unions merged to form the National Confederation of Peasants (the CNC). A second segment of the PDC peasant movement was organized by the leaders of INDAP, who, as we have seen, turned their efforts toward rural mobilization. INDAP unions became the bitter rivals of the CNC.

In spite of this heterogeneity, there is a certain sense in which reference may be made, at least initially, to the "union movement." In spite of their varying political orientations, the unions tended to resemble each other in both structure and social composition. At the organizational base of each sector of the union movement were locals, based in the various communes of the country. Such communal unions generally included workers from all strata of the rural lower class and of many different fundos; their total membership could range from one hundred to five hundred. Within a given province the communal unions were loosely grouped into provincial federations, whose leadership was drawn from the peasant leaders of the various locals. Provincial federations were, in turn, affiliated with one of the three major confederations — the FCI, the CNC, or the INDAP confederation — all of which tended to be dominated by men of rural, but middle class backgrounds.

Although ideology was clearly an important element of inter-union struggle at the national level, most observers agree that these considerations did not play a great role locally,[31] where political rivalries were based more on personality or power competition. Depending on local conditions, Marxist unions and Christian unions might cooperate or compete. Either might petition for expropriations, or strike for wages; and either might negotiate with

133

the landowners. In some respects, at both the local and the national levels the process of land reform presented the unions with a series of common problems and opportunities which did not depend on their political affiliations.

The temporary hegemony of one of these groups — the CNC — also simplifies an initial effort to generalize about the activities of the "peasant unions" during the early stages of the land reform. Of the 194 communal unions registered in the Ministry of Labor by the end of 1967, 60 listed their political affiliations. Thirty-two of these unions were registered with the CNC; 16 were listed as affiliates of the FCI; only 12 were INDAP associates. These data, of course, are quite fragmentary, and may tend to understate the actual strength of the FCI. In the provinces of Coquimbo and Curicó, where the FRAP was quite strong, the affiliations of the communal unions were not listed. Moreover, toward the end of Frei's term, the INDAP union, aided by its access to governmental resources, replaced the CNC as the largest union movement. Nevertheless, because of the clear financial advantages that the CNC enjoyed over the FRAP, and because of the head start it enjoyed over the INDAP unions, the CNC was far ahead in the organizational race until 1968 or 1969. Of the three union movements, the CNC was by far the most aggressive and the most successful in organizing wage strikes, which in 1966–67 sometimes involved as many as ten thousand peasants.[32] Their capacity to force communewide labor settlements rather than separate agreements from fundo to fundo showed a strength not yet attained by most of the urban unions and only approximated by the other peasant organizations. When one speaks of the union movement, therefore, it is impossible to ignore the central role played by the CNC.

None of this is to deny the significance of the differences within the union groupings or the importance of changes in the balance of power between them. All had considerable strength in certain areas, and in considering the political differences between the groups, the FRAP unions in particular deserve separate treatment, and will be discussed in Chapter 6. Here problems common to the union movement as a whole will be treated, with emphasis on those related to what was for most of Frei's term its largest single component — the CNC. All segments of the union movement — whether "Marxist" or "Christian" — viewed the redistribution of land as their most important single concern. All were active in the attempt to push the process along, through petitions, occasional land seizures, and demonstrations. At the same time, all of the unions were confronted with the task of reconciling this objective — of helping the peasants become landowners — with their other role as representatives of a landless, wage-earning rural class. At the local level the tension between these roles became especially important as the asentamientos were established. The principal issues were whether the unions would participate at all in the asentamientos; the sort of contributions the unions could make if they did participate; and the functions they would assume as the transitional period came to an end.

Their dual role suggests that the union structures were potentially capable of bridging the class cleavages that were accentuated in the process of selecting asentados. Possibly the unions could mitigate rural polarization between the afuerinos and the inquilinos by aggregating the interests of both. Early data gathered by the Ministry of Labor indicated that all of the unions included sizeable proportions of day laborers in their membership.[33] Presumably, in these cases, efforts to win higher wages for their constituents would tend to mitigate some of the exclusionary aspects of the land division process. In at least one case, the establishment of the asentamientos in the Choapa Valley (one of the first and largest areas of land reform), the local unions fought successfully for the inclusion of their constituents as beneficiaries of the reform.[34]

Yet caution must be exercised in drawing from this example the conclusion that the aggregating and brokerage role of the unions held true throughout the country. In areas with an excessive labor supply, union pressures for higher wages may well have induced employers to lay off their marginal workers or to avoid hiring additional ones. Clearly, the afuerinos, far more casually bound than the inquilinos to employment in a particular fundo, would in this situation be among the first to suffer. In at least some cases, unions attempted to *prevent* the hiring of new workers. One wage petition, written by the CNC in the province of Talca, asked that "outside personnel not be contracted, and in those areas where they must be hired, each one should be made to pay . . . ten escudos to go to the union committees on each fundo."[35] Thus, although in some

135

situations the unions may have acted as aggregators, in others the beneficiaries of their activity, like the beneficiaries of the land reform itself, were the inquilinos.

It is also important to note other points of conflict and cooperation between the unionization and the land reform processes. Whatever the types of peasant groups they represented, the unions were new and independent centers of power. As such, their interests and the aspirations of their leaders collided in many ways with the governmental reform apparatus, with the urban intellectuals who controlled this apparatus, and with the peasants on the asentamientos themselves. Some of these conflicts at the local level were noted in ICIRA's report on the position of the asentados toward union organizations:

With respect to syndicalization, the asentados have not defined themselves very clearly. All recognize that union participation was decisive in achieving the expropriation of some fundos where they worked as inquilinos . . . [But] in some areas the peasants fear that through the union, the occasional workers presently contracted by the asentamiento might gain the right to be incorporated into the asentamiento. In some asentamientos, unionism continues to play a role . . . In others it has lost its importance or it simply does not function, by the decision of the asentados themselves.[36]

These tensions should not, of course, obscure the importance of broad common interests and objectives which the unions sometimes shared with rival peasant and reformist groups. The capacity of the peasants to organize into unions, to present demands, and to create pressure for expropriations was clearly vital to any sustained reform process. Even after asentamientos were established, the unions sometimes assumed a complementary, rather than competitive, role. Union leaders became members of the asentamiento committees and chiefs of asentamiento. Union members were often the active and interested members of the asentamiento.

Another ICIRA study of two asentamientos in the Choapa regions, for example, found that the Marxist unions had performed precisely this role. From interviews of 75 (out of 279) asentados, the study made the following conclusions: (1) that peasants who participated in union activities were most likely to participate most actively in the running of the asentamiento; (2) that the syndicate acted as a communications belt for transmitting committee decisions to rank-and-file members of the asentamiento; and (3) that the union structures served as important checks against arbitrary exercise of authority by CORA officials or by asentamiento chiefs.[37]

Similar activities did not, however, pertain in all of the asentamientos throughout the country. In many, apparently, relations between local union leaders and the leaders of the asentamiento were as likely to be characterized by rivalry and tension as by cooperation. Interviews with union leaders at the national level — both Marxist and Christian Democrat — indicated that union organizers were often encouraged to stay away from the asentamientos and that, at times, they were even evicted from the settlement.[38] Among the persons interviewed, the consensus seemed to be that local relations between union leaders and asentamiento authorities could vary widely from region to region. In areas where the unions had built a strong local before the establishment of asentamientos, as in the Choapa Valley, relations were generally cooperative. In areas where unions had not yet been established and in areas where unions were weak, efforts to organize peasants were discouraged by local CORA officials.

It is difficult to go far beyond these broad generalities in discussing the local relations between the unions and the land reform institutions. What does seem clear is that the establishment of unions, like the establishment of asentamientos, generated tensions and cleavages, as well as support. Although the unionization and land reform processes were complementary in many important respects, they were competitive in others. Amorphous and ill-defined though this competition was at the local level, it constituted an important backdrop for a far clearer and potentially more dangerous power struggle at the national level, between the leaders of the CNC and the heads of the Christian Democratic reform agencies.

The CNC Leaders versus the Christian Democratic Left Wing: The Elite Struggle

At the national level, as in the countryside itself, much of the conflict revolved around who should control the reform. From the beginning of the reform effort it appeared that the CORA and

INDAP leaders intended to keep as much discretion as possible in their own hands. None of the leaders of the three national union movements was consulted about the drafting of the reform legislation. Although the unions were granted the opportunity to state their positions in the formal congressional hearings, they were unsuccessful in pressing for amendments that might have allowed them a greater voice in policy-making. For example, the leaders of the two reform organizations vetoed joint demands by the CNC and the FCI for legal representation on the CORA and INDAP governing boards, though even the SNA was entitled to one representative. Rather than coming from the unions themselves, peasant representatives were to be selected from among the asentados and the INDAP peasant committees, where presumably the CORA and INDAP leaders would have greater control. The "INDAP unions" were, not unexpectedly, somewhat less vociferous than the FCI and the CNC in demanding a voice in the reform process, but even they showed an occasional desire to establish their independence from the urban, middle class groups which controlled the reform administration. At a provincial peasant congress organized by INDAP in 1967, demands for a limit to the asentamiento period and for the establishment of individual parcels were pushed through against the wishes of the organizers of the congress.[39]

Although the leaders of all the unions shared in the rivalry with the reform administrators, it was the largest of the three, the CNC, which engaged in the most bitter competition. For obvious reasons the INDAP unions were in no position to take a consistently independent line. The FRAP unions conformed to the leftist politicians' desire to maintain a common front with the PDC left wing against opposition from the right. The leaders of the CNC, by contrast, had originally been recruited and were currently aided by Church and U.S. groups oriented toward the Christian Democracy but formally independent of the party itself. For the leaders of the Christian unions, the predominance of the CORA and INDAP in the reform process threatened their independence and their influence among the peasants; their battle with the Christian Democratic left wing, at first private and muted, became increasingly public and bitter.

Adding to the rivalry between the CNC and the CORA-INDAP

leaders were important social and ideological differences that tended to intensify the struggle. In a certain sense the rivalry reflected the cleavage between urban intellectuals, anxious to broaden the process of land reform into a reform of the larger society, and a more peasant-oriented elite, which viewed the reform as one among many steps that would aid their rural constituencies.[40] Although much of the CNC leadership came from the middle class and although INDAP and CORA had gained considerable support among the peasants, the CNC positions seemed more in accord with the pragmatic and immediate objectives attributed to peasants throughout the world than did the more abstract and idealistic concerns of the Christian Democratic left wing. The latter's willingness, for example, to leave open the possibility of collective property was vigorously opposed by the CNC leaders, who advocated the eventual establishment of individual parcels. From the point of view of making economic growth compatible with massive structural change, collectivization would appear reasonable enough. In view of the historic examples of peasant resistance to collectivization in the Communist world, however, the CNC's demand for individual parcels was probably an accurate reflection of the immediate aspirations of their peasant bases.

Deepening still further the cleavage between the Christian peasant movement and the reform administrators were quite different ideological conceptions of the role that the union movement should play in the process of reform. For the intellectuals in charge of the reform administration, the general process of peasant unionization had the express purpose of building a broad and unified base of support for a reformist or revolutionary elite. The leaders of the CNC responded to more pluralistic notions of unionism. Inspired in part by the example of American trade unions, and in part by the Church's reaction against the political ties of the Marxist movement, the CNC advocated unions that were not formally tied to any political party or subject to the paternalism of the government. Although their commitment to structural change as well as to higher wages remained strong, the CNC leaders viewed the ultimate objectives of both the land reform and the union movement as the achievement of the spontaneous and voluntary participation of the peasants themselves in modern society. For the CNC, many of the measures of state control that were proposed threatened "to lead to a real totalitarianism and to a denigration of the dignity of the campesino. He wants his own piece of land and the ability to work for himself. I think what these tecnicos want is a dictatorship run by themselves." [41]

These organizational, social, and ideological conflicts converged at a number of key points in the making of the PDC's agrarian policy. One such point was the process of unionization itself. CNC leaders lodged bitter protests over the INDAP's use of government funds to organize rival unions. Indeed, using government vehicles, credit, and other similar advantages, INDAP organizers had made some inroads into CNC areas, and had in some communal unions even succeeded in wresting control from the CNC.[42] Another such point was the framing of the new labor code, for which FRAP and PDC leftists advocated the formation of a unified movement that would have lumped together the Marxist and non-Marxist organizations and that would have given the government considerable control over policy and financing. CNC leaders vigorously protested these proposals, advocating instead union competition and automatic financing provisions that would have left the unions free from the threat of government control.

On those aspects of the land reform bill which tended to increase the actual or potential influence of CORA and to diminish their own, the reaction of the CNC leadership was equally vigorous. As we have seen, CNC leaders joined with their Marxist rivals in demanding representation on the councils of CORA and INDAP. Unlike their rivals, they also had serious reservations about the establishment of asentamientos. Although supporting the idea of a transitional period, CNC leaders were anxious to ensure that the period and the role of CORA would not be prolonged indefinitely. Accordingly, they joined with some PDC moderates and the right in an attempt to establish an absolute limit to the asentamiento period, after which the granting of titles of ownership would be compulsory. These efforts did not, of course, deter the CNC's strong general support for the reform effort or the reform bill; but it is noteworthy that one of the few criticisms of the bill by a PDC deputy within the Congress itself came from Deputy Emilio Lorenzini — one of the original organizers of the CNC. Referring to various provisions of the bill dealing with government controls over the formation of cooperatives, the sale by peasant beneficiaries of their land, and the asentamiento provisions, Lorenzini argued on the floor of the Chamber of Deputies, that unless changes were made "we can conclude that the peasants will never become landowners. We must make proprietors, dignify the peasant, and not leave him handed over to an institution in which he cannot resolve his problems." [43]

The CNC and the Christian Democratic Officialist Wing

In their bitter rivalry with the CORA and INDAP leaders, the leaders of the CNC found natural allies within the officialist sector of the PDC. Sharing with the government leaders a common ideological concern for a pluralistic reform movement and with the officialist deputies in the Congress a common antipathy to the left-wing leaders in charge of the reform, the CNC leadership frequently collaborated with the officialist wing. In the Minister of Labor, William Thayer, they found a strong supporter for their general efforts to organize for higher wages. The officialists' concern to achieve a greater equity for the expropriated landowners was, in turn, regarded sympathetically by the CNC leaders. The CNC and the officialists also coalesced around another common interest: meeting the competition from the FRAP. After winning large wage settlements of its own in Colchagua, for example, the CNC supported the Frei regime in its opposition to the still greater wage demands made by the FCI. The development of the pressures that eventually led to the defeat of the Marxist unions is described as follows by one observer:

. . . the [CNC] has been free in criticizing the government for moving too slowly in implementing agrarian reform . . . Nevertheless in the Colchagua strike, the [CNC] was forced to throw its full support behind the Frei regime by virtue of the fact that it could not afford to have its contract bettered by that of an opponent. On the other hand, however, there was another unlikely ally of the government, the landowners of Colchagua. Once again the converging interests resulting from a particular situation overcame the general atmosphere of mutual distrust.[44]

The alliance between the officialists and the largest peasant union against the intellectuals of CORA and INDAP and the

141

FRAP parallels similar alliances throughout Latin America, and it mirrors to some extent the larger urban-rural cleavage that the PDC faced in the electorate. Throughout the continent, the mobilization of peasant support for relatively moderate reformers has tended to outflank the urban intelligentsia, leaving them isolated and frustrated proponents of still more radical change. In the Venezuelan Democratic Action party, Romúlo Betancourt's strong hold over the peasant unions eventually drove the AD left wing into a desperate and unsuccessful guerrilla movement. The more recent failure of a guerrilla movement in Bolivia can probably also be ascribed to the links between the traditional peasant sectors and the older leadership of the Bolivian government.

These parallels, however, should not be carried too far. In Chile, unlike Venezuela and Bolivia, important factors limited the full development of such an alliance. Perhaps the most obvious was that the CNC probably could not hope to monopolize the peasants, any more than the land reform could be expected to allow the PDC to win the majority of votes in the countryside. CORA, INDAP, and the FRAP also enjoyed the support of significant segments of the rural lower class, and would continue to do so.

A more subtle but perhaps more important limitation was that neither the CNC leadership nor the officialists were fully committed to an alliance against the left wing. Although the officialists adopted a permissive posture toward union activities, they did not — like the Venezuelan leaders — take a direct hand in the organization process. CNC leaders, on the other hand, had been recruited under the sponsorship of Church and American organizations, rather than of the PDC itself. Dependent as it was on the officialist leaders for support and encouragement after 1964, the CNC nonetheless retained a strong interest in remaining formally independent from both wings of the party.

Perhaps the most important limitations on an officialist-CNC alliance were the commitments which the officialists had already made to the PDC left wing. The restrictions which these commitments placed on outside rightist groups tended to operate on the CNC leadership as well. The older party leaders could not accede to CNC demands for a voice in the land reform process without jeopardizing the allegiance that they had won from the left wing on other issues. Instead of a full CNC-officialist alliance which squeezed out the CORA-INDAP leaders, the Christian Democracy contained an uneasy triangular relationship among the three sets of leaders.

On matters relating to union (rather than reform) policy, the CNC generally prevailed over the party left wing. The new rural labor code was, for example, regarded by the CNC as a triumph. As presented to and passed by the Congress, it made possible the existence of competing and autonomous union structures, rather than the unified mass organization that the PDC left wing and the FRAP had demanded.

On matters relating directly to land reform, however, the CNC remained at the periphery of decision-making. The union was only partially successful, for example, in its efforts to establish a maximum time limit for the asentamiento period. The five-year period finally introduced in the law was far too long to be satisfactory to the CNC leaders. It meant that most asentamientos could be extended beyond 1970, when the FRAP or the PDC left wing, rather than the officialists, might control the reins of government. On other issues of collectivization, state controls, and the establishment of cooperatives, the CNC leaders enjoyed almost no success, in spite of the fact that they generally had the support of the officialists in the Congress and even of the SNA. Whatever role the CNC might play in wage policy, in getting out the vote, or in strike activities, the prospects for a large union voice in the land reform itself appeared dim.

For a time the balance between the three Christian Democratic groups seemed fairly durable. But the struggle that had developed between the CNC and the left wing over the control of the reform process and the reservations which kept the CNC from consolidating an alliance with the officialists remained difficult problems for both the Christian unions and for the Christian Democratic movement as a whole. Of the three groups, the CNC was in the greatest immediate danger, for the officialists' unwillingness to challenge the left-wingers' control over CORA and INDAP placed the Christian unions at a competitive disadvantage in the race to enlist members. Without full support from the Christian Democratic officialists over matters of agrarian policy, the CNC faced serious difficulties in maintaining and extending its organization.

The difficulties of the CNC, in turn, had important consequences for the Christian Democratic party as a whole. For one thing, they raised the question of whether the party could sustain its peasant base during periods when it would be out of office. As long as the Christian Democrats held governmental power, INDAP could be used in the place of the CNC as a vehicle for mobilizing rural support. This meant, however, that the party would rely almost solely on governmental resources, rather than on its own efforts, to create a union structure. Presumably many of the peasant recipients of such resources would be inclined to support any party that controlled the government, rather than the Christian Democrats themselves.

Finally, and most important from the point of view of our analysis, the divisions within the party's organizational base limited the internal political resources on which the Christian Democrats could draw during Frei's tenure in office. To be sure, the various Christian Democratic factions held together longer than had initially been expected. And the organization of a non-Marxist rural union movement, even with all of its fissures, increased the party's leverage in dealing with social and political forces operating outside the party framework. Yet this leverage alone was clearly not enough to ensure the Christian Democrats' continuation in office or the successful execution of an agrarian reform. The party had not been able to prevent a defection of its urban base of support; its electoral appeal in the countryside was limited; and it had not been entirely successful in integrating its organized support into the party framework. Although the Christian Democratic party was sufficiently strong and unified to establish the *terms* of debate over land reform, the *outcome* of this debate depended on the moderation and cooperation of other elements within the multiparty system. It is to this aspect of the politics of land reform — the reactions of the rightist and Marxist groups to the Christian Democratic effort — that we turn in the following chapters.

Part 3   Strategies of Opposition: Vertical Brokerage and the Maintenance of the Reform Coalition, 1964–1967

Chapter 5 The Right and the Christian Democratic Reform

Landowners react negatively to land reforms. But the nature of their reaction will vary with the options provided by the alignment of social forces and with the way conservative groups perceive these options. In revolutionary situations, landowners have had to choose between raising white armies and fleeing the country. In situations short of revolution, they may also be faced with disparate choices. An appeal to the military establishment and to the urban upper class appears to be the most prevalent mode of behavior throughout most of Latin America. At the local level the gendarmerie is called upon to quell peasant movements and to jail their organizers. At the national level the reaction is often to levy charges of Communism against a reform government, to rally other conservative social groups by raising the specter of disorder, and to conspire with sympathetic middle class military cliques. When the most likely and immediate alternative to reform appears to be revolution, landowners may conceivably feel impelled to accept a reform process as the lesser evil.

Although the ideological concessions of the Alessandri period had induced most Chilean rightist elements to profess their acceptance of rural change, they were virtually unanimous in their opposition to the Christian Democratic measures presented after 1964. Rational choices about the most effective *forms* of opposition were, however, far from obvious, and on this subject there was no unanimity. With the possible exceptions of the elections of 1920 and 1939, when new middle class groups first came into office, there was probably no period in Chilean history when the options of the landowners appeared as ambiguous as they did during Frei's term of office. For the landowners the election of the Christian Democrats posed a number of difficult strategic questions: What was the intention of the new government? Could this government be counted on to control the process of rural change once it was under way? Would a hard line of opposition draw other social groups to the defense of the landowners, or would it only hasten

147

the revolution? The nature of the rightist opposition was to depend heavily on the answers the conservatives were inclined to give to these questions.

At one level of analysis, the post-1964 situation appeared to reduce the chances for a successful hard-line defense of conservative interests. The representation of the rightist parties in the legislature had been sharply reduced. The immediate alternative to the moderate Christian Democratic government appeared to be the far more radical Christian Democratic left wing or the Marxist parties themselves. The repudiation of the right at the polls, the massive victory of the Christian Democrats, the growing dissatisfaction of urban and rural sectors of the society, all suggested that the landed elite had become isolated and weak and that the most rational way to defend landed interests was to move with the tide — moderating and channeling the process of change, rather than disrupting or blocking it.

This line had been advanced by Liberal and Conservative leaders before 1964. It was not, however, the only course of action open to landowning groups. Another set of possibilities lay in exploiting the organizational weakness of the pro-reform parties, in the intensified use of nonconstitutional resources, and in the effort to increase contacts between the landowners and various urban power groups. Between 1964 and 1967, peasant electoral support for the FRAP and the Christian Democracy had not been fully translated into organizational strength, and support for agrarian reform by urban unions was weak and uncertain. Meanwhile the urban and rural sectors of the upper class remained the most powerful economic forces in the society, controlling most of its wealth and capable of bringing a variety of pressures to bear on any political regime. By encouraging a polarization of political and social forces, rightist groups could reasonably hope that they, rather than the left, would win. Though such a strategy risked revolution, it held out the hope of forcing the PDC government to back down or, failing that, of replacing it by a more conservative civil or military regime.

In the fluid and shifting political context, much depended on the way landowners defined the Chilean "reality," and the ambiguity of this reality led, in fact, to several lines of opposition to land reform. Some conservative individuals, both inside and outside the major party and pressure group organizations, argued that landowning interests could no longer be defended primarily through normal electoral or lobbying techniques. To survive, the landowners would have to change the rules of the game, moving toward broader and more explosive forms of opposition. As in the Alessandri period, however, the leaders of the rightist parties and of the National Society of Agriculture (the Sociedad Nacional de Agricultura, SNA) tended to define their options in terms of the special resources and forms of access available to their organizations. Rightist party leaders, convinced that their earlier moderation had not led to satisfactory results, moved toward a harder line of opposition in the hope of attracting conservative electoral support. Leaders of the SNA moved in the opposite direction, moderating the SNA position in order to exploit the more limited channels of access then available within the Christian Democratic party. It is in the context of the debate within and between these various organizations that the complex behavior of the conservative opposition as a whole can best be understood.

The Interest Group Approach:
The SNA and Land Reform

During the first half of Frei's term, between 1964 and 1967, the National Society of Agriculture replaced the rightist parties as the leading representative of landed interests. The parties had received what many observers (mistakenly) believed was a death blow in the 1965 congressional elections, which reduced the right's congressional representation from forty-five seats to nine in the Chamber of Deputies and from thirteen seats to seven in the senate. Disorganized and confused by the sudden collapse of electoral support and congressional representation, party leaders perforce found it necessary to spend much of their time picking up the pieces, analyzing their mistakes, and debating about how to recoup their losses. The SNA was thus almost by default cast into a leadership role within rightist circles. To understand the manner in which the Society adjusted to this role, it is necessary to look briefly at its earlier relation to the political system and to the changes in this relationship that had occurred before the elections of 1964 and 1965.

149

Like the rightist parties, the SNA had emerged from the informal patterns of upper class rule that predominated in Chile during the nineteenth and early twentieth centuries. Historically, the Society was a faction of the aristocracy — a channel through which large, Central Valley landowners could gain special favors from governmental authorities and an arena in which individual aristocrats could advance their political careers. In contrast to the relatively autonomous associational interest groups of the United States and Western Europe, the SNA was intimately linked to other structures of power. Leadership roles within the SNA corresponded closely with governmental and party roles and with private positions of social power outside the formal, constitutional structures. Representatives of the SNA sat on governmental boards and filled positions within the executive branch. SNA leaders, or members of their family, or personal friends, were also leaders of the Liberal and Conservative parties. In collaboration with these parties and with other, lesser, landowning interest groups, the Society had enjoyed almost unchallenged power to block programs deemed repugnant by its leaders.

Well before 1964, however, the Society had developed into something more than a loosely structured veto group. Although the traditional patterns of behavior described above continued to predominate, the Society's need to operate within the relatively competitive urban world of twentieth century Chile induced certain countercurrents of action. These were accentuated after the election of the Christian Democrats and do much to explain the SNA's moderate response to the Christian Democratic effort at land reform. In the first place, with the rise of middle sector governments in the 1930s and 1940s, the SNA's ties to the central authorities tended to become more distant and less diffuse than in earlier decades. To be sure, on major questions concerning the rural social structure, the Society could not be challenged. But on less basic issues, concerning such matters as prices, credits, and taxes, the SNA was forced to compete with new groups emerging within the urban sphere and to supplement its traditional sources of influence with resources characteristic of interest groups in more developed countries. It tried to get along with governmental authorities by avoiding unreasonable demands and needlessly antagonistic postures. It sought compromises in cases of disagreement, and it developed a willingness to accept marginal defeats gracefully. Channels of access were sought where the chances to influence governmental decisions seemed most favorable.

A second trend, accompanying the adoption of a relatively pragmatic style in dealing with governmental authorities, was toward a greater organizational complexity within the SNA. During the 1950s and 1960s, the Society's leaders attempted to broaden the base of the SNA by considering the interests of regional as well as Central Valley farmers, by expanding its extension services, and by increasing technical studies designed to serve the needs of specialized producers. More attention was also paid to the problem of strengthening internal lines of authority and of formalizing and extending internal lines of communication. As a response to the FEDAGRI challenge of 1961, for example, the presidents of the specialized producers' associations had been incorporated into the SNA council. In 1963 a second vice presidency was created, to serve as a liaison office between the national leadership and the local agricultural organizations. In the early part of 1965, shortly after the election of the Christian Democrats, the presidency of the Society was transformed from a voluntary post filled by leading Central Valley landowners into a full-time, paid position.

Finally, during the late 1950s and early 1960s, a newer generation of professional men and agricultural experts were recruited into administrative positions within the Society. These men often worked full-time on the Society's technical and extension staffs and on the SNA journal, *El Campesino*; although they usually came from prominent aristocratic families, they adopted a relatively progressive orientation toward various questions of management-worker relations and toward newer production techniques. This tended to distinguish them from many of the older, more traditional agriculturalists who sat on the Society's general council. Luís Larraín, the president of the SNA between 1965 and 1967, was a good example of this more progressive type of individual. In the 1950s, Larraín had been a director of the Institute for Rural Education (IER), a Catholic organization devoted to the recruitment and training of peasant community leaders and, incidentally, a spawning ground for the Christian unions that emerged after 1964. In 1960–1962 he had served as the Chilean delegate to the

Latin American Common Market. In 1963 he became a vice president of the Society, and in 1965 he was elected to the presidency.

The electoral victories of the Christian Democracy caused the SNA to elaborate even further its interest group approach. For with a new reformist party in office and with their Liberal and Conservative allies reduced to a fraction of their former strength, the Society's leaders could no longer rely on their quasi-corporate links to governmental agencies or on their diffuse ties to governmental leaders to ensure a veto over policy. As never before, after 1964 the Society's influence within the system depended on the more limited resources available to normal lobby groups—strength of organization, command of technical skills and information, and the deployment of specialized personnel in positions designed to maximize access to governmental decision-makers. An account of Larraín's rise to the presidency of the Society illustrates the importance attached to such resources.

Shortly after Frei's victory in 1964, Victor Braun, then the president of the Society, held a meeting with Hugo Trevelli, the new Minister of Agriculture, to discuss the new government's program for land reform. Though little was apparently said in the meeting that the PDC had not reiterated many times before, the general proposals so alarmed the old SNA leaders that a strongly worded memorandum was circulated among the membership, harshly criticizing Trevelli, the government, and the reform plans. Relations with the new government, which were already strained, were virtually broken off.

To many members of the SNA council, however, the lack of communication with the new government made for an intolerable situation and considerable pressure built up within the organization for the resignation of the old officers. Attempts were first made to preserve a facade of continuity within the organization. Formal control of the Society was to remain in the hands of the old leaders, while the actual job of policy-making and of lobbying would be left to the first vice-president, then Luís Larraín, whose moderate views permitted him a more sympathetic audience within the Christian Democracy. This compromise arrangement was bound to be only temporary, and many of Larraín's active supporters within the council were still unsatisfied. One supporter, Aníbal Correa, the editor of the SNA monthly journal, published an open letter of protest calling for a more definitive solution to the problem of leadership. Correa pointed out that while the old directorate had served its purpose,

the times are now different and we, as a pressure group organization, have virtually no communication with the government . . . the current directorate is undoubtedly in a situation in which there is no clear and legitimate possibility of an understanding with the government. We know that [agrarian reform] signifies a profound transformation of the present structures, but in the SNA we have not been able to determine, for lack of contacts and information, in what form this step will be applied or proposed to the Congress.[1]

In April 1965 the Society's council acceded to this argument, electing an entirely new slate of officers. Not only was Larraín elected president, but the two vice presidential posts were filled by men of similar background. The first vice-president, Tomas Voticky, was only thirty-four years old at the time, a teacher at Catholic University, and a past president of a producers' association. The second, Gilberto Fuenzalida, forty-four years of age, had been active in student politics, was a teacher at Catholic University, and was currently serving as vice-president of the National Association of Wine Growers. The Christian Democratic government was quick to note and approve this change in leadership. As one editorial in the official government newspaper put it:

We previously criticized the closed attitude that had been adopted by the past directorate of the SNA toward all dialogue with the Executive . . . the new directorate . . . is free from these past criticisms . . . the point of view of the new directorate reflects an ample understanding of the historic moment in which the country is living . . . In not opposing these inevitable changes, but on the contrary, in collaborating with their execution, the farmers are demonstrating a valuable understanding of national necessities at a critical point . . .[2]

But the power struggle had by no means been completely resolved. The new officers continued to be answerable to a general council composed of many men who had opposed their election and of others who had supported them only tentatively. Shortly after the passage of the land reform law, dissent again emerged within the council, leading to the 1967 ouster of the officers elected in 1965. However, the election of the new officers in 1965 indicated the importance the broader leadership attached to the need to moderate their demands in order to retain their links with the government and to strengthen internal lines of authority in order to bargain more effectively. These steps followed a standard mode of operation which had already gained currency within the Society, and they permitted Larraín to act with great flexibility during the two-year course of his presidency. Thus, from 1965 to 1967 Larraín was able to extend considerably the concessions that had already been made on the subject of land reform and to use the machinery of the organization to silence more extreme dissidence both inside and outside the Society.

The SNA Strategy: A Moderation of Demands

From the beginning of Larraín's presidency the SNA tried to limit conflict with the Christian Democrats as much as possible. SNA declarations praised government efforts to increase agricultural prices; the Society's officers intervened in labor disputes and urged its membership to accept the new rural unions as legitimate bargaining agents. Although the Society was sharply critical of the new land reform bill, its leaders argued that agrarian reform was only one of many problems and possibilities facing the landed class. "It is an error to believe that the agrarian reform law will close, for good or ill, the door to agricultural problems," argued an editorial in the SNA's monthly journal. "The future will bring many surprises." [3] For this reason, the editorial continued,

our concern is concentrated not only on seeking improvements in the agrarian reform bill, but it is also designed to incite our farmers to an advanced and clear position, conscious of their duties to the rest of the rural collectivity . . . There is only one way that agriculture can avoid in the future the repetition of today's confusion: that is to prove to the country that the entrepreneur is the most qualified to make the land produce more. [4]

154

Underlying both the effort to stress agreement in other areas and the debate over the land reform bill was a set of assumptions that was described as follows by one of Larraín's close associates:

With a single party controlling both the executive and the congress, we can do little more than defend ourselves through the strength of our arguments. Our objections must be accompanied by proposals for modifications that are based on the Government's own general principles and that will attract the people within the Government who are willing to listen to us.[5]

Under Larraín's leadership the SNA became associated with a strategy of opposition resting on acceptance of the radical reduction in the right's political strength and on the assumption that landowners were becoming increasingly isolated from other social groups. Given this weakness, it was argued, the most rational course was to search for allies within the governing party itself — among Christian Democratic landowners, industrialists, and politicians — who might be inclined to listen sympathetically to SNA proposals which were not incompatible with the basic goals of the reform. At the same time, landowners should not succumb to fear and insecurity that might lead them to neglect production. Attempts should be made to rationalize management and increase investment. There should be a strict compliance with all social legislation, and efforts should be made where possible to go beyond such legislation in raising the wages and living standards of the rural workers.

By recognizing the limitations of the landowners' strength, by seeking allies within the government, and by reducing the level of open conflict, Larraín hoped to maximize the Society's remaining assets and to retain some influence in the process of change. Under such circumstances the SNA's command of funds and technical information could be used to offset its lack of broad popular support and add considerable force to its arguments within government offices. As a supplement to this approach, the news media might be used to present the landowners' case to the urban middle class, and the bargaining strength left to the Liberals and Conservatives in the Congress might be used to provide some muscle to the efforts at persuasion. But attempts to mobilize economic

155

or political pressures *against* the government would, it was felt, be counterproductive. Labor disputes, falling production, and categorical condemnations of land reform would only discourage moderates within the government and the middle class and would encourage more radical elements to turn the reform into a crusade against all members of the rural elite.

This general approach did not, of course, preclude SNA efforts to preserve the appearance of a united front with nonagricultural sectors of the upper class. For example, the Society argued that the land reform was a potential danger to urban as well as to rural property, and it consistently implied that food shortages resulting from the reform would harm the middle class as a whole. Nevertheless, the overall orientation of the SNA to the proposed Christian Democratic reform bill reflected the moderate strategy described above. Unlike other sectors of the opposition, Larraín and other SNA leaders scrupulously avoided inflammatory language and categorical condemnations of the government itself. The basically democratic orientation of Frei and other top Christian Democratic leaders was not questioned.[6] Moreover, although the Society strongly opposed various aspects of the reform law, most of its criticisms implied an acceptance of the basic assumptions of the bill and centered primarily on increasing the landowners' security within the general framework established by the Christian Democrats.

This can be seen clearly in Larraín's treatment of the provision which guaranteed to all reasonably efficient landowners the right to reserve the value equivalent of eighty hectares of agricultural land in Santiago province. Although Larraín objected bitterly to the way in which reserve lands would be determined and adjudicated, he did not challenge the provision itself. The conversion tables setting forth the amounts of land in various parts of the country that would be considered the equivalent of the eighty-hectare limit were viewed as inaccurate and unjust. The landowners, it was argued, had no protection in the selection of the portion of their land they would be permitted to keep. In many important instances, Larraín complained, decisions of the special local courts could not be appealed, even to the special appellate courts established in the land reform legislation itself.[7] Yet the idea of imposing an eighty-hectare limit on the amount of land that could be guaranteed to any proprietor was left unchallenged. As one leading SNA official stated in a private interview, "We are not really objecting to the limit of eighty basic hectares. The condition of payment for what is expropriated is of course important to us. But what we really want is to make sure that the efficient proprietor can keep, with security, the reserve land that is due him under the law." [8]

Similarly, important tacit concessions were implied in SNA's complaints about the provisions which would entitle an "exceptionally efficient" landowner to retain 320 rather than only 80 hectares of land. SNA officials argued that the criteria governing the identification of exceptionally efficient landowners were excessively vague, and in some instances unreasonable. It was pointed out that minor infractions of existing social security legislation or unrealistic provisions about the amount of land that had to be under cultivation would disqualify almost all landowners from being protected by the law. What was needed, according to Larraín, was a more exhaustive definition of efficiency, based on a detailed point system that would take into account both the quality of management and the social welfare of laborers.[9] No objection was made, on the other hand, to payment in bonds for property expropriated because of size or location. Nor was there any strong insistence that land be paid for at its commercial value. On this section of the bill, as on most others, SNA statements were as interesting for what they did *not* say as for what was actually stated.

Serious objections could, of course, still be raised to many of the criticisms that *were* made by the Society. In many instances the apparently harsh provisions of the bill attacked by the Society were designed to avoid legal obstacles that might be employed by landowners to slow the agrarian reform to a halt. Moderate though they were, SNA leaders such as Larraín were far from being in agreement with the Christian Democratic proposals. Yet few of the modifications which the SNA demanded — refinements in the conversion tables, improvements in the special courts system, or more precise definitions of efficiency — appeared seriously to jeopardize the government's flexibility in the expropriation of land. And while SNA leaders differed seriously with the government over the *degree* of security to which existing landowners were entitled, both sides agreed that some security was necessary if serious declines in agricultural production were to be avoided. In short, SNA criticisms of the Christian Democratic bill tended to be limited, reasonable, and directed primarily toward winning allies among those sectors of the Christian Democracy which "really wanted agrarian reform." SNA leaders had by no means abandoned the landowners' cause, but their strategy of opposition was clearly directed toward restraining conservatives as well as representing them.

The Independent Landowners

Although there was considerable opposition to Larraín's approach within the SNA itself, the most bitter opponents of the "soft line" came from the groups formerly associated with the FEDAGRI challenge — the directorate of the Consortium of Agricultural Societies of the South (CAS), men associated with the producers' associations, and various political independents who had formerly supported Ibañez and currently supported the heir to Ibañez's authoritarian personalist appeal, Jorge Prat.[10] From informal but extensive interviews with ten such individuals, it is clear that they rejected not only the role that was being played by the SNA, but also most of the assumptions behind Larraín's approach.

The chief tactical point of disagreement between this group and the SNA seemed to be whether the cultivation of allies within the Christian Democracy was worth the tacit concessions made by the SNA. Unlike the SNA, almost all the independents refused to accept the idea that the size of a property, rather than its efficiency, should be a criterion for expropriation: "The SNA position is that we should not make an issue of the 80 hectare maximum, but this is absurd. If a property is not farmed efficiently, let it be expropriated. But if it is efficient, it should be left in peace no matter what its size." [11]

Almost all members of the group also objected strongly to the SNA tactic of bargaining with the government behind closed doors. As another independent put it: "They think that they are shrewd puppeteers and that, by pulling strings, they can manage politics like a puppet show. Actually Frei has made vague promises, and then the Christian Democrats have turned around and done what they want about agrarian reform. It is the government that is fooling them and not the other way around." [12]

As the basis for these criticisms the independents offered three broader challenges to the SNA's role as the major representative of the landowners. First, behind their objections to the lobbying activities of the Society was a basic mistrust of the motives of the institution and of the type of people it represented. Leaders of the CAS, for example, who represented smaller, more commercial farmers in the south-central regions, had long been suspicious of the Central Valley "aristocrats" within the SNA. For the CAS, the SNA's efforts to amend the legislation would benefit only the rich and influential landowners, while the "real" farmers would still be left to suffer from arbitrary administrative decisions. "The SNA," argued one CAS leader, "is composed of politicians and not true farmers, they are using land for real estate, not for purposes of production, but they can be moderate because they think they will be able to escape the application of the agrarian reform." [13]

Second, many felt that SNA attempts to gain marginal concessions in the law were pointless, because the government would not be able to control the process of change once it had gotten under way. Whether or not the PDC officialists were sincere in their assurances that efficient proprietors would be protected, rising expectations in the countryside and political pressures from the PDC left wing would force the government to ignore any restraints that were actually written into the law. "Legal concessions," stated one critic of the SNA, "will probably not make much difference one way or the other. Politically, the Christian Democrats must move to the left, because they must outbid the FRAP for popular support." [14]

Finally, the independents tended to reject the SNA's assumption that hard-line resistance could lead only to a more massive reform, arguing that, on the contrary, the landowners would face peaceful but certain destruction if they failed to stand firm. Existing landowners would be deprived of their land without full compensation, while collectives would be established in the countryside under the euphemism of "communitarian property." Efforts to cultivate allies within the government would only blur this threat. On the other hand, by charging openly that there were Marxists within the PDC and by terming the government's program a totalitarian threat to liberty, allies could be rallied from sectors which appeared timid or neutral. Although there were obvious risks in this approach, few of the persons interviewed took seriously the threat of a FRAP victory. Several even claimed that they would welcome it as a means of drawing the battle lines more clearly. "If the FRAP had won in 1964," one volunteeered, "the only way we could have moved into a Marxist society is through civil war. Frei may do it peacefully. At least if the FRAP had won, the issues would have been clearer and the lines would have been more firmly drawn." [15]

The Role of the Urban Neutrals

The large urban property owners and the military were the "urban neutrals" most likely to be drawn into a battle of this sort against the PDC; and on the surface, the chances that their support could be attracted by a hard-line appeal seemed dim. Through 1967, neither had been major participants in the reform controversy, and both showed a clear reluctance to be mobilized into the arena of struggle. Leaders of the major industrial pressure groups had taken no public position on the land reform bill and had made only rare and cautious public criticisms of the constitutional reform proposals. The military had remained even more strictly neutral. Chilean officers had many years ago ceased to speak out in public on political issues that did not directly concern them, and none exerted the kind of day-to-day pressure that characterizes military behavior in other Latin American countries. Yet directly or indirectly, both were forces to be reckoned with by the Frei government, and both were prospective allies of the landowning opposition.

Industrialists, of course, operated in the political arena with far fewer restraints than did the military, and of the two sectors they were the landowners' most likely immediate source of support. Although there were exceptions to this rule, most large urban proprietors viewed the land reform as a threat to private property and to free enterprise, and many were fearful that they would be the next to suffer the burden of expropriations or property redistribution. One survey of 138 factory owners found that "less than one-fourth . . . were in favor of 'the government having powers to expropriate *latifundia*.' " [16] Informal interviews with the leaders of the Society for Factory Development (Sociedad de Fomento Fabril, SFF) indicated even stronger reservations about the proposed reform bills and about the SNA's methods of opposing them. "You can't work by agreeing basically and then trying to get minor change through private negotiations," one stated. "The thing to do is to defend private enterprise, without all these divisions between efficient and inefficient proprietors. That is not the real issue." [17]

The fact that these views were generally not stated publicly supported to a certain degree the SNA's assumption that the landed elite was becoming progressively isolated from the urban upper class. If urban proprietors were inclined to preserve their own status by staying on the sidelines of the reform struggle, then efforts to win their support did not warrant steps risking the landowners' loss of access to the government itself. But the private opinions of these urban proprietors did indicate that the assumption that the urban upper class would *remain* neutral was at least in part a self-fulfilling prophecy. In a situation in which these groups might feel impelled to take sides, there was little question where their support would go. By publicly condemning the reform, by complaining about the insecurity it brought with it, and by contributing organizational and economic resources to the landed opposition, these allies would be formidable indeed.

The possibility of military involvement on behalf of the landed opposition was far more remote. Only a few of the persons interviewed gave evidence of counting on this possibility in the immediate future. Nevertheless, a more active role for the Chilean military was not to be discounted entirely. Like similar social forces elsewhere in Latin America, the Chilean armed forces were well-organized and well-financed and commanded a large percentage of the Chilean budget. Like their brother officers in the larger Latin American countries, the Chilean officer corps was drawn from middle and upper middle class groups that were generally uneasy about large-scale mass mobilization and about the prospects of political disorder. In spite of its much vaunted professionalism, moreover, the Chilean military was not a stranger to plots and conspiracies. Military activity had resulted in coups in the 1920s and 1930s, and it persisted in some measure through the 1950s, when cliques of junior officers exerted strong pressures on the second Ibañez regime.[18]

In any event, plotting between the military and conservative civilians is only one of the factors that have made for military interventions in Latin America. Another, perhaps more important, factor has been the institutional vacuum left by the lack of strong party and governmental organizations capable of channeling or restraining the action of other social groups. Military interventions are as much the result as the cause of weak civilian political orders.[19] They may be viewed as "a response to the escalation of social conflict by several groups and parties coupled with the decline in the effectiveness and legitimacy of whatever political institutions may exist." [20]

Even though the independents stopped short of actual conspiracy, they were nonetheless willing to promote conditions of this sort in Chile. By advocating producers' strikes, by levying an all-out public attack upon the government, by ignoring the threat of retaliatory measures by opposing groups, the independents could hope to escalate conflict to the point that the Chilean officers would be drawn in in spite of themselves. As one of the independents interviewed put the matter, "We are moving into an institutional crisis, in which eventually the military may have to step in and take over. The real question is whether they would intervene on behalf of the right or the left. I think it would be the former." [21]

The SNA and the Coordinating Committee

During the debate over the land reform law, the most concerted effort to challenge the SNA's leadership and to press for a hardline, rather than a flexible opposition to the Christian Democrats, came with the formation of the Coordinating Committee of Agricultural Associations in October 1965. Its function was originally conceived as one of uniting the various regional and national associations, and there is no evidence whatsoever that it acted with conspiratorial intent. Nevertheless, its activities during 1965 and 1966 exemplify the tendency toward polarization that was implicit in the assumptions of some of the independents, while Larraín's effort to restrain this tendency is a good illustration of the manner in which the SNA's resources were used to dampen the conflict over land reform.

As the leading agricultural pressure group, the SNA joined in the formation of the Coordinating Committee. But control of the new organization quickly fell into the hands of the Society's most bitter critics. Along with the SNA, the constituent organizations included the CAS, the Society of the North, and various local associations, all of them responsive to the hard-line position of the independent landowners. Less visible, but with considerable influence in the Committee's formation, were rightist and radical politicians, who for reasons which shall be explained subsequently, had moved closer to the hard-line position themselves. Over the objection of Larraín, the man chosen to lead the Committee was Pedro Enrique Alfonso, a former Radical who currently headed the northern association.

The divergence between the Committee's approach and that taken by the SNA was apparent from the beginning. Whereas SNA editorials consistently argued that the landowners must win support by improving working conditions and by increasing production, Alfonso's first public statement asserted that private rural investment was impossible, as long as the government persisted in its plans for land reform and permitted general labor unrest. In contrast to the guarded criticisms made by Larraín in his own press conferences, the declaration which announced the formation of the Coordinating Committee warned that "even in democratic [i.e., PDC] sectors, there exist clear infiltrations of a totalitarian character that [tend] to subject agricultural activity to forms of collective exploitation and absolute state control . . ." [22]

The attack hardened after the text of the reform bill was published in November 1965. The general charge of totalitarian activity turned into a specific attack on the Institute of Agricultural Development (INDAP) and its head, Jacques Chonchol. "There is," complained the Committee, "a real technique of agitation in the countryside promoted by administrative functionaries." [23] "This agitation had been carried out by INDAP and other functionaries that are undubitably acting without the knowledge of those who have the over-all direction of the government." [24] Charges were also made that Chonchol was an "international agent," a "Marxist," and one of the leading figures in the Cuban agrarian revolution. Relations between the Committee and the government, which were bad from the outset, deteriorated completely during November and December. As Larraín had feared, Christian Democrats drew together to defend Chonchol. Officialists as well as left-wingers attended a series of public assemblies on Chonchol's behalf, and the president of the PDC, Patricio Aylwin — a major spokesman of the PDC moderates — engaged Alfonso in a bitter public polemic over INDAP's activities.

A number of other events charged the atmosphere further in the months following the introduction of the agrarian reform bill. In the Congress, the rightist senators — in the hope of gaining concessions on the constitutional reform — joined the Radicals and the FRAP in voting against key provisions of the government copper program; and both bills remained stalemated for several months in the Congress. In the fall of 1965 and the winter of 1966 the prolonged strikes in the copper mines accentuated the conflict. Considerably less serious, but adding to the tensions, were charges from the rightist press that the left was making "guerrilla strikes" and from the Communist press that the landowners were preparing for a coup d'état.

In March 1966, a meeting of the Committee's directors was held to assess the general situation. It was evidently at this point that the radical opposition decided to mount its most serious attack. Larraín's attempt to gain concessions from the government through negotiations, it was argued, had proven fruitless, and henceforth opposition would be conducted not through "trade association methods . . . but by political means." [25] Although the precise outlines of a "political" opposition were not spelled out, they apparently included efforts to organize regional demonstrations and rallies against the land reform, increased contacts with the business community, and the threat of producers' strikes.[26] The commitment to conduct an all-out opposition to the government became evident at the conclusion of the press conference held by the Committee's chairman, Pedro Alfonso. In some of the most provocative language that had been used in the public debate, Alfonso characterized the Frei regime as a "totalitarian government that represents the will of a single party . . . It is precipitating Chile toward Communism and will end in an abyss that will provoke disaster for the country . . . it has created a great political machine managed by Mr. Trevelli [the Minister of Agriculture] through CORA . . ." [27]

Without the SNA's support or at least acquiescence in such activities, however, the efforts of these substantially poorer, more loosely structured associations could not succeed. In fact, Alfonso's press conference marked the effective end of the Committee's activities, rather than the beginning of a new, accelerated phase of opposition. Larraín, of course, could not explicitly state his disagreement with Alfonso's charges without breaking the facade of public unity that was supposed to exist among the agricultural groups but, in a symbolic gesture, he showed his disapproval by not joining Alfonso and the presidents of the two other main agricultural societies at the press conference.

Far more than symbolic gestures were involved in the SNA effort to restrict the impact of the Coordinating Committee. Throughout the period in which the relations between the PDC and the Committee had been deteriorating, the SNA leaders had continued to lobby within the administration and the Congress, pressing for a number of limited, detailed amendments to the reform bill. As has already been noted, several of these were championed by individual Christian Democratic congressmen, who were inclined to favor the Society's position, while Frei and members of his cabinet gave assurances that at least some of these amendments would be incorporated into the project. These assurances were used to good effect by Larraín to head off dissidents within both the Coordinating Committee and the SNA itself. As one councillor was to complain later on, the Committee failed "principally because it lacked the support of the SNA directorate, which preferred to deal with the administrative authorities and with the government party . . . When it was requested at that time that either the SNA or Alfonso initiate a public campaign, the [officers] answered that they would see later on. Nothing was ever done. The Society's Executive Committee always preferred to continue talking with the President, believing the formal promises that he was making to them." [28]

With support at least temporarily consolidated within the SNA council, the Society's officers were able to turn the Society's administrative apparatus and prestige against the hardliners. Without fanfare, the Coordinating Committee was denied access to the

Society's staff and funds, and the Committee's activities came to a halt. Unable to sustain the costs of a publicity campaign, and lacking the organizational resources to promote local demonstrations and strikes, the Committee gradually ceased to be a factor in the reform debate.

This did not of course mean that the hard-line opponents of land reform had been eliminated from the political scene. After the passage of the reform law, they along with many SNA councillors and some rightist politicians claimed that Larraín's approach had failed and that the law had not been amended to their satisfaction. But in the critical period in which the law itself was being considered in the Congress, the restraints imposed by the Society's leadership had contributed significantly to a deescalation of general tensions. In May 1966, as the reform law was about to gain its initial approval in the Chamber of Deputies, the change in atmosphere had become so noticeable that the weekly news magazine *Ercilla* commented: "The attacks . . . have lessened their heat . . . The [Coordinating Committee] has made a truce in the duel of insertions that it had made with the government . . . and the SNA itself has adopted a more lenient attitude with respect to what officials may say or do." [29]

The Rightist Politicians and the Reform

The position of the rightist politicians can be located somewhere between the soft line adopted by the SNA and the more radical opposition of the Coordinating Committee. In the course of the Frei regime the parties' attack on the land reform increased in harshness and their relations with the Christian Democrats grew increasingly strained. At the same time, however, interviews with ten rightist party leaders indicated that a variety of restraints continued to underlie their behavior. These men continued to work within the parliamentary framework; and unlike the hard-line independents, they showed a disposition to compromise that added an element of stability to the reform process.

The crushing electoral defeats suffered by the two rightist parties in 1964 and 1965 provided the major impetus for a closer cooperation with their erstwhile independent adversaries. In the first place, the uneasy relations between the younger, relatively advanced members of the party elite and the older, more traditional leadership became still more strained by the recriminations which followed the losses at the polls. For the more conservative rightists, these losses confirmed their suspicion that a reformist posture was, for the right, politically unfeasible, while the threat posed by the PDC reforms convinced them that it was time for all of the conservative elements — whether party politicians or independents — to close ranks. In April 1966, after a year of negotiations, the older leaders of the Liberals and Conservatives, and the adherents of Jorge Prat (a major independent leader) agreed to merge to form the National party (the PN). This move alienated the moderates still further and, after 1965, many dropped out of politics entirely. Although Prat himself also later dropped out of the new party (it was not sufficiently authoritarian for his taste), his top lieutenants assumed key positions in the new leadership structure; one former *pratista,* Victor Garcia, was in 1967 made president of the new party.

Like the hard-line independent opponents of land reform, the party politicians tended to be skeptical about the efficacy of the "interest-group approach." Such an approach, it was argued, would not be effective in protecting landed interests, unless supplemented by additional bargaining weapons. And as they were deprived by their electoral losses of the strength that had formerly been provided by a large congressional delegation, many party leaders were inclined to look sympathetically on efforts to mobilize other types of power resources. As one Conservative politician phrased the problem:

The SNA has been acting like a beggar. It has no parliamentary strength. Personally I think they have been in error. What they should do is to organize a huge publicity campaign, and public meetings to put added pressure on the government. Then they should go to the President and say, "Look, we are not doing this to obstruct your program. This can help you to control your own left wing. We want our conversations to continue." [30]

The most important basis for the right's new hard-line approach, however, did not lie in going outside constitutional channels but in manipulating the electoral resources remaining at its disposal to alter the current balance of power. Specifically, this approach rested on an attempt to capitalize on the yearning for national authority and order that allegedly existed within broad segments of the urban society. Whereas in the period from 1960 to 1964 the right had collaborated in the first land reform bill in order to offset Christian Democratic gains within the middle class, it now opposed the PDC land reform measure as one which would bring hardship, higher taxes, and inflation to this same group. The appeal to the "neglected" rather than to the "reformist" middle class thus became central to the strategy and the rhetoric of the new leaders of the National party. This class, according to one of these leaders, had been "ignored by both the Government and the FRAP . . . If we are successful in gaining their support, we will have captured one-third of the votes and we will be able to play a powerful role. The FRAP and the PDC can fight it out for the lower class vote if they want, perhaps with a Marxist appeal. But we will have a powerful role." [31]

This approach was opposed by some within the National party, and most Nationals continued in their professions of support for the "idea" of agrarian reform. Nevertheless, the new party's public statements tended increasingly to reflect this hard-line electoral appeal. Emphasis was given to the "collectivist" nature of the new reform and to the prospect of falling food production, massive diversion of expenditures, and the general disorder that would "inevitably" follow the Christian Democratic effort. These burdens, it was argued, would fall primarily upon the middle class. The official PN statement after the passage of the constitutional reform of property rights appealed "especially to the middle class for a serene meditation about the evident existence of a plan designed basically to destroy it, and with it, the liberty of all Chileans." [32] Another National politician — a major spokesman for the hard line within the party — added: "No one disagrees with the need to raise the living conditions of the most postponed sectors of the society. But we see no reason why this makes necessary a levelling toward the bottom, depressing the middle class, reducing its income, weakening its sense of independence, scorning its moral strength, subjugating it, humiliating it, and impoverishing it." [33] This was indeed a very different tone from the one that had been struck by the rightists in the debate over the Alessandri reform law. However, underlying the increasingly vituperative relationship between the right and the Christian Democracy were a variety of important restraints that tended to limit the conflict. Notwithstanding their broad attack on the Christian Democratic bill, the rightist politicians seemed more willing than the independents to accept the need for further concessions in their position.

For one thing, almost all of the former Liberals and Conservatives had already been involved in the support of one land reform law, and they were in no position to deny the basic legitimacy of land expropriation or of payment in bonds. After 1964, the independents tended to regard the PDC initiative as a confirmation of the predictions they had made during the Alessandri period — that modest concessions in principle would lead to further, more radical measures. The rightist politicians were, on the other hand, forced to defend the existing legislation and to concede the Christian Democrats the right to seek improvement in its details. Thus, in spite of their bitter condemnation of the new proposals, Liberals and Conservatives continued to show an inclination to compromise on its specific provisions.

Unlike their new National party allies, moreover, former Liberals and Conservatives were long accustomed to operating within the confines of the electoral and congressional arena, an experience which tended to tie the politicians closely to the general political system and to the actors within it. Almost all of the politicians interviewed spoke of friendship and respect for particular persons within the PDC, and very few were willing to charge that there were Marxists in the government. In fact, despite their general opposition to the government, many of the politicians interviewed admired individual Christian Democratic policy initiatives. Several singled out its massive educational reform, and another cited the mobilization of the youth. A third remarked: "In many respects, I am very optimistic about the way this government has acted. Industrial production was up last year [1965] and unemployment is down. Much of this, of course, is due to the work that was done under the Alessandri government, but this government has done a good job too." [34]

Finally, the "career politicians" denied neither the importance of gaining amendments to the bill nor the role of the SNA in negotiating with the government in order to win these amendments. All shared Larraín's assumption that legal modifications

169

could be of prime importance in restraining the actions of the government, and several reiterated assurances, made by Christian Democratic officialists themselves, that the government would administer the law with prudence.

The Nationals' argument for a broader form of opposition, therefore, did not mean that the politicians belittled the need for bargaining with the government or for using allies within official circles. Unlike the independents, none of the politicians argued that the acceptance of the current government implied peaceful but certain destruction of the landowning class; and none was willing to admit that a FRAP victory in 1964 might have served the interests of the landowners better than did the actual result. Several politicians felt that a strong, categorical challenge to the government's bill would be understood by the government not as the beginning of a total break, but as an initial position that would be moderated by compromise. As one Liberal politician admitted when questioned about a particularly broad public exchange on agrarian reform: "That is the way our country is. You know, for example, that we Liberals were in the cabinet with the Communists, and we had pretty good relations with them too. One day we can attack the president bitterly, and the next day we can deal with him." [35]

In a sense the former Liberal and Conservative leaders can be characterized as the manipulative core of the conservative opposition, willing to employ simultaneously a number of approaches and appeals. Faced with the desire to alter the existing balance of congressional and electoral power and, at the same time, with the need to maximize advantages within the existing balance, the rightist politicians' behavior was marked by a complex mixture of radicalism and flexibility. Their attempts to mobilize a broad urban electoral front against the Christian Democrats created severe problems for the government. Yet the pressures from the right almost always stopped short of the point at which they might have created complete polarization within the system.

Congressional Conflict and Bargaining:
The Copper Dispute and Agrarian Reform

This mixture of radicalism and flexibility was evident in the way the National party used its congressional bargaining strength throughout the passage of the reform bill. In spite of their relative weakness within the Congress, the Nationals were not without important means of putting pressure on the government. A variety of weapons were available for delaying, altering, or obstructing major pieces of legislation. To understand the nature of the right's congressional bargaining strength, it is necessary to describe briefly the procedures by which a bill moves through the two houses of the Chilean Congress. Simple majorities of both the Senate and the Chamber of Deputies must first approve "in general" any bill proposed. At this point, the bill passes back and forth between the two houses until disagreements on the specific content of the bill are resolved. The initiating house can "insist" on its version by a simple majority, and if one-third of the members of the second house support this version, it will become law. If a bill were to be introduced in the Chamber of Deputies, for example, the process of insistence would be as given in Table 15.

Table 15. The insistence process in the Chilean Congress

Chamber of Deputies	Senate
First passage: The bill is approved in general by a simple majority.	*Second passage:* The bill and changes in detail are approved by a simple majority.
Third passage: The Deputies can override the Senate by a simple majority.	*Fourth passage:* The Senate may override the Chamber and insist on its original version with a *two-thirds* majority.
Fifth passage: The Deputies may eliminate the disputed provisions from the bill by a *two-thirds* majority. Otherwise, the Senate version becomes law.	
Presidential Veto: This is an item veto which can be overridden by two-thirds of both chambers.	

Strategies of Opposition

The nature of the insistence process gave the Christian Democrats, with their absolute majority in the Chamber of Deputies, a tremendous legislative advantage; for once majorities in both houses had given general approval to government measures, the government could determine the substance of the legislation by gaining the support of only one-third of the Senate. This was, however, not as easy as it sounded, for the Christian Democrats' thirteen senators were still three votes shy of this one-third total. To save its legislation from emasculation in the Senate, the government thus had to seek the help of some of the opposition senators. All of this put the right potentially in a strategic position. Its seven senators were not enough to provide the government with a majority in that chamber, but they were sufficient to provide it with a one-third voting block. On the other hand, in collusion with the other opposition parties, rightist senators could frustrate many important aspects of the government's legislative program.

An opportunity of this sort became available to the right during the first half of 1966, in the course of the passage of the Christian Democratic copper reform bill. This legislation, introduced in March 1965, was initially approved by a Christian Democratic-Radical coalition in both houses of the Congress. As noted in a previous chapter, however, the Radical senators, who were moving toward a political alliance with the Marxists, refused to support several key provisions of the legislation regarding Chilean tax concessions to American investors. In the latter part of 1965, therefore, these provisions, after being passed by a Christian Democratic majority in the Chamber of Deputies, were rejected by an opposition coalition in the Senate. The Chamber of Deputies then insisted on its version, and the provisions returned to the Senate, where their fate depended on the right's willingness to provide the government with the necessary one-third total vote. The right was thus presented with a formidable bargaining weapon that could be wielded in opposition to land reform. The manner in which it employed this weapon is the most important illustration of the general character of rightist behavior that was described above.

Actually, the Christian Democratic government had hoped to avoid such a predicament by postponing the debate on land reform until the copper legislation had been passed. It delayed publication of the land reform bill for over a year after coming to office. The important constitutional reform of property rights (which removed the remaining restrictions on expropriation processes) had been published as part of an omnibus measure dealing with a large number of constitutional issues, but the government appeared content to let this measure bog down in a Senate committee until the copper question had been settled. These plans were frustrated, however, by the Christian Democratic left wing and by the Marxists. The former impelled the government to publish its land reform bill in November 1965, and a series of parliamentary maneuvers by Marxist senators placed the constitutional reform bill on the Senate agenda for immediate debate, just as the copper legislation was coming up for consideration. The position in the Congress of the copper provisions, the constitutional reform bill and the agrarian reform bill in January 1966 are summarized in Table 16.

Table 16. The status of copper, agrarian reform, and constitutional reform in the legislature

---

Copper Provisions

In its fourth passage in the Senate. These could now be upheld in the Senate by one-third of the senators, a total which only the right was likely to provide.

Constitutional Reform

In its second passage in the Senate. This was awaiting the approval of a majority to be provided by the FRAP and the Radicals.

Agrarian Reform

This was in its first passage in the Chamber of Deputies awaiting the approval of a simple majority which could be provided by the PDC alone.

In anticipation of gaining concessions on agrarian reform, the rightist senators announced that they would withhold support on the copper bill, and for the first four months of 1966 the situation appeared stalemated. As time passed, it became increasingly clear that the right intended to engage the Christian Democratic government in a bitter war of nerves. This war involved dangers for both sides. On the one hand, whichever way the right voted on

173

the copper question, the Christian Democrats had the votes to push through their land reform bills, since both the FRAP and the Radicals had promised their support. On the other hand, the right was in a position to retaliate against the Frei regime by withholding, once and for all, support for the copper program. Equally serious penalties could have been imposed on the government if the right had chosen to demand sweeping modifications in the land reform legislation as the price for its support on copper, for such modifications would almost certainly have increased the level of tension within the Christian Democracy, where the left wing strongly supported radical land reform measures and was highly unsympathetic toward the copper program. For several months it appeared as if the right did indeed intend to force the regime into a choice between its two major programs. "The true function of the copper program," argued one Liberal senator, "is not only the development of the copper companies, but the destruction of the right of property, the agrarian reform, agitation in the countryside, the instability of law . . . Our vigorous and active middle class, that immense social group in which the best hopes of the country lie, are the principal targets and victims of this policy." [36]

From the beginning of the controversy, however, there were signs that the rightist politicians had planned to use their leverage in copper for purposes of bargaining, rather than total obstruction. In spite of bitter public polemics, both the PDC and the right were careful to maintain more quiet contacts as well. Private conversations about a favorable vote on copper continued from January to March 1966, while the question of possible amendments to the constitutional reform of property were raised by Francisco Bulnes in the Senate.

A number of factors provided the basis for what was, from the PDC's point of view, a successful end to these negotiations. Although they have already been discussed or implied, it is useful to reiterate them. First, in contrast to their more militant colleagues, rightist politicians believed that even limited legislative concessions could be worthwhile as restraints on the Christian Democratic government. They also tended to believe that the government would be willing to compromise. One of the chief negotiators asserted toward the end of the controversy, "We put pressure on the government, but I think Frei was a little startled by the way the project had turned out and wanted to make some changes anyway." [37] Finally, though the right was able to force some absolute choices on the Christian Democrats, the PDC's capacity to command a majority on the land reform bills also presented the right with difficult choices. If the Nationals persisted in their war of nerves, they risked losing the chance to exert any influence over the details of the land reform legislation. Their other alternative was to support the copper program, and to settle for whatever concessions they could get on land reform, even if these concessions did not meet their basic objectives.

Characteristically, the second option was selected. "It was obvious," stated one politician in an interview, "that we would eventually vote for copper. The question was one of getting the maximum mileage out of that vote." [38] Direct conversations between the rightist political leaders and Frei himself finally broke the impasse on April 1, 1966. The following day the copper provisions were supported by the right in the Senate, and shortly afterward a series of changes were made in the constitutional and agrarian reform bills.

It is interesting to note the low price which the rightist senators finally accepted in return for their support on copper. The most important government concession in the Senate centered on the constitutional amendment. Initially this had left the terms of indemnity and the form of adjudication over expropriated property entirely to congressional discretion. In the Senate, however, the property clause was changed to read that indemnities had to be determined "equitably" and that all tribunals had to "judge conforming to law." With these concessions, it was possible for expropriated landowners to make legal protest against particularly harsh terms of payment and to conduct limited appeals from the special courts to the Supreme Court. Though these changes did leave an opening wedge for delay and litigation in the expropriation proceedings, they by no means crippled the overall process of expropriation. Even with the changes, the government would still be permitted to expropriate at tax value, to establish a strong system of special courts, and to set the terms on which the value of bonds might be readjusted to compensate for inflation. When compared with the earlier debate over deferred payments during the Alessandri era, there is little question that the right had come a long way.

In spite of the limits of the government's changes, Francisco Bulnes could still argue in the Senate:

The long campaign . . . to show the government and the PDC the range and effects of the reform . . . have produced results a little late, but positive . . . I am glad . . . that the final result, without being fully satisfactory . . . constitutes a sufficient definition in favor of private property and even a minimum safeguard in cases of expropriation.[39]

In the agrarian reform bill that passed the Chamber of Deputies, the government also introduced a number of changes which attempted to answer at least some of the original criticisms made by the SNA. Included in the amendments passed by the Chamber were: alterations of the tables of land equivalents to the eighty basic hectares, in order to give some types of landowners a large area of reserve;[40] an expansion of the jurisdiction of the special appellate tribunals;[41] and — subject to a variety of restrictions — a new provision permitting an expropriated landowner to choose the portion of land he might keep.[42] Also added to the bill were new clauses concerning compensation for expropriated property, which allowed a landowner to invest his bonds in nationally owned industry.

The period of good feeling produced by these changes was not to last long. When the constitutional reform bill was sent back from the Senate to the Chamber of Deputies, the government reneged on some of the agreements it had made with the rightist senators. Though the concessions made by the PDC had been extremely limited, the government wished, understandably, to eliminate even the slightest possibility that the constitutionality of its land reform bill might be challenged. Equally understandable was the bitterness that this decision evoked on the part of the rightist senators, who returned to an all-out attack against the government. Another six months were to pass before the constitutional reform finally became law, and an even longer period of time was required for the land reform bill itself. Nevertheless, the copper agreements marked a decisive turning point for all of the major government bills. With all of the details of the copper legislation finally passed, the rightists could only fight a rearguard action over the details of the other major bills, for which the government could count on the support of the other opposition parties. Although the relations between the PDC and the National party continued on a rough and erratic course, the right's flexibility at a critical point in the legislative process ensured that all three governmental measures would become law in essentially the form in which they had been presented to the Congress.

Rightist Opposition Since the Passage of the Reform Laws: The Parties and the SNA

Until the summer of 1967, when the agrarian reform bill was finally passed, the moderation of the SNA leadership and the relative flexibility of the rightist politicians tended to be the predominant theme in the overall opposition to the land reform. After that time, the moderate voices, though still audible, grew considerably fainter; and the conflict between the Christian Democrats and the various landed groups appeared to intensify.

The ouster of the SNA officers in July 1967 appeared to be the pivotal event in this shift in emphasis. Until May 1967 there was relatively little sign of dissidence within the SNA council about the manner in which Larraín and his fellow officers had conducted themselves toward the government. As the passage of the land reform legislation drew near, however, the resignations in May of three influential councillors signaled a growing dissatisfaction with the Society's officers. Internal debate within the Society continued, and two months later the officers themselves resigned. In the late summer of the same year, the Society's leadership passed back into the hands of older, more conservative men, most of whom were leaders of the rightist parties.

From that point on the Society and the Nationals tended to move in closer step with the other, more radical segments of the opposition. The hardening attack was evident both inside and outside the Congress. In the legislative arena the rightist senators provoked a minor storm by joining with the left and the Radicals to deny Frei the constitutionally required Senate permission to visit the United States. Outside the legislative arena the rightists adopted a variety of tactics designed to harass the government and

177

to dramatize their opposition. In 1968, for example, rightist politicians persuaded the inquilinos on two fundos to lock out CORA officials who had been sent to take possession of the land. During the fall of 1967 and the winter of 1968, SNA and party officials organized a series of regional rallies of landowners, at which the government and the land reform were attacked in harsh and uncompromising language. Throughout this period the SNA officials continued to engage in private dialogue with government leaders, but the frequency and content of the Society's public declarations against the land reform had clearly changed from what they had been during the Larraín period. Like the rightist party leaders, SNA officials began to give exaggerated emphasis to the costs of the Christian Democratic reform and to the burdens it would bring to the urban population. An SNA advertisement stated in February 1968:

The program of 100,000 families will have the fabulous cost of 1,700,000 escudos. This would mean that *for five years, one of each five escudos disposable for any investment whatsoever, private as well as public, whether it is for schools, roads, hospitals, or new industries, will have to be diverted to land reform* . . . The Agrarian Reform is not adjusting to its legitimate objectives of better production . . . and it is tying up the resources of the entire country.[43]

It is tempting to account for this shift in terms of the change that had simultaneously occurred in the reform process itself. In the summer of 1967, about the time that Larraín was replaced as president of the SNA, the reform laws had at last been passed, and the struggle over land reform moved from debate within Congress to a more direct focus on expropriations in the countryside. The shift from legislation to implementation of the reform meant that, henceforth, the "real" sacrifices would begin for the landowners. As might be expected, this prospect tended to encourage an intensification of the opposition and a quest for new means of defense.

The importance of the final passage of the reform law in driving the opposition toward a harder line can, however, easily be exaggerated. The Christian Democratic government, it may be recalled, did not wait for the passage of its own law to begin the actual process of expropriation and division of land. This had begun almost as soon as Frei had taken office. The *pace* of expropriations, it is true, did accelerate somewhat after the final passage of the new law. In 1965 and 1966 the number of new families settled on asentamientos reached only around 2,000 per year. In 1967 the number was closer to 4,000. Clearly, however, the reform process was still far closer to the gradualism promised by the officialists of the PDC than to the massive goals of the party's left wing. The shift in the arena of struggle from the Congress to the countryside was gradual, and it is unlikely that this alone can explain the changes in the behavior of the opposition.

A full understanding of the change in the oppositions' approach must thus take into account other factors. Throughout this chapter it has been argued that the nature of the opposition depended on the types of options that were open to the representatives of the landed class. It was suggested further that choices would be defined by these representatives according to the way they had customarily mobilized the resources of the landed class and the types of tools they had used to influence Chilean political decisions. As an interest group, the SNA responded to the access that was available to it within other parties and within the administration itself. Between 1964 and 1967 this led it toward a moderate form of opposition. The rightist parties, which related to the political system through the electoral mechanism and which competed directly with other parties for control of the government, responded to the Christian Democratic challenge with a less moderate, although still flexible, form of behavior. The shifts that transpired after 1967 responded as much to changes in the lobbying and electoral possibilities as they did to changes in the reform process itself.

One aspect of the post-1967 situation which clearly affected the position of both the new National party and the SNA was the inability of the Christian Democratic officialists to deliver fully on *their* earlier assurances that limited concessions would be made in the land reform legislation. There were a number of reasons why delivery on these assurances was difficult for the government. In the first place, any changes in the legislation designed to accommodate the right — no matter how limited their substance — were bound to risk the suspicion of the party left-wingers, some of whom were prepared to regard even the slightest gesture of accommodation as a "sell-out." Secondly, in spite of the moderation of many of the right's demands, there was still considerable distance between the changes it had asked for and what the government was willing to concede. In part, no doubt, government officials acted out of the legitimate fear that even modest modifications in the law might someday prove to be annoying or obstructive loopholes. Thus, while officialist leaders did seriously study many of the proposals made by the SNA and although they did incorporate some of these proposals in the course of the copper agreements, the final law left many of the Society's objections unanswered.

This proved disappointing to the moderate leadership of the SNA. In the summer of 1966, after the reform bill had completed its first passage in the Chamber of Deputies, an SNA statement admitted that the bill rectified "some of the innumerable points that were objected to when the project was published." [44] It added, however, that "it could by no means be argued that that [bill] assures the possibility of realizing an agrarian reform with respect for efficient proprietors . . ." [45]

The sharpest reaction, however, was produced by the government's decision to revise the agreements it had made on the constitutional reforms in the Senate in order to gain the right's acceptance of the copper law. When the constitutional bill returned to the Chamber of Deputies, the PDC introduced special provisions concerning the expropriation of rural property that were designed to eliminate any chance that the constitutionality of its reform law could be challenged. This unilateral revision of the government's part of the copper agreement stirred angry protest from the SNA, which charged that the PDC had "discriminated" against agricultural property. The rightist politicians reacted even more sharply, since they considered the government's move a betrayal of trust and confidence on the part of the PDC officialists. The reversal prompted one of the remaining moderates within the Nationalist party to remark in an interview that "from now on, any time we go to the Moneda [the presidential palace], it will be through the front door and publicly. No more of these back-door deals, because the president will not keep his word." [46]

These reversals on the part of the government indicated at least one difficulty in the process of accommodation between reformist and antireformist elements. In spite of the considerable moderation on both sides, the gulf between the two was not easily bridged. Each side had legitimate interests and concerns which came into serious conflict with the other's position. In itself, however, this may not have been sufficient to deter further efforts at accommodation. The government had, after all, granted *some* concessions which had been viewed with approval by the SNA and which had been important in deterring the challenge of less moderate elements within the opposition. To understand the general widening of the gulf between government and opposition, therefore, it is also necessary to consider still another factor: the organizational and electoral recovery of the rightist party organization.

The weakness and confusion of the former Liberals and Conservatives was one of the conditions that had made the "interest group" approach attractive to members of the SNA. Between the disastrous defeats of 1965 and the passage of the law in 1967, however, some of this weakness and confusion had been overcome. By April 1966, conversations and negotiations between Liberals and Conservatives were concluded, and the National party was formally constituted. By the same month of the following year, the results of the 1967 elections offered additional hope to the strategists of the National party that their hard line might restore their electoral fortune. In its national percentage, the right gained only slightly in the 1967 elections over its totals in 1965, going from about 12 to 14 percent of the total vote. In the first and second districts of Santiago, however, which comprised most of the central city, the rightist vote jumped almost 5 percentage points, from about 9 percent in 1965 to almost 14 percent in 1967.[47] Although it is difficult to determine conclusively where these urban votes had come from, there were some indications that the Nationals' decision to appeal to the "neglected" middle class was beginning to pay off. The rightists lost slightly in such working class districts as San Miguel and Quinta Normal. On the other hand, their voting percentages in the middle class urban communes of Providencia and Los Condes rose considerably, from 23 percent to 36 percent in the first, and from 20 percent to 33 percent in the second.[48] In contrast to the periods following the congressional races of 1961 and 1965, in which rightist politicians had engaged in sharp internal debate over the reasons for their losses, the 1967 election was heralded as a forerunner of further gains — an interpretation which was reinforced by electoral advances for the right in the 1969 congressional elections. Pointing toward the coming 1970 presidential contest, the public pronouncements of the National party leaders appeared to become still harder and more vituperative in tone.

In the summer of 1967, all of this placed Larraín and his fellow SNA officers in a politically fatal scissors-hold. They had come into office, in the words of one of their major critics, when "the Society's directorate was not being received by the administrative authorities" and when "the politicians had lost an election, leaving the agriculturalists . . . bereft of administrative protection . . ." [49] Contacts with the government and the weakness of the rightist parties had been Larraín's trump cards in dealing with dissident conservative elements. But the Nationals had now begun to regain strength, while "no more constitutional procedures remain[ed] in which the situation of agriculture could be improved in the agrarian reform bill." [50] It was the loss of these trump cards that made Larraín's position untenable. Buoyed by their successes in the April elections, the rightist politicians on the SNA council joined forces with the harder-line independents to eject the officers. Within the SNA, as well as the National party, the old-line politicians once again assumed the leadership of the opposition.

Access, Electoral Support, and Rightist Moderation

Conservative groups thus spoke in a variety of ways — sometimes harmoniously, sometimes discordantly, but always shifting in approach and emphasis. Taken together, the variety of approaches and appeals made by conservative groups presented reformist elements in the system with a formidable challenge which tested the mettle of even the most skillful among them. Indeed, the difficulties of coping with landed opposition, both in Chile and elsewhere in Latin America, have led a variety of writers to characterize landowners and their representatives as a "blind" and reactionary group, disposed to stop reform at any cost. From this, the conclusion is sometimes drawn that if change is to be effected within the rural social structure, the opposition must somehow be destroyed or eliminated from power. "If agrarian reform is to be made within a democratic system," Jacques Chonchol has argued, "it has to have political support of such a nature that the affected minorities are no longer in a condition to oppose." [51]

In part, of course, the validity of this statement rests on the definition of "change" itself. If reform is defined only in terms of a rapid and drastic modification of the rural social structure, then it is not likely that it can be accomplished without finding a way to overpower the opposition. The more radical the reform, the more "closed" the opposition is likely to be. If, however, relatively moderate reform is involved, then this study of the Chilean right would suggest that the stereotypes of a blind and stubborn reaction must be revised and refined if both the problems and the possibilities involved in standing-off opposition are to be understood.

For one thing, as Hirschman points out, the successful initiation of reform may depend as much on the reformer's capacity to outwit and persuade his adversaries as on his capacity to overpower them. The Chilean case suggests further that the relative flexibility of rightist organizations themselves may also be of considerable importance for the initiation of reform. The capacity of these representative institutions to regulate the landowners' role in the reform process worked to mute the impact of dissident sectors of the opposition and in many important instances added a stabilizing element to the conflict. The brokerage functions assumed were toward a softening of the conservatives' orientation toward rural change. In 1958 most rightist forces would not acknowledge the legitimacy of reform. In 1961, as a result of the effort of the rightist parties, the major issue was whether to accept deferred payments as compensation for the expropriation of abandoned and inefficient rural property. By 1967, due to SNA efforts, many conservatives were concentrating on the amount of land that efficient landowners would be allowed to keep. These shifts in the terms of debate helped to keep open the lines of communication to the Christian Democratic government, and in many ways they helped to save the government from having to choose between abandoning its land reform or relying solely on the left and the Radicals for support of its general legislative program. Even though agreement between the government and the right proved elusive, the capacity of rightist organizations to exert influence within the congressional and administrative arena helped to discourage broader conflicts elsewhere in the system.

This is not to deny, of course, that the influence of conservative elements must be reduced if change is to be effected. What is suggested, rather, is that even while the grip of rightist sectors within the system is being loosened, the retention of at least some channels of access and some representation may be essential if the system is to be spared the threat of a broad, paralyzing reaction. The problem is one of striking a balance — between restricting the power of conservatives and retaining some access for them. It is apparent that the influence of rightist organizations *does* slow reform, and as the need for reform increases it may become increasingly difficult for rightist organizations to be felt in policy decisions without unduly clogging the governmental machinery. Yet as rightist organizations move farther from the centers of power, they may lose both the incentive and the capacity to moderate the interests of their constituents.

Whether these conflicting needs can be met will depend on a variety of factors. One of the most important of these, however, may well be the *type* of organizations and the *type* of power resources that are used to defend the interests of conservative social forces. The contrasting responses of the rightist parties and of the SNA to the decline in their strength after 1964 suggests that interest groups, rather than parties, may ultimately prove the best instruments for representing landowners without at the same time jeopardizing the process of reform as a whole. In the case of parties, dependence on an electoral base may lead to an exaggeration of differences between opposing groups and to the obscuring of points of agreement between them. It was apparently for this reason that the line of the rightist parties grew relatively less moderate after 1964. A mildly reformist appeal had not won them votes, while a harder line seemed to be paying off. As an interest group, on the other hand, the SNA leaders depended less on the mobilization of electoral support than on the ability to gain access to important decision-makers. With the rise of the Christian Democrats to power, therefore, they were inclined not to exaggerate differences but to seek governmental allies — to emphasize quiet lobbying as a means of influencing political decisions.

The fact that these techniques could not be maintained after 1967 indicates that the need to strike a balance between reducing rightist influence and retaining some political access was a dilemma that was not easily solved. It could perhaps be argued that even after the fall of Larraín, the role of party politicians continued to provide some elements of stability within the system. Former Liberals and Conservatives were still distinguishable from their new National colleagues by their commitment to bargaining within the parliamentary framework; and they were inclined to aim their appeal at a broad middle class electoral base, rather than at more limited power groups within urban society. Nevertheless, party efforts to force bargaining at the congressional level proved clumsy and obstructive in many ways, while the appeal to the middle class voters clearly increased the degree of tension and conflict at the electoral level. The prospects after 1967 were for sharpening conflict between the right and other sectors of the system.

Whether this was the last word about the behavior of the conservative opposition, however, was difficult to predict. In view of the fluidity of Chilean politics and the shifting quality of political alignments, the reform controversy was likely to be characterized by both an ebb and flow of controversy and by periods of rapprochement and polarization. In this shifting situation the opposition could become still more disruptive and authoritarian, or it could soften its line once again. Particularly toward the end of the reform process, if reformist parties are able to establish an organized peasant mass base, the interest group approach developed by the SNA might conceivably reemerge as an appropriate means of self-defense. This will depend on the evolving relationship between rightist pressure group organizations and parties, on the flexibility and behavior of the reform movements themselves, and on the critical "swing" position of the Chilean urban sectors.

Chapter 6 The Chilean Left and Agrarian Reform

After the bitterly fought electoral campaigns of 1964 and 1965, the two parties of the left, the Communists and Socialists, became the major competitors of the Christian Democratic government. In the presidential contest the leftist candidate, Salvador Allende, had been the only other serious contender, and the results of the congressional race made the Communist-Socialist coalition, the Popular Action Front (FRAP) the second largest political force in the country. In view of these developments, it is not surprising that general relations between the Marxist left and the reformist government were characterized by antagonism and rivalry. Of considerably greater interest, however, was the fact that this rivalry was not infrequently punctuated by cooperation between the two groups — most notably on the question of agrarian reform. Although the politicians of the FRAP were not entirely uncritical of the Christian Democratic initiative, their behavior throughout the passage of the reform bill and through the initial implementation period was marked by strong, almost unconditional, support.

Although the *fact* of this support was indisputable, its *meaning* was shrouded in considerable ambiguity. The almost instinctive response of many American observers (including the author) is to view the behavior of the Chilean left in terms of the classic patterns of confrontation between reformers and radicals. The starting point for analyzing this confrontation is the assumption that Marxist radicals are driven by the single-minded pursuit of total change.[1] Instances of compromise between reformers and radicals, therefore, provoke questions about the "special circumstances" that lead to this cooperation; about whether this cooperation is lasting or temporary; and about future leftist efforts to broaden or capture a reform process.

These assumptions are reinforced by an examination of the strategic questions asked by the Chilean leftists themselves: Is the "revolution" to be achieved through conflict or cooperation with moderate groups? The answers given by different segments of the

Chilean left are somewhat surprising; for in Chile, the highly nationalistic Socialist intellectuals, and not the Moscow-oriented Communists, consistently take the more radical line.[2] When confronted with the Christian Democratic challenge after 1964, the Communists advocated a strategy of selective opposition, in which the left would support "positive" government initiatives that might ultimately lead to broad structural change. Socialist politicians, on the other hand, argued that the left's opposition should be "irreducible, because it does not admit concession, and it [should be] indivisible because it is the overall action of this government . . . that merits our repudiation."[3] Judging from their rhetoric, however, both Chilean Marxist parties appeared to share a concern for promoting change in the society. The assumption that the left seeks to overturn the social order, often accepted as a "given" by outside observers seeking to understand leftist behavior, was also at the heart of the debate within the left itself.

But whatever the validity of this "given" may be elsewhere in the world, it is not a reliable premise on which to begin a discussion of the Chilean Marxist parties. In Chile the left has traditionally collaborated closely with other groups in the system in order to gain limited objectives; only rarely have the Communists or the Socialists moved into a position of intransigent isolation. Although in their writing and in their internal debate the Marxists are among the most astute and observant critics of the Chilean system, their ideological rhetoric is misleading if it is taken as a guide to their behavior. Thus, in spite of the revolutionary themes in Marxist ideology, the specific behavior of both parties appears to respond closely to the incentives provided by the system itself. Though there have been changes in this behavior that cannot be ignored, the FRAP's cooperation with center groups has, historically speaking, been the norm rather than the exception.

The distinction between the Chilean left's ideological criticism of the system and its pervasive ties to that system is thus crucial to an understanding of its specific role in the Christian Democratic reform effort. By taking the former as a starting point, a false impression results that in backing the PDC initiative the left had somehow been grudgingly brought to accept a "half a loaf," or that its support had been predicated on the hope that it could capitalize on a Christian Democratic failure. By taking the latter as a starting

187

point, a considerably different picture emerges: in some respects, the Marxists' acceptance of the PDC initiative resembled a somewhat desperate attempt to keep up with developments which threatened to pass them by. Whereas the "revolutionary" premise seeks to understand how the Marxists might work to crush the political order, the premise that the Marxists had become a part of that system points to the possible contributions they might make to its maintenance.

The Communist and Socialist Parties and the Chilean Political System

If the reflex of some Americans is to accept the revolutionary premise about the Chilean left, many Chileans assert unequivocally that the left has become part of the "Establishment." Pointing to the Marxists' readiness to abandon their quest for peasant support after the Popular Front victory of 1939, to their general reluctance to engage in violent or conspiratorial activity, and to their stubborn defense of certain "privileged" industrial labor sectors, Osvaldo Sunkel has concluded that the "left wing parties, including the Communist Party, as well as the trade unions, have . . . become increasingly incorporated into the political Establishment, and that their existence and influence depend on the maintenance of this system." [4]

Although this conclusion is much more plausible than the revolutionary premise, it is nonetheless debatable. Aside from important differences within leftist circles, there are a number of other considerations which must also be taken into account before leaping from the rather obvious point that the left has not engaged in violent revolutionary activity to the assertion that it is a part of the system. As James Morris points out, for example, the mere fact that a leftist party accepts constitutional limitations on its activity while it is in opposition by no means ensures that it will respect these same limitations once in power. Only when political groups give clear indication, through their statements and their behavior, that they will accept alternation in office as a concomitant of competition can it be reasonably ascertained that the "rules of the game" have become internalized.[5]

This point is an important one, because it is by no means clear that once elected either the Communists or the Socialists will be entirely willing to relinquish their hold on the government. This suspicion is shared not only by the conservative and moderate elements of Chilean society, but sometimes by the non-Marxist radicals themselves; and it adds an acrimonious note to the relations between the Marxist and non-Marxist parties that prevents each from fully acknowledging the legitimacy of the other. While this caveat should be borne in mind, however, it is somewhat irrelevant to the present purpose — which is to examine the behavior of the Marxists while in opposition to the Christian Democrats.

Another consideration, far more relevant to the discussion, is that the nature of the leftist *opposition* itself appeared to grow more radical in the years preceding the 1964 elections. This radicalization became visible at least as early as the mid-1950s, when the Communists and Socialists formed the FRAP coalition devoted to a victory for the left. Before that time violent rivalry, occasionally interrupted by periods of collaboration, had marked the relationship between the two parties. Afterward, though tensions persisted, the coalition lasted for over a decade. Unlike earlier periods of collaboration, moreover, in which Marxist unity was based on the support of centrist candidates, the FRAP coalition was dominated by the Marxists themselves, with small, non-Marxist splinter groups playing only a marginal role.

Also in evidence in the late 1950s was the inclination of Communists and Socialists to repudiate their past moderation, to raise new, explosive issues, and to seek as constituents the marginal groups which had previously been considered "off limits" for the left. After the Cuban revolution, the Socialists developed a vocal "pekinista" wing, which advocated emulation of the Cuban guerrilla movement in Chile. After 1959, the FRAP coalition also began to raise the question of agrarian reform and nationalization of the American copper mines with increasing urgency. Even the relatively cautious Communists, who stopped far short of many Socialists in their revolutionary rhetoric, advocated a more aggressive effort to mobilize peasants and urban slum dwellers and criticized their own neglect of these groups during the 1940s. Looking back on the days of the Popular Front from the perspective of 1967, the

189

man who had been the Communist Secretary General during the earlier period admitted the "error of accepting, finally, the paralyzation [of rural unions], motivated by the purpose of 'not creating difficulties for the government.' " [6] By the 1960s, both the Communists and the Socialists had abandoned some of the tacit restraints that had previously been the condition for their entry into the electoral process.

The characterization of the left as "part of the system" would be misleading in the extreme if it did not take these factors into account. Also important to note, however, are the positive advantages that had been gained by both parties in their long years of participation in the constitutional order. For the elites of both parties, elected positions had become important bases of personal advancement and valuable means of exerting political influence. Party energy and attention, therefore, had always been geared primarily to achieving these objectives. Although Marxist leaders did act aggressively on behalf of a limited proletarian constituency, their concern for broader segments of the lower class had been mostly restricted to the election period itself. Representation of these groups in interelection periods was characterized by occasional legislative initiatives or by interventions within the bureaucracy. In spite of the left's increasingly militant programs and its renewed interest in marginal groups, these features of Marxist behavior had changed only slowly. The co-optation of Marxist leaders into the system during the 1940s put powerful brakes on the subsequent trend toward radicalization.

The assertion that the leftist leaders had been co-opted is, of course, easy to make but difficult to document. Duverger furnishes one useful criterion with his distinction between parliamentary parties and those which had originated outside the legislature.[7] In the former type of party, power accrues to parliamentary notables, even after the party has expanded its electoral strength. The latter types, on the other hand, tend to take a more reserved position toward legislative activity. Even when these parties participate in such activity, legislative posts are usually assigned to secondary party figures. The major decision-making power remains in the hands of leaders who remain outside the legislature entirely or who base their authority on positions within the party structure.

According to this distinction, the Socialists — who are ideologically the more radical of the two Marxist sectors — would appear rather well integrated into the arena of multiparty competition. The major Socialist leaders, without exception, held positions in the Congress and frequently had independent and personal bases of electoral support. The Socialist presidential candidate, Salvadore Allende, held no formal position within the party from 1958 to 1968. He had served as a cabinet minister, however, between 1939 and 1944 and had been a senator ever since. Over one-half of the fifteen-man Socialist Central Committee elected in 1964, and all of the major party officers, were also elected to congressional posts.[8] In spite of their radical rhetoric and their occasional statements of contempt for parliamentary activity, the Socialists were probably far closer to being what Neumann has termed a "party of individual representation" — based on the leadership of notables — than they were to being a revolutionary "party of integration." [9]

It is probably not too much of an exaggeration, in fact, to draw a comparison between the Socialist party and the Radicals — the patronage party par excellence. Like the Radicals, the Socialist elite has generally been composed of upwardly mobile white-collar workers, seeking security through government employment and political advancement. Twenty-three percent of the Socialist congressmen elected in 1965 had been functionaries within the Chilean administration. Of the five other major parties, only the Radicals' 37 percent was higher. The pattern of advancement for these Socialist sectors also resembled that among the Radicals.[10] In both parties it was common for militant young leaders to challenge their elders, to replace them in top party positions, to achieve congressional posts, and then to become more moderate themselves over time. Without denying the sincerity of many individual Socialists who espoused revolutionary objectives, the latent function of ideological militancy appeared to be one of rotating leaders and of providing room at the top for newer groups of politicians. "Those who arrive in Congress," complained one Socialist senator in 1961, "become professionalized, mechanized in their conduct . . . Few escape the links that this atmosphere creates. A kind phrase, a pat on the shoulders . . . they almost always end the combative vigor of the most intransigent." [11]

Communist leaders appeared somewhat less subject to this type of co-optation. Power and prestige continued, in large measure, to be based more on positions within the party organization than on parliamentary activity. The Communist party was the only one of the six major parties to pay the salaries of its congressional delegation out of the party treasury. Moreover, the Communists' close ties to the Soviet Union and their strict, secretive, internal discipline were regarded uneasily by other political formations, including the Socialists themselves.[12] For this reason, the Communists were the occasional objects of repression. Between 1948 and 1958, the party was prohibited from running candidates under the Communist label, although party members did run under different party names and were permitted to operate their newspaper and their trade unions.

Nevertheless, when the Chilean Communists are compared with other Communist parties — including those of Western Europe — their willingness to cooperate in broad coalitions and to operate within the framework of constitutional norms in order to achieve limited objectives appears to have no precedent. The decade of experience in center-left governments, beginning in 1939, had enabled the party to build up a certain reservoir of "respectability" and some important stakes in the existing order. All major party leaders held seats in the Congress. Even more than the Socialists, the Communists were inclined to seek allies from anywhere on the ideological spectrum, including the far right, in order to maintain this advantage. For a brief period in 1946, the party shared cabinet positions with Liberals and Radicals. Using the prerogatives of legality, moreover, the party had been able to consolidate its internal organization to a degree matched by few other Communist parties in Latin America. After thirty years of participation within the system, the party had built up a strong base within the trade union movement, a network of commercial enterprises that provided an important source of domestic financing, and a widely read newspaper.

These bases of strength were challenged, but not destroyed, during the decade of illegality beginning in 1948. When that period ended in 1958, one of the party's main preoccupations was to avoid any further imposition of legal restrictions on its activities. For the next decade the Communists scrupulously refrained from any provocation that would again make them scapegoats for the rest of the system. In this respect the Communists appeared far more "constitutionalist" than the Socialists.

Turning from apparent contrasts in the ideological orientations of the Communist and Socialist leaders to other characteristics of behavior, moreover, many of the differences between the two parties tend to disappear. The two Marxist elites resembled each other (and many other centrist and rightist groups), for example, in the manner in which they sought the support of labor groups and in the way they represented these groups within the system. Like other centrist and rightist politicians, the leftists often reflected in their behavior a paternalistic orientation toward lower class groups and an apparent lack of interest in the formation of a revolutionary mass base. Although the rank and file of both parties had long been drawn out of lower class groups, blue-collar workers still did not usually reach the highest levels of leadership. About 70 percent of the Socialist deputies and about 80 percent of the Communist deputies elected in 1965 came from non-blue-collar backgrounds.[13] These middle class congressmen were closely involved in the direction of the Marxist trade unions, but their leadership resembled the paternalistic, brokerage role, characteristic of other middle class political groups within the system. In major wage conflicts, bargaining with employers, and intercession with government authorities, the role of union spokesmen was generally assumed by these middle class congressmen, whose education and polish permitted them to move more comfortably at the upper levels of Chilean society. Like the congressmen of other parties, the Communists and Socialists spent much of their time receiving petitioners, intervening in the bureaucracy, or pushing through legislation designed to satisfy the grievances of particular clienteles.

It is not surprising, in light of this activity, that the organizational base of both Marxist parties remained fragmented and weak. Although individual components of the Marxist labor movement — the coal and copper miners, construction workers, and so forth — were well organized, the strength of the labor movement as a whole had not markedly improved in the past thirty years. The Central Confederation of Workers (CUT), which was dominated by the Marxist parties, was "weak in the extreme. It ha[d] little control over affiliated local, national, and provincial unions, and what centralized authority it [did] have derive[d] from a similarity of party allegiances among leaders at various levels of the structure, and not from economic strength or statutory grants of authority as such." [14] In the main, Marxist union activity tended to provide the major benefits for a small "labor aristocracy," whose wage increases and social security gains often came at the expense of more loosely organized, or unorganized, members of the working class. In this sense, argues Osvaldo Sunkel, the left had developed "into a formidable obstacle to the rationalization of the political structure and of economic and social policy." [15]

It should be pointed out, of course, that the blame for these developments cannot be placed solely on the Marxist elites. In their organizational efforts, leftist leaders faced a variety of difficulties, which included the threat of repression, a severely restrictive labor code, a lack of financial resources, and the traditionalism of many lower class groups themselves. By the same token, however, it is at least a plausible proposition that the Marxist leaders' deep involvement in electoral and congressional activities had diverted their energies and resources from a concentrated effort to overcome these obstacles.[16]

At least in part, this proposition is supported by the left's tacit acceptance of upper class control in the countryside after 1939. More generally, however, unionization of all workers — urban as well as rural — leveled off after the election of the Popular Front. According to the statistics of the Ministry of Labor, shown in Table 17, the percentage of legally organized workers in the total labor force remained almost constant between 1941 and 1959, after a period of rapid growth during the 1930s.

These figures, of course, do not tell all of the story. Aside from the growth of legal unions, which Table 17 depicts, workers organized into de facto associations must also be taken into account. Morris and Oyander estimate that in 1959 approximately another 4 to 6 percent of the labor force fell into the de facto category, bringing the total percentage of organized workers up to around 16 percent.[17] Even after taking this additional estimate into account, however, it is probable that the unionization process had not reached even those workers normally considered organizable. The census of 1960 shows that the workers in the secondary sector (presumably those most susceptible to a Marxist appeal) consti-

Table 17. Growth of the Chilean union movement, 1932–1959

Period	Percent of labor force unionized	Number of unions
1932	3.0	421
1940	9.0	1,888
1941–1945[a]	11.4	1,684
1946–1950[a]	12.3	1,831
1951–1955[a]	12.4	2,048
1956–1959[a]	10.8	2,037

Source: James O. Morris and Roberto Oyander, *Afiliación y Finanzas Sindicales en Chile, 1932–59.* Instituto de Organisación y Administración (INSORA), Publicaciones INSORA, Editorial Universitaria, Santiago de Chile, 1962.

[a] Average for each period.

tuted about 24 percent of the total active population, a figure well above the maximum of 16 percent actually organized. Since only about one-half of all organized workers were actually affiliated with one of the two Marxist parties, it would appear that the Marxist leaders had not been particularly energetic in the task of building an organized base of strength.

This behavior had admittedly changed during the 1960s. Attempts by the leftist politicians to win the votes of the marginals through the advocacy of structural change were accompanied by important efforts to organize these marginals and to bring them into the political order. Especially after 1964, the leftists were active in organizing peasant unions in the countryside and neighborhood councils, mothers' committees, and party cells in the urban slums. What was also clear, however, was that the left had "something to lose" in this process. Mass mobilization threatened the position of the established union leaders and politicians at the apex of the narrowly based and exclusivist labor movement. Revolutionary activity jeopardized the status and emoluments of congressional office the Marxist politicians had long enjoyed. Broad, categorical demands for modernization went against the left's characteristic habit of seeking short-run, immediate advantages for its established constituents. Important though it may have been, the new radicalism that the left exhibited in the 1960s thus went against the grain of its own deeply rooted habits and interests.

It is against this general background that the left's increasing advocacy of agrarian reform and its growing interest in the peasants as a base of support must be considered. By the end of the last decade, the FRAP could lay reasonable claim to being the first group seriously to raise the question of land reform and to challenge the hold of the upper class over the rural workers. At the same time, however, it is also clear that Marxist efforts on behalf of the peasants were not intended to go far beyond the values and expectations of their non-Marxist competitors. By the time the first national congress of the FCI had been held in 1961, the organizational efforts of Christian Democratic-oriented groups were also well under way. If anything, the overall organizational efforts of the Marxists lagged somewhat behind other groups. The first large-scale wage strike among peasants had occurred some seven years before 1961, and had been organized by non-Marxist intellectuals, who later became affiliated with the PDC.[18]

At the national level, the FRAP's proposals for land reform were more clearly at the forefront of debate on the subject. The specifics of these proposals were, however, always kept well within the shifting mainstream of debate. In 1954 a land reform bill presented by the Socialists to the Congress was one of the first of its kind, but by the standards of the 1960s, the provisions of this bill were quite modest. The state was to acquire abandoned land and auction it off to the highest bidder. The proceeds were to be used for further land acquisitions to be redistributed among peasants. During debate on the Alessandri bill, the right seized rather gleefully on the existence of this limited proposal, pointing out that the Alessandri measure went far beyond the Socialist one.[19] The FRAP politicians responded by repudiating their own earlier measure; but even this repudiation in some measure reflected their commitment to the congressional rules of the game. The 1954 project had been presented, argued Socialist Senator Almeyda, "in accordance with the political conditions of that period, so that it could be successful as a legal initiative within the Congress." [20]

The left's new proposals, made in preparation for the presidential campaign of 1964, contained a much broader vision of change. Even these, however, did not go beyond similar proposals made by the Christian Democrats themselves. Like the PDC, the FRAP proposal eschewed the idea of total collectivization, advocating in-

196

stead a "mixed form of individual holdings, cooperatives, and state farms." Also like the Christian Democrats, FRAP congressmen promised "concessions to the owners of latifundia of a land surface sufficient to work and to live with their families. The poor and medium peasants and even the rich farmers who work their land rationally have nothing to fear. On the contrary, they will count on the aid of the State to achieve an increase in the productivity of their land." [21]

Thus, while the land reform question had explosive implications for the Chilean political system, the way the FRAP raised this question did not. On the contrary, the substance of the left's pre-1964 proposals and the method by which it sought to gain peasant support reflected its own profound ties to the existing order. These ties, it seems, continued to constitute the main motor of leftist behavior between 1964 and 1970. The incentives of the electoral and congressional system — far more than the pursuit of long-range revolutionary objectives — were the factors that most consistently explained the FRAP's congressional support of the PDC initiative, and the left's new effort to build a base of rural strength tended to reflect traditional patterns of representation already established in the cities. At both the congressional and the local level, FRAP efforts were directed, as in the past, toward gaining immediate benefits for its new peasant following and not toward exploiting the new social cleavages emerging within the countryside.

The FRAP and the Agrarian Reform:
The Congressional Level

Within days of the publication of the Christian Democratic agrarian reform legislation, both major parties of the left announced that they would vote in favor of the Christian Democratic initiative. The Political Committee of the Communist party stated that "although we do not agree fully with its details, it constitutes a good basis to begin the solutions of the agricultural problem, in accordance with the current conditions under which it has been proposed." [22] The Socialists announced that they also would support the bill, "because of the correct diagnosis [of land concentration] on which it is based." [23] Whatever the differences that lay between the relatively moderate Communists and their more radical

Socialist allies, both Marxist groups followed through on their general announcements of support with favorable votes on the general legislation.

In itself, of course, there was nothing in this support that might be taken as a necessary indication that the FRAP lacked revolutionary fervor. There were many good reasons why the most militant group might have been brought to support the Christian Democratic effort. It weakened an important segment of the Chilean "oligarchy," and it helped along a process of mobilization which the left might ultimately have hoped to capture. At the same time, there were also good reasons why the Christian Democratic reform effort could have been characterized as a devastating threat to the prospects for broader change, in the larger society and in the countryside itself. Throughout the course of the land reform bill's passage, moreover, there were a variety of ways in which a revolutionary group, acting on these reasons, might have hoped to embarrass or obstruct the reform initiative. What stands out as distinctive in the FRAP's congressional behavior is not that it rejected these reasons and these opportunities, but that they were not even seriously considered.

Among the arguments that might have been marshaled by the FRAP in opposition to the reform measures were, first, that it was a direct challenge to the left's earlier gains in the countryside, and second, that the Christian Democratic *administration* of the law threatened to defuse rural unrest at a point far short of a total restructuring of agrarian society. By the time the reform bill was presented to the Congress in November 1965, it was clear that the Christian Democrats' command of government funds, as well as the additional resources available to them through American sources, had given them a clear lead in the effort to organize rural workers. The Christian Democrats' position as the initiators of land reform and the distributors of land offered them the opportunity to consolidate this lead, particularly through such instruments of potential political control as the asentamiento, which all of the opposition parties had reason to fear.

Perhaps a still greater reason for FRAP concern was the direction in which the Christian Democratic reform appeared to be moving during the first years of the Frei administration. The actual scope of the reform was destined to be far more restricted than the original Christian Democratic promises had indicated. It had been directed, moreover, toward the most "traditional" sector of the peasantry, and pointed toward the creation of a new rural power stratum with strong vested interests in preventing further change. In this respect, the Frei regime might be said to have represented a far greater challenge than did the Alessandri administration to the egalitarian and revolutionary objectives that were supposed to inspire the left's behavior. With a far greater will and incentive to do so, the Christian Democratic regime threatened to accomplish what the Alessandri regime had proposed: an adjustment that might strengthen, rather than weaken, the "capitalist" aspects of the Chilean social order.

Had it chosen to frustrate such developments, the FRAP's options would not have been limited only to the risky attempt at revolutionary activity in the countryside. The left's thirteen senators constituted the largest single voting bloc in that chamber. If the leftists had voted against the Christian Democratic reform bill, moreover, they would probably have drawn the Radicals along with them; for the left wing of the PR was anxious to move into an electoral alignment with the FRAP, while the right wing was opposed to the bill in any case. Thus, the FRAP was in a position to command a majority in opposition to the Christian Democratic reform. In addition, by this same majority the left had already managed to gain control of the major leadership positions within the Senate and the Senate committees. With the help of Radical votes, Salvador Allende had been elected president of the Senate. The Committee on Agriculture, which was in charge of the initial hearings and recommendations on the land reform bill, was composed of four FRAP senators, two Radicals, two Christian Democrats, and one senator of the right. It was chaired by the Socialist Senator, Salomon Corbalán. Although these positions did not have the same importance as similar posts within the United States committee system, their occupants were in a position to delay passage of measures and to influence their details.

Thus, in terms of its alleged objective of promoting sweeping alterations in the rural social structure and of bringing a leftist government to power — the left's most "rational" line of behavior was quite unclear. In spite of this ambiguity, however, there is no evidence that either of the two Marxist parties proposed the more radical course of action, even as one of several alternatives.

Of the two leftist parties, the Socialists might be considered the most likely to have urged opposition to the Christian Democratic measure. In their general strategy of opposition to the Frei regime, the Socialists had publicly differed from their Communist allies, calling for a "categorical" opposition that would include all government initiatives — even those which "superficially" appeared to be "positive." On the floor of the Senate itself, Socialists occasionally argued that the Christian Democratic land reform bill was "directed toward strengthening the present system." [24] At no point, however, did the Socialists appear inclined to draw from these principles the logical conclusion that the reform bill should therefore be opposed. In practice, the Socialists as as well as the Communists appeared firmly committed to supporting the initiative.

When questioned in interviews about the apparent inconsistency between their general line of closed opposition and their support of the land reform project, the Socialist leaders tended candidly to admit the existence of a gap between their "rhetoric" and their "action." Indeed, although the Socialists had often bemoaned the fact that they talked one way and acted another, few appeared genuinely concerned about this in private. In spite of their public criticisms of the bill, all of the Socialists interviewed maintained that it was a "good law" and that they were proud of their collaboration in its passage. As one Central Committee member put it when asked about the inconsistency: "We could not simply sell out the interests of the lower class by making things worse. We are basically a democratic party. Maybe some people can argue that the best revolutionary course is to increase the misery of the people. But Chileans are basically a rational people, who repudiate such radical adventures." [25]

There is no simple explanation for the persistence of this gap between theory and practice. Some observers have attributed it to the Marxists' inclination to import radical ideologies from abroad, without really relating them to specific Chilean conditions.[26] Earlier in this chapter it was suggested that ideological militancy was useful in internal power struggles, as well as in forging a line of action toward nonleftist groups. Perhaps also, the gap between theory and practice was not always as broad as it appeared to be on the question of land reform. Clearly, however, the profession of revolutionary objectives and the general advocacy of a "closed" opposition to Christian Democratic initiatives did not have great relevance to the Socialists' behavior on land reform. It is necessary, therefore, to cut through their somewhat irrelevant rhetoric and to search for other incentives which moved both leftist parties to action.

Some of these incentives were apparent in interviews with leftist leaders. The most important of these was the obvious threat of electoral sanctions that the left might have incurred had it openly opposed the Christian Democratic measures.[27] The FRAP could justify its opposition to the Alessandri measures by pointing to the conservative character of both the regime and the reform, but these arguments were far less credible in the case of the PDC. Moreover, the Christian Democratic initiative paralleled the FRAP's own campaign proposals in many of its details; and though the FRAP did criticize the Christian Democrats "from the left" once the latter had come to office, it is probable that the disagreements did not go very far. For most leftists the land reform bill was a good law and deserved to be supported.

For a complete understanding of the nature of this support, however, it is necessary to consider the types of incentives faced by the FRAP as one group within the multiparty system. Although few FRAP politicians would admit it, it may be speculated that their actions were not based primarily on the expectation of winning a majority of the vote; for this type of objective rarely enters into the calculations of the actors in a multiparty system. What is generally sought in this type of system is a level of *minority* strength sufficient to permit influence within a governing or an opposition coalition. In Chile, where coalitions shift freely and where even opposition politicians can hope to share in the policy-making process, the line between "victory" and "defeat" is especially thin. There is some truth to the expression, heard after almost every Chilean congressional election, that "everybody wins."

Inasmuch as the FRAP acted on the basis of these expectations (and the history of its activity within the system suggests that it did), then the gains it could ultimately expect from the Christian Democratic reform initiative did not depend entirely on the losses of the Christian Democrats themselves. The "zero-sum" competition, sometimes attributed generally to the "race" between radicals and reformers, did not fully apply in Chile. On the contrary, in the 1967 elections there were many rural communes in which the FRAP or the PDC had won or lost together. While undoubtedly both groupings hoped eventually to win the race, it is nevertheless important to observe that the FRAP stood to gain something even if the PDC gained still more. Even if it finished second best, the FRAP would still augment its overall strength by championing the cause of disaffected peasant minorities and by gaining benefits for a limited peasant clientele. From the point of view of promoting revolutionary rural change, the FRAP's most rational course was ambiguous. It might have sought to oppose or support the Christian Democratic initiative. Inasmuch as the left's interest was in augmenting its existing base of electoral strength, its best course of action pointed rather clearly toward a positive, unconditional support of the reform.

On the whole, the FRAP's congressional behavior was consistent with this second interpretation of its interests. Throughout the passage of the law, the support given by the Communists and Socialists suggested a strong, positive desire to push the Christian Democratic initiative through the Congress as rapidly as possible. Although some FRAP proposals for amendments to the bill provoked debate with the government, these appeared designed more for public consumption than for the purpose of imparting a more radical content to the measure. One FRAP amendment, for example, proposed to reduce the right of reserve from eighty to forty hectares. After this was voted down in the agricultural committee, however, it was not raised again on the floor of either chamber. FRAP congressmen did object to one article which denied land titles to peasants who had seized land by force; but other "conservative" aspects of the bill were not challenged at all. There were no recorded objections from the left, for example, to the provisions which gave preference to resident farm workers in the selection of asentados, even though this provision worked against the interests of the Marxists' afuerino constituents.

The leftists were inclined, moreover, not only to avoid divisive confrontations with the Christian Democrats, but to collaborate closely in the day-to-day task of steering the bill through the senatorial labyrinth. One indication of the degree of this collaboration can be gleaned from the minutes of the Senate Committee on Agriculture. There, it will be recalled, the FRAP representatives outnumbered those of all other parties, and the chairman was the Socialist, Salomon Corbalán. Table 18 shows the alignments on

Table 18. Voting alignments on amendments to the land reform bill in the Joint Senate Commission on Agriculture

| Voting alignments | Voting distribution | | Frequency of alignment, in percentages[a] |
	With FRAP	Against FRAP	
FRAP v. PDC-PR-PN	4	5	33.3
FRAP-PDC v. PR-PN	6	3	23.8
FRAP-PDC-PR v. PN	8	1	7.1
FRAP-all	9	0	9.5
FRAP-PR v. PDC-PN	6	3	9.5
FRAP-PR-PN v. PDC	7	2	7.1
FRAP-PN v. PDC-PR	5	4	9.5
			99.8

[a] There were 42 amendments in all.

forty-two amendments brought to a vote within the committee. On one-third of the votes, the FRAP position was successfully opposed by a majority composed of the Radicals, the PDC, and the right. At the same time, however, the FRAP voted with the PDC over 40 percent of the time, and on 23.8 percent of the votes a FRAP–PDC alignment provided the majority against the Radicals and the right. When the bill finally emerged from the Congress, the Socialist chairman of the committee was thanked personally by the Minister of Agriculture for his help in the passage of the measure.

The persistence of this collaboration was all the more remarkable when the larger political context in which it occurred is considered. The left's initial announcement that it would vote for the agrarian reform was made in November 1965, a period when the Marxist copper unions were also engaged in their first bitter strike against the Christian Democratic copper initiatives. The ensuing period of cooperation in the Senate Committee on Agriculture came only months after a second copper strike had been quelled by the dispatch of government troops and by the shooting of nine

203

civilians. Evidently the FRAP considered the advantages to be gained from the land reform too important to permit even these incidents from deterring its passage.

Only one major incident between the FRAP and the PDC appeared to suggest the contrary conclusion. Because it calls into question some of the major theses advanced here about the nature of the FRAP's incentives and about its interest in land reform, this incident will be examined in some detail, even though some of its aspects have already been discussed in other connections.

Between October 1965 and January 1966, a period in which the PDC copper bill appeared to be nearing passage in the Senate, four FRAP senators insisted that the constitutional reform of property be placed on the Senate agenda for immediate debate. For a number of reasons, the FRAP initiative proved bitterly embarrassing to the Christian Democratic government. The latter had originally introduced the property amendment as a part of a larger omnibus constitutional reform that also included changes in the civil service requirements, new voting qualifications, and substantial increases in the formal powers of the president. If the property amendment were treated separately, as the FRAP had proposed, the government feared that the other measures would languish indefinitely in the Congress. Far more important, however, was the fact that the Christian Democratic government had attempted to hold back discussion of land reform legislation until it had successfully obtained the right's support for copper. By insisting on the "premature" discussion of the property amendment, the left threatened to ensnarl the fate of the two measures and to jeopardize the passage of both. When the FRAP efforts to place the amendment on the Senate agenda became successful in January 1965, some of these problems materialized. As already noted, the FRAP initiative did result in an increase in the right's bargaining leverage. The Liberals and Conservatives withheld their support of the copper initiative until limited concessions were made in the property amendment. Somewhat later, on the other hand, the FRAP attempted (unsuccessfully) to introduce amendments into the constitutional property provisions that would have abrogated all of the copper reforms which had just been enacted. Thus, with the help of the Radicals in the Senate, the FRAP introduced into the constitutional reform the provision that all mining enterprises were to be nationalized within a period of five years, provisions which the Christian Democratic majority subsequently eliminated in the Chamber of Deputies.

From the point of view of the PDC officialists, then, the FRAP initiative had some clear obstructionist implications. It had maneuvered the government into a difficult position within the Congress and within its own party. It had increased the bargaining leverage of the right and the left. And in the event that the government chose to make concessions to the right, the maneuver appeared to pave the way for the FRAP to withdraw its promise of support on land reform.

The general argument that the FRAP had as its major objective the purpose of pushing through the land reform legislation as quickly as possible would perhaps be stronger if this controversy had not taken place. This case, however, was the only serious controversy between the PDC and the FRAP that marred their congressional collaboration on land reform. Moreover, even in this one case it is doubtful that the left seriously intended to use its votes on land reform as a means of blocking the copper legislation, and it is still more doubtful that the leftists seriously considered blocking the land reform bill itself. On the contrary, while leftist pressure for immediate discussion of the property amendment provided the government with some difficulties, it was conducted with considerable elements of restraint.

Let us first consider the FRAP's attempt to abrogate the PDC copper initiative by introducing amendments into the constitutional reform of property. In fact, these amendments which had been introduced in the Senate had little chance of surviving in the final legislation. The PDC's majority in the Chamber of Deputies and the broad veto powers of the president ensured that these nationalization clauses would be eliminated, a fact of which the skilled parliamentarians of the left were well aware. Only by threatening to withdraw their support of land reform, which had not yet come to a general vote in the Senate, could the FRAP have hoped to deter the government's copper initiative. This was apparently too high a price for the left to pay, for there is no evidence that such a threat was even considered.

The other "negative" effect of the FRAP's initiative was that it forced the government to make limited concessions to the right in order to gain its final support on the copper legislation. Here again, however, the FRAP leaders were aware that any crippling concessions made by the government could be undone in the Chamber of Deputies. To be sure, the fact that any concessions were made at all provided the left with great propaganda material. The Communist newspaper, *El Siglo,* seized upon the copper accords as proof that "Frei had bent before the pressure of the Liberals and the Conservatives." [28] Once again, however, public rhetoric must be distinguished from actual behavior. Interviews conducted with both FRAP and PDC politicians indicated that the former were not interested in using these accords as a pretext for withdrawing their support or for forcing through amendments of their own. Privately, the FRAP assured the Christian Democrats that "all they had really wanted to do was to hurry the project along." [29]

The FRAP's stated purpose of "hurrying the project along," finally, should not be underestimated as one of the primary objectives behind its initiative. From the beginning of the controversy, FRAP politicians had argued that the property amendment would get nowhere as long as it remained tied to the larger omnibus measure in which it had been introduced. By moving to detach this amendment and to consider it immediately, the FRAP had accomplished precisely what it had proposed. It forced the government to set priorities and to make decisions that it had previously hoped to avoid, helping in the process to impel this vital piece of reform legislation through the legislative process. By the end of 1967, when all of the major pieces of copper and agrarian reform legislation had already been passed, the other proposals included in the original omnibus measure were still mired in the Senate. Without the FRAP's effort to detach the property section, that complement to the land reform measure might well have been stalemated along with these others.

The FRAP and the Agrarian Reform: Peasant Mobilization

In many respects the left's behavior in the countryside resembled its behavior in the Congress. Its major emphasis there, as in the Congress, appeared to be directed toward pushing the reform along and toward enlarging a peasant constituency by forcing the government to live up to its promises. Somewhat more than in the

206

Congress, this emphasis was mixed with some instances of sharp rivalry between the FRAP and the Christian Democrats, especially in the field of wage demands and wage settlements. Mutual accusations of "scabbing," of presenting exaggerated wage demands, or of reaching separate settlements were not uncommon. On the whole, however, and in spite of strong competition, the left and the PDC each seemed, at the very least, willing to coexist with the other; and at times there were some notable examples of cooperation to gain mutual objectives.

This conclusion, of course, must be considered far more tentative than conclusions drawn earlier about the FRAP's behavior within the Congress. Whereas research on the FRAP's legislative behavior covers a completed phase of reform, discussion of activity within the countryside confronts a process that, even without the FRAP's victory in 1970, would have been subject to considerable change. Among the factors that had relatively unforeseeable consequences for the behavior of the FRAP was the passage of the new unionization law in 1967. By providing funding to all of the new rural unions, the new law promised to eliminate the left's financial handicap in the competition with the Christian Democrats and offered it the opportunity to overcome the PDC's lead in the field of union organization. The changing attitudes of the peasants themselves, who in the early stages of the land reform were only gradually discarding their traditionalist orientations, provided still another indeterminate variable, which no political elite could control completely.

In spite of the ambiguities, however, two more or less distinct patterns of behavior appeared to be associated with the left's effort to gather rural support during the Frei administration. At the level of mass voting, the left was increasingly able to appeal to the most alienated sectors of Chilean society. In their efforts to organize and represent these interests, on the other hand, FRAP leaders appeared far more concerned with exploiting those channels of access opened to them by the PDC government and the Christian Democratic party than they were with consolidating the class base of their electoral support through organizational efforts that could be directed against the system as a whole.

The patterns emerging at the electoral level will be considered first. In a discussion of the development of rural political consciousness, Petras and Zeitlin point to two important correlates of the FRAP vote. They found that in the presidential elections of 1958 and 1964, among male voters, the left was most likely to equal or exceed its national percentage in two types of rural communes: those which were adjacent to mining centers, and those with low percentages of rural proprietors. Their major conclusion was that "the mining and adjoining areas develop a distinct political culture, radical and socialist in content, that tends to eliminate the importance of class differences in the peasantry and unite the peasants across class lines." [30] In other areas, they suggest that "class position is a major determinant of peasant political behavior and that the rural proletariat, as distinguished from peasant proprietors, is apparently the major social base of the FRAP in the countryside." [31]

The Petras-Zeitlin analysis may be extended by adding a further hypothesis. When speaking of the "rural proletariat," it is necessary to distinguish broadly between the inquilinos and the afuerinos. As observed earlier, the latter were the most disadvantaged stratum of the rural population, both under the old latifundia system and under the new social structure being encouraged by the Christian Democratic land reform. Thus, this important subsector of the landless rural workers might be expected to constitute the most important basis of the radical vote. Table 19 supports this contention. In the presidential elections of 1958 and 1964, the FRAP increasingly tended to equal or exceed its national vote in communes with higher percentages of afuerinos. More than 60 (60.7) percent of the rural communes in which the labor force was over 40 percent afuerino gave the FRAP a high vote in the 1964 elections; only 27.7 percent of the communes with the lowest percentage of afuerinos gave the FRAP a high vote during the same election.

Neither the Petras and Zeitlin data nor our own permit conclusive inferences about all of the determinants of peasant radicalism. Aside from the class and locational factors, possibly intervening variables related to education, crop patterns, and historical loyalties might also influence the situation. However, the data do permit the conclusion that the FRAP did penetrate electorally into the lowest strata of the Chilean social structure. More important, the data indicate the feasibility of a FRAP effort to forge an electoral

208

Table 19. Afuerino support for the left, 1958 and 1964

| Percent afuerinos in communes | Percentage of communes with a "high" FRAP vote[a] | |
	1958	1964
40+ (N = 61)	47.5	60.7
30–39 (N = 44)	42.7	50.0
20–29 (N = 35)	20.0	42.1
0–19 (N = 37)	29.1	27.7
	$(p > .05)$	$(p > .02)$

[a] Communes in which the FRAP equaled or exceeded its national voting percentage.

alliance between the two labor groups presumed to be the most disaffected with the Frei administration — organized proletarian labor and unorganized rural day workers and migrants.

Turning from electoral alignments to more direct forms of representation undertaken by FRAP politicians, however, it was evident that a quite different pattern had emerged. For one thing, at the trade union level, close cooperation failed to materialize between worker and peasant sectors associated with the left. The Marxist peasant union, the FCI, was formally affiliated with the CUT, and rural organizers were sometimes taken on a part-time basis from the urban unions. In private interviews, however, both Communist and Socialist congressmen admitted that the task of forging an alliance between workers and peasants had met only partial success.[32] The difficulty was not surprising, in the light of the nature of the CUT itself. Financially weak, internally divided, unable to consolidate even the various urban local unions into a centralized structure, the Confederation could hardly be expected to serve as the basis for a strong effort at rural mobilization. Complaints about the lack of urban support from the Marxist peasant leaders, therefore, were not uncommon. While acknowledging some instances of urban-rural cooperation, FCI president José Campusano also noted that there were "thousands of unions that should have helped to develop the peasant movement. Especially lacking in this respect are the nitrate and copper organizations." [33] This criticism of the miners was particularly interesting, since they were among the strongest of the FRAP unions.

In the countryside itself, it was evident that neither the Communists nor the Socialists were particularly interested in directing their attention to the afuerino stratum. The rural Marxist movement instead showed a tendency to go in the other direction — toward a more "vertical" pattern of mobilization, which combined some segments of the afuerinos with higher strata of the peasantry. In an early article on agrarian reform, the Communist Secretary General, Luís Corvalán, stressed the importance of an *inclusive* form of rural organization, wherever that was practical. "We Communists believe that the best form of organization is that of the independent union, with headquarters in the village, in which are grouped the workers from various *fundos* and all of the modest sectors of the rural population, from the wage hand to the small proprietor, including the sharecropper, the poor peasant, etc." [34]

Whether it was from the Marxists' actual policy or from the imperatives of local conditions, the FCI unions did appear to approach the objectives sketched out by Corvalán. After admittedly impressionistic but nevertheless long observation, members of the ICIRA staff indicated that the FCI unions did not differ markedly in their social composition from either the CNC or the INDAP unions. Although the rank-and-file membership of the Marxist rural organizations included afuerinos, the unions did not represent the exclusive interests of that stratum, and their local leadership was drawn almost entirely from higher levels of the peasantry. Some figures from the Ministry of Labor give further support to this contention. In the FCI's provincial federation in O'Higgins, almost one half (48 percent) of the original 954 members were day laborers. Of the twelve members of the provincial board, however, only two were afuerinos, while the rest were inquilinos.[35]

Other, less formal means of bringing the peasants into the political process reflected the same tendencies. In local areas, the Marxist politicians elected to municipal councils frequently built amorphous lower class clienteles by taking up the cause of individual peasants before the local police, landowners, or government agencies. On the national level, several Socialist deputies were also noted for their capacity to establish close, personal ties with a heterogeneous peasant following. A good example of this type of leader was Oscar Naranjo, the Socialist deputy from Curico. As a doctor, Naranjo developed a strong local base of support by giving free medical care to needy peasants. After his election, "much of his time in Curico and Santiago [was] spent helping the peasants to penetrate the bureaucracy by opening the doors for which only an elected official has the key." [36] Most of the Marxist elite performed similar brokerage functions; large numbers of peasants could usually be seen in the waiting room of most Socialist and Communist congressmen, awaiting their help in obtaining the payment of social security benefits, protesting a dismissal, or securing a property title, through a phone call to officials in the CORA or the Ministry of Labor.

Such activities did not, of course, prevent other, more radical confrontations between the FRAP and the PDC. On a few occasions between 1964 and 1967, Communist and Socialist congressmen were also active in organizing the occupation of fundos. Although these instances were rare (there had been four in the four-year period), they were nevertheless explosive; for they kept alive the possibility of direct action on a more massive scale, and they challenged a government commitment to prevent such action by denying ownership to peasants involved in the seizures. Even in these instances, however, the efforts of the FRAP leadership were generally confined to the resident workers of the fundo, and they usually involved brokerage as well as "agitation." In a case study of the seizure of the fundo "Los Cristales," for example, Terry McCoy points out that neither the government nor the left was willing to push their demands to the farthest extremes.[37] An agreement reached after negotiations between CORA and various Socialist leaders conceded to the peasants their right to keep the owner off the property and provided that INDAP would assume the management of the fundo. At the same time, however, the Socialists tacitly dropped their demands that the fundo be formally expropriated. The INDAP management was undertaken "on behalf" of the old owner, who was allowed to share in some of the profits from the estate. Though the peasants had been granted a de facto control, the government was permitted to keep its commitment to deny them formal ownership:

While Naranjo [the deputy who led the seizure] and the Socialist party occasionally confront the government with the problem of "Los Cristales," they seem satisfied enough with the present situation not to press for a formal, fixed solution. For the time being, the Socialists have ignored the options of further revolutionary action and confined their activities to the conventional channels of protest, such as petitioning the government to incorporate "Los Cristales" into the official agrarian reform program.[38]

The more formally organized Marxist unions often engaged in similar brokerage activities; because they cut across most rural strata, this brokerage in some instances worked to the advantage of the normally excluded afuerinos. In the badly overcrowded fundos of the Choapa Valley, one of the first "pilot projects" of the land reform, this appeared to be the case. Because the Choapa region had been owned by the state, Marxist unions had been permitted to operate there; for the same reason (it did not involve the expropriation of private lands), this area was one of the targets of the older, Alessandri reform. In 1964 Alessandri's administration moved to transfer jurisdiction to CORA, which was then expected to parcel the land out into individual plots. Because of the population density of the region, the distribution of economically viable parcels would have required the expulsion of a significant proportion of the peasants. By a series of strikes and demonstrations, therefore, the Marxist unions were able to block the transfer of the Choapa lands to the CORA, and the situation remained stalemated through the end of the Alessandri period.

After the election of Frei, however, negotiations were begun with the new leaders of CORA. The resulting agreement involved the establishment of asentamientos, in which at least some of the day workers were to be included as asentados and in which others were to continue to be contracted from the outside.[39] The difficult question of selection had thus been postponed, but as a short-run arrangement, the results of the negotiations appeared to satisfy both sides. ICIRA studies, made two years later, showed that the wage differential between inquilinos and afuerinos had narrowed since the establishment of the asentamiento. The Marxist union leaders, in the meantime, had themselves been elected to the asentamiento committees, and were reported to have established good working relations with the officials of CORA.[40]

In distinguishing between the FRAP's apparently broad class-based electoral support and these more "vertical," particularlistic forms of representation, one cannot ignore the possibility that the latter will disappear as the workers and peasants become more class conscious and more disaffected. The type of brokerage described above can be effective only so long as it involves a limited number of workers of all social strata, since fundo seizures and the inclusion of afuerinos in overcrowded areas on a broad scale would be neither politically nor economically feasible. At the same time, however, the obvious similarities between these forms of representation and the FRAP's own earlier behavior in the cities suggests that they may be an enduring aspect of the Chilean political system.

Sidney Tarrow's study of a similar phenomenon in Italy gives some comparative support to this contention. In Southern Italy, Tarrow argues, a Communist effort to mobilize the peasants resulted in a fusion between the *form* of a mass organization and the reality of "clientele" politics, paralleling the older relationship between patron and peasant.[41] If it cannot be stated with confidence that a similar adaptation will be made in Chile, neither can it be denied that these "traditional" linkages between patron and client often reappear, even in the most "modern" institutions and processes. To the extent that this was true in the Chilean countryside, the FRAP's behavior as an opposition party had a "safety-value" effect, relieving tensions by accommodating some parts of all social strata and defusing a potentially revolutionary and alienated sector of the peasantry.

The FRAP and the Copper Dispute

The discussion of the left's support of the Christian Democratic land reform would not be complete if it failed to take into account the left's strong opposition to other policies of the Frei regime. Throughout the Frei administration, the FRAP attacked the government for its failure to control the urban monopolies and to mobilize the urban poor. Both Communists and Socialists sided with Cuba in the polemics that erupted between that country and the Frei government, while the Socialists joined the Cuban-oriented Organization of Continental Solidarity and helped to establish its headquarters in Santiago.[42] Finally, the left's opposition to the "Chileanization" of the copper companies led eventually to prolonged strikes and to violence. Were these forms of opposition also best explained in terms of the FRAP's continuing ties to the existing sociopolitical order? Or did they represent a process of radicalization that transcended the limits and incentives that appeared to operate in the FRAP's collaboration on land reform?

There can be little question that on many of the issues that divided the FRAP from the Christian Democracy, FRAP leaders were driven — as they were in the process of peasant mobilization — in part by a serious concern for establishing a genuinely nationalistic and popularly based movement and by a profound desire to move away from the errors of the past. In their opposition to the copper reforms, which provoked the most bitter confrontation between the left and the PDC, Communists and Socialists argued with some justification that the stock purchases and long-term tax concessions envisioned by the Frei regime formed a step which would only consolidate the position of the American companies and forestall the prospects of outright nationalization. It is probably no accident, however, that of the many disagreements which permeated the relations between the left and the government, it was the copper issue which induced the most bitter confrontation. As the conflict developed, it became apparent that what was at stake was not simply the question of nationalization, but also the interests of the copper miners — one of the FRAP's strongest and most "established" constituencies.

In addition to the strong opposition carried on by the FRAP leadership in the Congress — an opposition which has already been discussed — the copper dispute involved two work stoppages, each of which was of unprecedented length and each of which involved the workers in all of the major mines. The first strike began in October 1965 and lasted through November of the same year. It was initiated after it became clear that the FRAP would not be able to block the general congressional approval of the copper agreements. The second strike (which lasted through January and February of 1966) began in the Chiquicamata mines, owned by Braden Copper Company, and had as its origin a genuine wage dispute between the miners and the employers. Almost immediately, however, sympathy strikes were organized in the other mines, in partial protest against an annual wage readjustment bill then being debated in the Congress. Although the second strike appeared to be more directly concerned with the question of wages, it renewed the question of the copper agreements as well; for attached as riders to the readjustment legislation were the important details of the copper legislation that had been at issue in the bargaining between the government and the right.

It is of some interest to note that both strikes were technically illegal and that this was the pretext used by the government to arrest the leaders of the first strike and to dispatch troops to end the second. In this respect, however, it was probably the government rather than the FRAP that had departed from the accepted norms. Unions frequently engaged in, and Chilean governments usually tolerated, activities that were formally prohibited by the restrictive Chilean labor code. More important as an indication of the FRAP's increasing militancy was its apparent willingness to engage in prolonged stoppages, designed in part to attain manifestly "political" objectives. Normally, even strikes that were strictly limited to trade union questions were settled in a matter of days or weeks, rather than months. And while stoppages protesting broader governmental policies were not unknown, they were usually restricted to a limited time period, often twenty-four hours, announced beforehand by the union or party leaders. The copper strikes of 1965 and 1966, by contrast, were clearly related to the issue of nationalization, and were initiated with a commitment to continue the stoppages for an undefined period of time. For these reasons, the officialists of the Christian Democracy accused the left of a new and reckless disregard for the national economy, while editorials in the conservative newspapers, *El Mercurio* and *Diario Ilustrado,* tended to view the strikes as the Chilean version of "guerrilla warfare."

Although the FRAP's commitment to nationalization had undoubtedly increased, it was not clear that their activity represented as abrupt a departure from their earlier "constitutionalism" as the polemics had indicated. In many respects, both their objectives in 1965–66 and the means they employed to attain these objectives were ones which had long been associated with their role within the system.

It is probably true that the FRAP's determination to pursue extended strikes was a serious provocation to a government attempting to reform the economy; but it was government troops, not the miners, that had initiated the actual violence that erupted in the copper strikes. There is thus reason to believe that the bitterness involved in the confrontation stemmed as much from the government's decision to act with unusual (and perhaps unwarranted) firmness, as from an increasing rebelliousness on the part of the FRAP. In any case, limited forms of direct action in order to achieve trade union objectives had always been a part of the left's arsenal of political weapons, even in the most moderate phases of its history.

At the same time, the Communist and Socialist leaders were clearly reluctant to permit the unleashing of broader forms of violence over which they could not exercise control. This reluctance had long been a characteristic of the left's political behavior and continued throughout the Christian Democratic period. Leftist leaders cooperated with governmental authorities, for example, in helping to restore order after the devastating Santiago bus-fare riots of 1957.[43] Again, in 1961, the leaders of the FRAP collaborated to purge the CUT of anarchist elements, which had advocated efforts to direct the workers' movement toward a form of urban guerrilla warfare.[44] After a radical fringe group initiated a series of bombings in 1967–68, leaders of both established Marxist parties issued statements of public condemnation, deploring the acts as "adventuristic" and "un-Marxist." [45]

More important perhaps than the elements of continuity in the *means* employed by the FRAP was the nature of the *objectives* they sought. Whatever the left's ideological commitment may have been about nationalization and imperialism, its continuing concern about more concrete benefits for its mining constituency should not be underestimated. In spite of their apparently categorical condemnation of the government's proposals for stock purchases, leftist congressmen sought to incorporate into the copper bill itself a variety of welfare provisions for the mine workers — a forty-hour week, extended housing and pension benefits, and other similar measures. Only after some of these provisions were eliminated from the law in the Chamber of Deputies did the first copper strike begin. The second strike, as noted earlier, was still more directly concerned with wages. In that case the FRAP objected to the government's offer of a 25 percent readjustment in mining wages — a raise equal to the official figures on price increases for the preceding year. Instead, the left demanded a 40 percent readjustment, a claim that was by no means unreasonable when it is considered that the official figures on inflation were generally acknowledged to be below the real increases in price levels.

Throughout both strikes the leftist leaders themselves strongly denied the "political" character of the strikes and insisted that they were strictly unionist in nature. "The copper strike," a Socialist declaration stated during the first stoppage, "is exclusively unionist [gremial] and it conforms to the legitimate right of these workers to struggle for gains against the obstinacy of companies . . . who refuse to accept the social welfare amendments included in the Senate." [46] Similarly, the Communists maintained that the strikes were meant to ensure that the "benefits won with great difficulty in the long years of struggle will be respected." [47] Their claims were reinforced by the fact that the question of nationalization never entered into the negotiations or the settlement of either strike. The relatively peaceful settlement of the first strike was limited strictly to salary issues, and was heralded by the Communists and Socialists as a victory for the workers. The complaints raised after the repression of the second stoppage did not mention the copper agreements. More conventionally, they were directed against the government's abrogation of the "right to strike."

This is not to say that the FRAP's opposition to the copper agreements was merely a facade. There was no necessary incompatibility between the left's demand for outright nationalization and its attempt to gain welfare concessions for the copper workers. On the contrary, in any process of change, labor's bread-and-butter interests often overlap with ideological radicalism. Still less can it be denied that, for whatever reasons they were undertaken, the copper strikes represented considerable obstacles to the government's attempt to encourage investment by the copper companies. But however much the FRAP's militancy may have stemmed from these more radical objectives, it also stemmed from a stubborn defense of and a desire to extend gains already won within the framework of the established system. On occasion, the government itself recognized this "conservative" component of the FRAP's radical behavior. "The FRAP," it claimed, had "abused its union's

217

power by trying, through prolonged strikes, to obtain a preferential and exceptional treatment and break the basis of what should be a unified national effort, to the disadvantage of the rest of the workers." [48]

Although the discussion of the FRAP's copper opposition thus tends to support part of the earlier interpretation given to its role in the land reform, it does, however, call into question some aspects of the safety-valve role earlier ascribed to the left's activity. There can be little question that the copper strikes were enormously costly and disruptive to the national economy. Estimates of the cost of the strikes in terms of production and foreign exchange reached 70 million dollars, while the cost of the actual delay in initiating the copper programs was probably still greater. In this sense the left's tendency to engage in an aggressive pursuit of wage demands threatened to contribute to general instability and to a climate of increasing conflict.

In a second, more subtle sense, the left's opposition to the copper reforms illustrated another way in which it challenged the land reform process. The concern for protecting or extending the benefits of various labor groups tended to compete with the land reform process itself for governmental funds and attention. However willing the FRAP may have been to support the government's land reform effort, it was not willing to allow the cost of this effort to fall upon its organized labor constituency. By pressing simultaneously for wage benefits and for structural change, the FRAP tended to pull the system in two opposing directions. As long as it remained in opposition, the left could probably move in both directions without any political cost to itself. In the event of its rise to power, however, the left — no less than the Christian Democrats — would be faced with the need to reconcile these quite different, and contradictory, expectations. This conflict between the interests of organized labor and the governmental commitment to land reform became still clearer during 1967–68, after both the copper and the land reform legislation had been passed.

Part 4 The Urban-Rural Cleavage, 1968–1970

Chapter 7 The Urban Radicals and Land Reform

Land reform usually requires a coalition between peasants and at least some discontented sectors of urban society. The role of peasants in this coalition has received the most attention and there is little doubt that some pressure from the peasantry is necessary for a thoroughgoing redistribution of property. Nevertheless, it is from urban society that the peasants draw leadership, support for their demands, and legitimation for their actions. Without the aid of dissident urban groups, dissatisfied peasants are likely to be repressed. With such aid, other things being equal, they are likely to succeed. Having examined eight separate land reforms, Elias Tuma concluded that "the more dissatisfied the middle class, the more likely the reform." [1]

In the early 1960s, many of the conditions for an urban-rural coalition appeared to be emerging in Chile. Intellectuals and middle class politicians began to move into the countryside, to organize peasants, to promise them land reform, and to seek their electoral support. Broader sectors of urban society, suffering under the weight of economic stagnation and rising prices, appeared receptive to this effort. "As of 1960," Frederick Pike has written, "there were many signs that middle groups might be seeking an alliance with the lower classes . . . Stung by inflation and with their hopes for expanding opportunities frustrated by Chile's lack of real growth, some middle-class supporters of the Christian Democratic Party, of the activist wing of the Radical Party, and of the FRAP . . . seemed intent upon siding with the lower mass in a genuine attempt to alter the traditional sociopolitical structure." [2]

Within Chile, the reform-minded elites themselves were also highly sensitive to the possibility and importance of this alliance. Justifications of land reform proposals invariably stressed the benefits that such a program would bring to the urban population. A redistribution of rural property was to bring higher productivity, more and cheaper food, and expanding economic opportunities for city dwellers, as well as land for the peasants. The view of the left-wing sector of the Christian Democratic party in this respect reflected the strategy and the hope of much greater numbers of political leaders. "The concrete objective," stated the Chonchol Plan, "should be to reduce the right to the exclusive support of the oligarchical sectors and the latifundistas, in accordance with the objective criteria of the distribution of land and income . . . *We must consolidate a stable social and electoral support through the creation of an alliance between the people and the progressive middle class.*" [3]

But even while these words were being written, hopes that the Christian Democrats could maintain such an alliance were fading. The municipal elections of 1967 were marked by a significant falling off of the Christian Democrats' urban support, by a continued growth of leftist party strength, and by a turn to the right among at least some city voters. What had gone wrong?

Disappointed U.S. officials, political commentators, and frustrated Christian Democratic politicians themselves often answered this question by pointing to the mistakes of the Christian Democratic regime. According to their ideological predispositions, critics argued that the regime had moved too quickly or too slowly; that it had frightened away its more conservative followers by rash action; or that it had disappointed its more radical followers by making promises on which it could not deliver. It is extremely doubtful, however, that the causes of urban disaffection can be attributed entirely to the political mistakes of the regime. In point of fact, the regime had by 1967 begun to deliver on many of the promises it had made upon coming into office, and it had acted in a way which might have been expected to maximize rather than alienate the support of city dwellers. The period from 1964–1967 had been marked by a reasonable rate of economic growth, by a reduction in the rate of inflation, by the passage of major reform laws, and by the beginning of a modest, but not insignificant, land redistribution program. The regime may well have made some errors in its effort to consolidate an urban-rural coalition, but it is likely that its failure was due to broader difficulties that would be faced by almost any regime which came to power in Chile. The possibilities of an urban-rural alliance in Chile, in short, may have been badly overestimated in the first place.

The Difficulties of an Urban-Rural Coalition

When parallels are cited between the potential role of the city in the Chilean land reform and successful urban-rural alliances in other countries, at least one important difference is sometimes overlooked. In most other countries the alliance had been formed during the early stages of modernization, at a time when the middle class was still a relatively small counterelite seeking to displace a dominant rural oligarchy and when the peasants were still an overwhelming majority capable of providing the support necessary to achieve this objective. Only Cuba, with its long subjugation to the United States, its semiproletarian sugar workers, and its unusually repressive military dictatorship is an exception to this rule. In Bolivia, Mexico, Russia, and China, where the formation of an urban-rural coalition resulted in revolution, the leadership was provided by a small intelligentsia and by a somewhat larger commercial sector, both of which had previously been excluded from the existing system of power and status. This was also true in most countries where land reform was instituted by steps short of revolution. Egypt and Pakistan, for example, undertook land reforms at a much earlier stage of development than Chile's. And in Venezuela, now a highly urbanized country, the urban-peasant alliance originated in the 1930s, when the middle class was also quite small.

In the 1960s Chile's urban society was, by contrast, large and heterogeneous — which tended to affect the composition of a prospective urban-rural coalition and to alter the conditions in which it could be maintained. The rural oligarchy, which elsewhere had been the target of urban and rural dissatisfaction, had in Chile long ceased to function as a dominant ruling class, and peasants were already a minority of the population. Chilean middle and working class groups had, on the other hand, grown enormously in size and political influence. To maintain itself in power, therefore, a Chilean reform government required more than the support of peasants and middle class intellectuals. It needed mass support from the cities as well. And in view of the multiplicity of interests, functional groupings, and ideological outlooks that existed within this urban world, the task of winning and maintaining the allegiance of significant numbers of Chilean city dwellers was far more complex and difficult than it might have been in simpler societies.

One possible source of support were the urban marginals — a loosely defined group which presumably included recent migrants to the cities, unskilled and nonfactory labor, and people who lived in urban slums. This subproletarian lower class had grown enormously in recent years, and it figured prominently in the electoral calculations of the Christian Democrats and the left. Nevertheless, the political importance of this sector has probably been exaggerated. Recent studies of urban marginals — and particularly of the new migrants into the cities — have all strongly downgraded the revolutionary potential that was once thought to exist within this sector.[4] Several studies have noted contrary tendencies, toward relative satisfaction, awe and respect for established authority, and general political passivity. In some Latin American countries, slum dwellers have provided strong support for right-wing personalist leaders. And in Chile itself, the paternalistic and authoritarian appeal made by Jorge Alessandri apparently had an impact among the urban poor. Besides the peasants themselves, the urban marginals are the most tradition-bound group in Chile, and the most difficult one to organize. Therefore, while the urban marginals may or may not provide votes for a reformist movement, active backing for such a movement would probably have to come from or be supplemented by more organized and influential segments of the city population — white-collar workers, small merchants and proprietors, and factory workers.

By the late 1950s and early 1960s, these urban strata had grown increasingly dissatisfied with their situation, which led them initially to join the peasants in supporting the Christian Democrats and the FRAP. There was reason to believe, however, that much of this support was politically unstable and difficult to translate into effective backing for broad programs of economic development and structural change. Unlike "emerging" urban groups in countries still dominated by old rural aristocracies, and like the middle sectors in other advanced Latin American countries, much of Chile's city population had already been granted a degree of power and status. Struggles characteristic of countries at early stages of urbanization had, in Chile, already been resolved without recourse to an alliance with peasants. Political power and limited social mobility had been afforded to members of the propertied middle class. The right to organize and to strike for wages had been granted to industrial and white-collar workers. These gains had been limited by the continuing influence of the older aristocracy, and were jeopardized by the inability of the economic order to continue the rapid expansion of the 1930s and 1940s. But the resulting frustrations of the "established" urban strata stemmed less from their *exclusion* from the existing system than from the *erosion* of the gains they had already made. This distinction can profoundly affect the nature and direction of urban protest.

It is plausible, for example, to assume that an erosion of previously-won gains incline many middle class Chileans to support the far right, rather than the reformist center-left. In Argentina and Brazil, nationalist military coups are said to have had the backing of these sectors. Although the left-of-center Christian Democrats also enjoyed considerable middle class support, this may well have resulted more from a fear of Communism than from a strong backing for developmental and reformist objectives. In any case, the widespread popularity of Ibañez and Alessandri during the 1950s and the gains of the National party in 1967 indicated that the potential for antireformist protests was quite high in Chile, particularly among the propertied sectors of urban society.

The dissatisfaction of white-collar and factory workers flowed in a somewhat different direction. With their wage benefits eaten away by inflation, with jobs rendered insecure and mobility limited by slow economic growth, these groups seemed to be solid supporters of change-oriented parties and the most likely urban allies of the peasants in their demand for land reform. But the discontent of these sectors also meant important difficulties for a government interested in promoting rural change. These groups frequently protested against price increases and job insecurity, but their claims on the system rarely crystallized into demands for changes of specific aspects of the existing social order. What was at stake for urban radicals, as for the more comfortable elements within the city, was the extension of benefits already established within the system — better wages, more social security, more comfortable housing. White-collar and factory workers were unquestionably dissatisfied in a vague, general way with the existing state of affairs in Chile, and they were inclined to press aggressively for measures which affected their immediate interests. But they appeared to be relatively disinterested in broader ideological and structural issues.

Support for this contention can be found in attitude surveys of blue-collar workers conducted separately by Alex Inkeles and Henry Landsberger in the city of Santiago in the early 1960s. When asked what degree of change Chile needed in order to advance, 33 percent of Inkeles's respondents answered that "total and immediate change" was necessary, while only 1 percent felt that no change was necessary. But the general desire for change was not normally translated into protest against specific aspects of the socioeconomic structure. Only 8 percent of the labor leaders, for example, found that foreign capital had done "much harm." Sixty-eight percent felt that foreign capital had been beneficial, or that it had done neither good nor harm.[5] The study conducted by Henry Landsberger produced similar results. In the Landsberger sample, 34 percent of the respondents felt "total and immediate change" was necessary for progress, and only 1 percent felt none was needed. On the other hand, 73 percent of the union respondents found relations with management either "very good" or "more good than bad." Only 3 percent described their relations as entirely bad, while 23 percent felt they were "more bad than good." [6]

Both surveys indicated that blue-collar groups were most easily mobilized over questions of immediate economic interest, rather than broad, ideological issues. In the Inkeles study, 89 percent of the union leaders felt that the most important task of the union was to improve the economic position of the workers through wages and pensions or to improve the physical conditions of work. Only 11 percent felt that the union should be primarily interested in "broad programs and social activities" or in awakening "strong political attitudes and consciousness." Ordinary union members and workers who were not unionized exhibited an even more overwhelmingly "economistic" orientation. Ninety-seven percent of the former and 100 percent of the latter group felt that the most important goal of the union was better wages or improved conditions of work. The Landsberger study of union leaders found that 62 percent of the workers felt that in the next three to five years the unions should concentrate on salaries, severance pay, pensions, and so forth; only 1 percent felt it should stress political consciousness; only 8 percent gave priority to improving the education and spiritual development of workers; and only 10 percent opted for a goal of "unification and strengthening of the union movement in Chile." [7] The remarkable fact, Landsberger notes, "is that 43 percent of the union leaders professed to be sympathetic to the two Chilean Marxist parties, the Communists and Socialists; yet they did not see the union in Marxist terms. And 23 percent of the leaders professed sympathy toward the Christian Democrats; yet few emphasized education." [8]

Similar tendencies can be noted among white-collar workers, the most politicized and "radical" component of the urban working class. Like the blue-collar laborers, white-collar sectors were militant in their efforts to win bread-and-butter gains, and there is evidence that this militancy increased in the course of the Frei regime. In the four-year period from 1962 through 1965, the number of man-days lost through white-collar strikes multiplied almost seven times — from 27,332 in 1962, to 215,103 in 1965.[9] Yet there is little in such militancy to suggest strong feelings of solidarity with peasants, a sustained commitment to broad, developmental programs, or a deep interest in rural reform. On the contrary, the available data point in the opposite direction. One study of various strata of public employees, for example, found that while 66 percent of the sample favored "change," no more than 18 percent of the various white-collar strata attached a "high degree of importance" to agrarian reform and from 56 percent to 76 percent of the different strata felt such reform was of "low" importance.[10] The behavior of white-collar unions appeared to reflect such attitudes. Although white-collar leaders and trade union congresses occasionally made favorable comments about agrarian reform in speeches and declarations, this rhetoric was not transformed into contributions toward peasant organization, or into sustained lobbying efforts within the government.

This does not mean that the "progressive" urban mass played no positive role in the land reform process. These groups, after all, voted for leaders who espoused the redistribution of rural property and who sought to mobilize the peasants. Their general dissatisfaction with the state of affairs in Chile undoubtedly contributed to a crisis atmosphere in which "reform" was considered necessary in order to avert "revolution." It is probable, moreover, that a side effect of this dissatisfaction was to increase the popularity of land reform as a symbol of change, as an attack on the "oligarchy," and as a dramatic step toward progress. At the same time, however, the concrete demands that were actively pursued by these groups tended at many points to conflict with the necessities of a land reform program. A government which spent time resolving wage disputes had less time to spend on the agricultural sector; funds spent on urban jobs, social security, and pensions meant fewer funds for expropriation of rural property and for the disbursement of credit and extension aid to peasants. A general urban interest in cheaper food conflicted in the short run with the need to provide market incentives to old and new rural proprietors. The paradox of urban society was that while a majority was probably weakly inclined toward land reform, it was strongly opposed to paying the costs that would be incurred in such a program.

The role of the "progressive" urban social forces in the politics of land reform was thus an ambivalent one. It varied with the level on which political activity occurred and with the different stages of the process of land division. The role was obviously most positive at those levels and stages where the costs of the program were least apparent. Early in the land reform and within the Congress, urban dissatisfaction undoubtedly contributed to the landowners' sense of isolation and encouraged the urban upper class to remain on the sidelines. As the reform moved to the administrative level and as urban sacrifices became necessary, however, the behavior of the different city sectors became negative. Though many of these groups did not explicitly abandon the rhetoric of reform, it became increasingly difficult to channel their behavior in directions that did not seriously detract from meaningful change.

The Radicals and the Urban Paradox

The "natural" beneficiaries of urban dissatisfaction were the opposition parties. In the municipal elections of 1967, all three opposition sectors made gains in the cities which exceeded their national percentages. From the perspective of 1967, it was still far too early to determine the extent of the trend toward the opposition parties or which opposition sector would ultimately gain the most. One thing, however, was apparent: directly or indirectly, the appeals made by these urban opposition sectors tended to have an undermining effect on the Christian Democratic effort at land reform. This effect was, of course, clearest and most direct in the case of the right. The National party attempted to take advantage of unrest by stressing the costs of agrarian reform and by promising a return to order, stability, and national unity. The left and the Radicals supported the idea of broad, dramatic change, but they also sought to capitalize on urban unrest by sustaining a militant defense of immediate trade union interests that often retarded such change.

The paradox of urban discontent was expressed in its purest form by the Radical party. The Radicals had the fewest ideological and political interests in land reform and the closest ties to the heterogeneous urban middle sector. Unlike the Communists and Socialists, the party had not established a solid base of peasant support; and it had not attracted the type of intellectual who served in the Christian Democratic party to elaborate detailed developmental programs and who pressed for structural change. At all levels the Radical party was rooted solidly in the propertied and salaried sectors of the middle class. Its organization and behavior thus tended to reflect their tensions, anxieties, and outlooks.

At the height of the Radicals' power in the 1940s, the party leaders had managed to unite these groups into a solid electoral and patronage machine. Provincial businessmen seeking favors, white-collar workers seeking jobs, and even rival politicians seeking support turned to Radical congressmen and executives for aid. A wide network of local and provincial asembleas — each a combination social club, employment agency, and electioneering organization — linked national party leaders closely to local notables and white-collar associations and provided the latter with considerable leverage in national politics. As Federico Gil has noted, "No leader can hope to maintain his influence without immediate connection with the asembleas, since these bodies often enough can manage to make or unmake candidates by their stubborn resistance to submit to impositions from above." [11] By working with the support of these local units, individual Radical leaders could parlay themselves into high governmental office and from there, through connections and power, into positions of social status and economic wealth.

Bitter dissension and hard in-fighting were almost inevitable in a party with this type of social composition and organization; and like the Christian Democrats, Radicals sometimes divided into what can be roughly categorized as left and right wings. The bases of Radical factionalism, however, were not primarily ideological or programmatic. The concerns of local middle class groups, disputes over the spoils of office, personal political rivalries, and the electoral necessities of the moment played a far greater role within the Radical divisions than they did within the Christian Democracy. Although some Radical leaders were, of course, deeply committed to various structural issues, the party's internal disputes were generally characterized by the rapid formation and dissolution of cliques, small-scale rebellions and reconciliations, and abrupt shifts in the allegiances of individual leaders and party groups. Thus, a leader like Pedro Aguirre, the first Radical to be elected to the Chilean presidency, could strongly oppose the Popular Front alliance in 1937 and assume the leadership of the alliance in 1938. A Gabriel Gonzalez, another Chilean president, could urge close ties with the Communists in 1946 and could initiate the move to outlaw the party two years later.

By the mid-1960s the Radicals had been out of the presidency for over a decade. Their once formidable political machine had become worn, and the factional struggles had become somewhat more intense. Nevertheless, the composition, organization, and outlook that had characterized the party during its heyday continued in large measure to shape its behavior. Because of their continued congressional strength, the Radicals remained in a position to act as brokers for a variety of middle sector groups. This, in turn, helped to provide the party with a remarkable staying power, which generally defied predictions about its imminent collapse or disintegration. At the same time, precisely because their constituents had limited, nonideological concerns, party leaders were consistently able to take on or discard "collectivist" rhetoric or to change alignments as circumstances dictated — without basically altering their fundamental orientation within the system. Drifts to the left or right stemmed, in Kalman Silvert's words, from "the necessity to take color from coalition rather than from inner conviction directed outward in convincingly proposed policy." [12]

It is in this context that the post-1964 behavior of the Radicals

230

must be viewed — both with respect to their general alliance formed with the FRAP and with regard to their position on land reform. The Radicals' post-1964 alignment with the left abruptly reversed a drift toward cooperation with the rightist parties that had begun in 1948 with the outlawing of the Communists and culminated in 1962–63 with the formation of the Democratic Front. Needless to say, a shift of such magnitude could not have been accomplished without serious internal difficulties. The shift began shortly after the PR's defeats in 1965, when angry delegates of the Radical National Assembly rejected the official reports of the right-wing executive committee, prompting five of the most prominent members of this committee to resign from the party in protest. It was consolidated in 1967, when Alberto Baltra, a long-time member of the far-left wing of the party, became the Radicals' presumptive presidential candidate and their leading spokesman in the preelection period. Also catapulted into important positions of leadership in the course of this transition was a small group of young Radical lawyers, two of whom were installed as the Secretary General and Treasurer of the party. Drawing from what they felt to be the example of the early Falangists, these leaders hoped to establish a new "doctrinal" orientation for the Radicals and to transform the party into a disciplined cadre, unwilling to sacrifice "reform" for electoral expediency. "It is time," argued the new Secretary General, "to abandon the belief that we belong to a party equidistant from the left and right. The PR belongs to the forces of labor and as such it has one common ancestral enemy — the exploiting classes." [13]

Notwithstanding the rotation of leaders at the top of the party structure, however, these hopes were not likely to be realized. Two important obstacles blocked the way. First, the "purge" of right-wing members of the executive committee did not fully extend down into the congressional or local bases of the party membership. Most of these sectors could now agree that the center-right strategy had been a political mistake, and many were willing to acquiesce tentatively to the leadership of such men as Baltra. For the core of congressmen and local leaders who constituted the major center of power within the party, it is likely that the shift was motivated more by tactical expediency than by a recognition of the importance of a broad reorientation of doctrine. To regain

the presidency the Radicals needed allies. A center-right alliance
had, however, already proved ineffective, and a coalition with the
Christian Democrats would inevitably be dominated by them. This
left the Communists and Socialists — an alternative that was not
unacceptable to the pragmatic elements within the PR as a means
to regain office. One provincial leader who supported the move
toward the FRAP justified his support in the following manner:
"In order to channel its practical action, the [Radical party] must
circumstantially collaborate with other political forces. Within the
national political mosaic, it might happen that the only force with
which we can collaborate would be the FRAP . . . They consider
us 'fellow travelers.' We have the same idea about them. We can
go together part of the way. But as soon as our interpretation of
the political reality becomes incompatible, nothing will stop us
from becoming adversaries." [14]

A second limitation lay in the composition and outlook of the
Radical left wing itself. As among the Christian Democrats, this
loose and amorphous sector had always constituted a powerful
force within the Radical party. Unlike the PDC left wing, however,
the source of Radical leftism was not the universities, the student
movements, or the personnel of technical, advisory bodies, where
the PR as a whole enjoyed little support. It came instead from the
ranks of the lower middle class — primary school teachers, government bureaucrats, and white-collar employees. On the whole, this
meant that the Christian Democratic left-winger was "in general
intellectually superior to his counterpart in the Radical party," [15]
and presumably more attuned to the ideological issues of the day.
Radical leftists, moreover, were generally at least a generation older
than the Christian Democratic "rebels," many of whom had entered the Congress in their late twenties and early thirties — fresh
from the battles of the universities themselves. Often actual veterans of the days of the Popular Front, the Radical leftists tended
to identify with the older issues of that period — public education,
industrialization, state ownership of industry, and social security.
Though these Radicals were also open to the advocacy of other
measures such as land reform, much of their rhetoric continued to
fight the battles of the 1930s. A declaration of the Radical youth
division in 1966, for example, called upon the party to promote
three "fundamental" objectives: "(1) the nationalization of trans-

portation; (2) the nationalization of Chilean education and the elimination of all private [i.e., Catholic] schools in the country; (3) fundamental changes in the social security system." [16]

These limitations should not be lost from view in evaluating the Radicals' role in the land reform controversy that took place after 1964. On the positive side, it is probable that the ascendency of the Radical party's left wing helped to assure the PR's support in Congress of the Christian Democratic agrarian measures, for the right wing of the party was clearly reluctant to accept rural change. Although the latter group had initiated the Alessandri legislation, it had strong private reservations about the implementation of even these modest measures, and during the Frei period, several of these right-wingers moved into open opposition to the PDC legislation. Some, like Pedro Alfonso, had resigned from the Radical party to assume the leadership of the most militant segments of the opposition. Others, like Julio Durán, remained in the party and voted for the land reform bill in the Congress, but otherwise joined in the general chorus of public criticism. The new left-wing Radical leaders who controlled the executive committee after 1965 were, on the other hand, clearly more favorable to the idea of land reform; and they readily followed the FRAP's lead in supporting the Christian Democratic measures.

The importance of these votes should not be underestimated. The PR's support of the PDC initiative helped to solidify the government's Senate majority. It contributed to the isolation of the right within the Congress. And it provided the Christian Democratic government with some flexibility in dealing with the other opposition parties.

Outside the legislative arena, however, the PR made few positive contributions to the redistribution of rural property or to the mobilization of peasants. Unlike the Christian Democrats, who drafted much of their complex reform law while they were in opposition to the Alessandri regime, the Radicals showed neither the interest nor the ability to elaborate the details of a reform program. Unlike the Christian Democrats and the FRAP, the Radicals were not active in mobilizing peasants, in pressing for the passage of the bill, or even in drumming up support for the reform within the cities. Through 1967, no Radical peasant organization had come into existence. Nor did the Radical politicians show any signs of having thought systematically about how the interests of their salary-earning supporters might best be defended within the general context of a reform program. If Radical right-wingers appeared basically opposed to changes in the rural social structure during the Christian Democratic period, the leftists who controlled the party appeared basically disinterested.

In these respects, then, the Radicals' backing of the land reform was superficial. Their desire to defend the competing welfare claims of the urban middle class, on the other hand, was profound. And this desire was shared by all sectors of the PR leadership. Even the conservative elements that prevailed during the Alessandri period were unable or unwilling to ignore such pressures for special welfare benefits and subsidies. Between 1958 and 1964, the Radicals constantly tried to chip away at Alessandri's austerity measures, in spite of the strain this placed on their coalition with the right. Although this coalition survived almost to the end of Alessandri's term, a decision by Radical congressmen to support the wage demands of striking public health workers did, late in 1963, provoke the resignation of the Radical cabinet ministers and the withdrawal of the party from cabinet-level positions.[17]

The Radical shift to the left after 1964 moved the party toward an even more militant posture on these welfare issues. After 1964, leaders of white-collar associations were given a greater voice within the executive committee. In the unions themselves, Radicals and Communists frequently ran combined slates against the Christian Democrats. The Radical leaders of the Association of Public and Private Employees (ANEF and ANEP) were encouraged to work closely with the Communist and Socialist leaders of the blue-collar confederation, the CUT. The PR protested the alleged persecution of Radical civil servants; it condemned efforts to restrict wage and salary increases; it attacked the PDC for permitting inflation to continue and for allowing the workers to suffer under the weight of "unjust" taxes.

All of this placed the Christian Democratic government in a complex and difficult cross fire. Although the Radicals professed a desire for land reform, they refused to engage in broad cooperation with a government promoting this program. Although the party leaders echoed diffuse demands that everything must change, they

pressed most aggressively for claims that diverted energies and resources from the effort to change anything at all.

The focus has been on the Radicals as the principal expression
of this paradox, though this form of behavior was by no means
limited to them alone. On the contrary, the tendency to adopt progressive formulas while seeking security at the expense of others
was in many ways ubiquitous. It could be glimpsed not only within
the Radicals, but in the left, the Nationals, and even within the
Christian Democracy itself.

The Readjustment Controversy and Agrarian Reform

The dilemma posed by this type of opposition was not an unusual one for Chilean governments. All of the regimes that pre-
ceded the Christian Democrats had had to face protests over rising prices and even stronger protests over austerity measures designed to halt these price increases. Although almost everyone in
the market economy was hurt by the erosion of wages and by the
uncertainties of the money market, each major social group attempted to protect itself by pressing for special compensations
designed to shift the burdens of inflation onto others. Businessmen
sought more credits and a relaxation of price controls. Labor
groups sought annual readjustments of wage and salary levels
through government legislation. Inevitably the result was that
everyone lost and the spiral started again. Politically the loser was,
of course, the regime in power, for it was in trouble if it refused to
grant special compensations and it was in trouble if it did not.

The Christian Democrats planned to avoid this predicament in
two ways. In the long run the Frei government hoped that such
measures as the agrarian and copper reforms would strike at the
roots of the inflationary spiral by eliminating the structural bottlenecks that impeded the development of the Chilean economy. In
the short run it was hoped discontent could be alleviated by spread-
ing out the costs of the developmental programs and by offering at
least some benefits to most of the major groups in the society.
Thus, the Christian Democrats anticipated and tried to head off a
strong urban reaction to land reform by tempering the pace and
scope of the redistribution process. At the same time they avoided

the harsh austerity measures imposed by the Ibañez and Alessandri regimes by substituting a more gradual attack on inflation. In contrast to earlier regimes, the Frei government had from 1964 to 1967 permitted wage and salary readjustments equal to the official price increases of the preceding year. By increasing taxes and by keeping readjustments equal to, instead of more than, the cost-of-living increase, the government hoped that over a period of five years it could reduce yearly price rises while at the same time pushing forward with its program of structural reform.

During its first three years the Frei regime was successful in maintaining this delicate balance. It was aided by rising copper prices and by the utilization of plant capacity left idle during the Alessandri period, both of which tended to buoy up the economy. As this era came to a close, however, the balance appeared to be breaking down. By the end of 1967 existing plant capacity was being fully utilized and copper prices began to level off. The growth rate, which had during 1965–66 been at the level of 5 and 6 percent, tapered off to 3 percent in 1967. The rate of inflation increased from 17 percent in 1966 to 22 percent during 1967.[18] When compared to the runaway inflation and economic stagnation of the 1950s, this was far from a crisis situation. Nevertheless, for the leaders of the officialist wing of the Christian Democracy, the danger signals were clear. It was argued that if programs of structural change were to remain compatible with the objective of price stability, some additional sacrifices would have to be imposed on the urban population. A number of measures were envisioned, including cutbacks on welfare spending, additional tax increases, and the encouragement of private savings. But the most controversial aspect of this "consolidation" (as the program was termed by government officials) was an attempt to place new restrictions on wage increases. The failure of this attempt — and the reaction which it provoked from organized sectors of urban labor — illustrates some of the difficulties involved in the Christian Democratic effort to sustain the momentum of rural change within a primarily urban social setting.

The controversy began in October 1967 when Sergio Molina, then the Minister of Finance, proposed that the government abandon its policy of granting wage increases that came to 100 percent of the previous year's cost-of-living increase. The bill he presented constituted a forced savings plan, in which all cash wage increases would be held to about 75 percent of the previous year's price rise. The remaining 25 percent would be paid by private or public employers into a "fund for national development," and the workers would receive savings bonds redeemable over a period of three years. In addition to reducing wage-cost pressures, Molina estimated that this savings effort would provide roughly 600 million extra escudos for development purposes — a sum equal to about 7 percent of the proposed 1968 budget. Through this fund, it was implied, the government would be able to maintain the rhythm of "some programs that are [already] in execution, such as the educational plan and the agrarian reform." [19]

Within the PDC the left-wing reaction to the forced savings initiative was strong. Several months were to pass (October through December 1967) while it was debated within the party. Predictably, however, these differences were eventually ironed out. Through the pressure of the left wing, clauses were added to the bill providing for additional employer contributions to the forced savings fund. At the same time, many Christian Democratic left-wingers were disposed to accept the general argument that the workers, as well as the propertied groups, should share in the costs of development. Indeed, the Plan Chonchol, which has been quoted in other parts of this volume as representative of Christian Democratic left-wing thinking, had itself made forced savings proposals similar to those now being raised by the officialists.[20] Thus, while the program stirred bitter controversy within the PDC, the most prolonged attack once again came from the opposition parties.

In the Congress the readjustment bill came under fire from all parts of the political spectrum. Not unlike conservative politicians in the United States, the Chilean right insisted that it could not support the measure until government expenditures had been drastically cut back. It was assumed this meant that the right would not support forced savings unless the government curtailed or abandoned its reform program. The Radicals, Communists, and Socialists, on the other hand, championed the cause of the salaried groups affected by the savings plan. Ignoring, for the most part, the government's argument that forced savings would provide funds for development, these opposition parties contemptuously dubbed the savings bonds with the epithet "chiribono" — the Chilean slang expression for a bad check — and vigorously rejected the proposal. Faced with the prospect of certain defeat in the Senate, Frei withdrew the proposal in January 1968, and a new Minister of Finance, Raul Saez, was appointed to work out a new readjustment bill that would conform more directly to the dictates of political reality.

The second proposal for readjustment was presented in March 1968. In general it represented a considerable retreat from the measures envisioned in the earlier initiative. With respect to most of the workers, efforts to hold the cash readjustment below the 20 percent price increase of the previous year were abandoned. Some measures in the new proposal did, however, reflect an attempt to salvage at least some of the earlier forced savings ideas. The most controversial of these was a provision which made the wage readjustment a *maximum,* as well as a *minimum,* pay raise for all workers in the private sector. Any gains made through collective bargaining that exceeded 20 percent would, as before, be paid into a development fund — this time for workers' housing. At the same time, for about one-third of the better-paid public employees, wage readjustments were, as in the first bill, to be held down below the 20 percent level. The differences between the Saez proposal and the initial forced savings plan are shown in Table 20.

Table 20. Provisions of the readjustment bills submitted by the Frei administration to the Congress, 1967–1968

| | (1967 inflation = 20 percent) | | | |
| | Public sector | | Private sector | |
	Cash	Bonds	Cash	Bonds
First bill	15% increase	5% increase	15% increase	5% increase
Second bill	2/3 of sector 20% increase 1/3 of sector 12.5% increase	7.5% increase	20% increase	Extra wage gains made through collective bargaining to be paid in bonds

Retreat on the forced savings idea was accompanied by further attempts to consolidate public expenditures and by a renewed effort to increase the confidence of private investors. Along with his new readjustment bill, Saez also proposed to cut some 434 million escudos from the Molina budget. Added to the general economies already initiated by Molina himself, this meant an overall reduction of about 13 percent from the 1967 levels. These cuts brought with them a subtle but important change in the government's earlier orientation toward reform. Though Molina had urged a cutback in government expenditures, he had implied a distinction between wage, salary, and welfare expenditures on the one hand, and programs of structural change on the other. Saez, in contrast, warned that structural changes would also have to be slowed down:

Nowadays, revolution, rapid change, structural modifications and other similar expressions have become common language, but not always with a complete understanding of the precise meanings of these terms . . . or with a defined means of achieving these objectives . . . Chile has raised its current expenditures and its social investments which are not immediately reproductive farther than the growth of its economy would permit . . .[21]

The agrarian question was now singled out for special attention. In a major policy address to the nation, Saez stressed themes designed to appeal to the landowning class. Implicitly discarding earlier emphasis on massive expropriations and the possibility of collective farming, Saez advocated a "gradual improvement in the productive levels of land through the expropriation of badly worked property and through the formation of new, small entrepreneurs." He reaffirmed the importance of "defining the form and conditions in which the efficient entrepreneur can continue to work." [22] Finally, the minister warned that the standards of efficiency should not be applied too rigorously to the agricultural sector:

In a developing country such as ours, where only the great mining enterprises and a few state enterprises have achieved high scales of production and efficiency . . . , it would not be just to pretend that our agriculture should be evaluated . . . by [standards] that are only obtained in countries with high levels of economic and human development. These results cannot technically be achieved even in other national activities which do not confront the difficulties that are special to agriculture.[23]

Although Saez promised in his policy address that the size of the land reform would not be reduced from its past levels, this promise was open to considerable question. As part of the new budget economies proposed, CORA and INDAP budgets were to be reduced by some 25 percent, or almost twice the general level of budget cuts.[24] Had the proposal been allowed to stand, it would have severely crippled the momentum of the land reform expropriations. After three years of effort, a large percentage of the total land reform budget was necessarily committed to aiding asentamientos already established. Cutbacks would have had to come, therefore, from those sections of the budget allocated to establish new asentamientos. CORA officials thus estimated that Saez's reductions would have permitted them to settle only one to two thousand peasants during 1968 — between one-quarter and one-half of their annual totals during the period from 1965 through 1967.[25]

It is probable that the cutback in the land reform was motivated by more than a simple concern for balancing the budget. The need for fiscal economies, after all, gave the officialist wing of the party a good opportunity to trim the sails of the CORA and INDAP leaders and to reaffirm explicitly their own, more moderate reform objectives. The cutback might also have been considered one way to restore the confidence of urban investors, who had frequently complained about the general climate of insecurity in which they had been forced to operate. The background of the new Minister of Finance and his earlier role in the Christian Democratic factional struggle suggests that he may have acted at least in part from these motives. Still formally an independent, Saez had enjoyed high positions under Alessandri and Ibañez as well as under Frei. His relative orthodoxy on economic policy issues had won him considerable respect from the right and from the United States and had, at the same time, made him the object of bitter attacks by the Christian Democratic left wing, which questioned the sincerity of his commitment to structural change.

Yet it was still correct to say that the government could not simultaneously meet urban demands and the costs of land reform without the risk of a considerably accelerated inflation. In general terms, the need to allocate resources and to set priorities left only two alternatives. One was an additional tax increase, which would channel more funds from the private to the public sector. But taxes had already risen by almost 70 percent between 1964 and 1967, and the government had legitimate reason to fear serious economic and political repercussions from further increases.[26] The alternative was to reallocate public outlays themselves. But many sectors of the vastly expanded government budget — public works, housing, and public debt payment — constituted relatively fixed expenditures. In view of the loss of revenue brought about by the failure of Molina's development fund proposal and considering the political weakness of the peasants, the land reform appeared a logical area for reduction. Although personalities and extraneous concerns had some influence in the cutback, it is reasonable to assume that the government had been motivated principally by the need to choose between these competing objectives.

For the most part, however, the necessity of choice was simply ignored by most of the opposition sectors. The white- and blue-collar interest groups made little mention of the agrarian question, concentrating most of their attention and energy on eliminating the forced savings provisions that still remained in the new readjustment initiative. Only the FRAP, with interests in both the urban and the rural sectors, paid attention to both questions, but it did so without explicitly drawing a connection between the two. The leftist press criticized government plans to "abandon" the land reform, but it was even more vehement in its opposition to the government's "antiproletarian" readjustment measure. The implications of urban protest thus had a strange effect on the debate over issues which seemed intimately intertwined. Apathy about structural change and the great importance attached to wage readjustments made urban labor's response to Molina's original proposals a foregone conclusion. The same priorities now forced the government to defend its new proposals on two essentially separate fronts and in two separate political arenas.

The Christian Democratic party and cabinet were the primary focal point for the struggle over the land question. Neither peasant organizations nor the opposition parties appeared to play a particularly large role in this struggle. The FRAP and INDAP peasant unions did organize some one-day work stoppages to protest the reduction in financing; scarcely noted in the press, these were not felt within the cities at all, where attention continued to be riveted almost exclusively on the issues of readjustments. The role of the peasant organizations was reduced even more as a consequence

241

of the rivalry between the Christian unions and the leaders of the reform administration. Although they were disturbed about the cutbacks, the union leaders had also been distressed about the earlier use of CORA and INDAP funds to build rival unions and to increase the power of the agencies at their expense.[27] Thus, no public statements were issued by the leaders of the Christian unions throughout the controversy, and these leaders expressed only mild objections to the funding decision in private.

The major task of defending the land reform budget therefore fell to the activists within CORA and INDAP and their allies within the PDC left wing. The latter, through the party's peasant department, leaked an angry memorandum to the press, warning against the "freezing of agrarian reform." [28] More quietly, Chonchol, Moreno, and other top CORA and INDAP leaders combined threats of resignation with efforts to find alternative sources of financing. In the final compromise between these reform administrators and the other cabinet officials, the agencies' budget cuts were reduced from 25 percent to 15 percent — a figure more in line with the overall budget economies. More important, CORA officials were dispatched to Washington to negotiate a 20 million dollar loan from the United States. By the middle of 1968 these compromises enabled the reform officials to argue publicly that past levels of expropriations would be at least temporarily maintained.

The arena in which the struggle over readjustment occurred extended well beyond the cabinet and into the streets. The question that continued to draw large segments of the organized urban population into the melee was Saez's effort to salvage at least some of Molina's earlier forced savings provisions. In spite of the fact that it appeared to contain some broad concessions to wage earners, the second readjustment bill continued to provoke bitter opposition.

Although most workers and salary earners had been granted a full 20 percent readjustment, they objected to the provisions which made this a maximum, as well as a minimum, increase. For many unions in the private and public sector, legislated wage readjustments were customarily only a starting point in a larger collective bargaining process; by establishing that workers could not be paid in cash for any increases over the 20 percent figure, the new readjustment bill virtually eliminated the use of the strike as an effective bargaining weapon. Most leaders argued that even a wage increase that equalled the official inflation rate did not really compensate the workers in full for the deterioration in their living standard, since the official figures on inflation were felt to be below the "real" rise in the cost of living. Thus, the unions of the Workers Confederation, the white-collar associations of private and public employees, the FRAP, the Radicals, and the Nationals again announced their rejection of the bill.

By the middle of March 1968 the situation again appeared stalemated, and tensions had visibly increased in Santiago. For the first three months of the new year, the government had been unable to provide what most citizens regarded as a basic service — protection against the effects of inflation through wage readjustments. Street demonstrations by various labor sectors were almost a daily occurrence, and both the FRAP and the Radicals appeared to be mobilizing for a general strike. An even more ominous note was added by rumblings from the military. Reports of resignations among junior officers, themselves anxiously awaiting wage readjustments, appeared in all of the major newspapers. Cabinet leaders began to mention the possibility of a "breakdown in the institutional order," and Frei conferred on an almost daily basis with the leaders of the military establishment.[29] Although these rumors may well have been exploited by the government in order to frighten the opposition, it is probably no exaggeration to say that Chile was in March 1968 closer to a coup d'etat than at any time in the last decade.

What followed was in many ways characteristic of the Chilean political system. Just as the conflict appeared to reach the point of no return, the interests of various sectors in the preservation of the constitutional order became evident, and important compromises were reached. The first and most important of these was between the PDC and the Communist party. In return for the government's promise to remove its limitation on the bargaining power of the private sector workers, the Communists agreed to vote in favor of the readjustment bill in the Senate. The Communists justified their move by pointing to the concession that they had wrested from the PDC.[30] Socialists and Radicals, on the other hand, argued that the Communists had in fact been frightened by the prospects of continuing disorder and that their decision had been motivated, as in the past, by the desire to avoid any action that might provoke a new ban on their legal activities. Whatever their motives, it is clear that the Communist action was viewed as a "betrayal" by most of the party's allies and supporters. For the first time in ten years, the Socialists and Communists voted on different sides of a major issue. Even more unprecedented was the fact that the Communists on the CUT council publicly rebuked the party's leaders for their decision and declared that they would continue to side with the other opposition parties.[31]

At this point, however, the Christian Democrats found allies from another strange quarter — the National party's congressional delegation. Disturbed by the PDC's willingness to accept Communist support and frightened by concurrent rumors of a larger Communist-Christian Democratic alliance, the rightist congressmen moved to relax the tensions that appeared to be driving those two groups together. In defiance of orders from their more hard-line executive committee, the Nationals, instead of joining with the opposition as they had done before, abstained from the voting. This abstention, along with the Communists' positive support, at last furnished the Christian Democrats with the necessary Senate majority.

Although several months were to pass before the readjustment finally became law, the immediate crisis had passed. But the passage of this bill was no victory for the Christian Democrats. For one thing, until the bill's final passage in the late spring of 1968, strikes, street demonstrations, and occasional violence continued more or less unabated. More important still, unlike the land reform and the copper legislation, the readjustment bill had been emasculated in the bargaining process. The legislated wage increases for all but one-third of the public employees contained almost none of the provisions originally deemed essential for an anti-inflationary effort. Although the compromise with the Communists had earned them the repudiation of the leftist urban sectors, it had left the Christian Democrats almost exactly where they had started, before Molina had made his first forced savings proposal. To Saez himself, the compromise appeared so crippling that he tendered his resignation after less than three months in office.

The Problem of Urban Cooperation

The foregoing account illustrates the larger arena of conflict in which the land reform controversy was unfolding. Because the question of readjustment raised a wide variety of issues, and because it involved broad sectors of the political system, it can be viewed from a number of different perspectives. On the one hand, the immediate outcome of the land reform budget decision gave grounds for some optimism. The pressure of the Christian Democratic left wing and the fortuitous intervention of the United States government meant that, at least temporarily, land division would continue to receive the funding necessary to continue expropriations at a moderate pace. Between 1968 and 1970, the basic rhythm of expropriations was maintained, with from four to six thousand peasant families receiving land during each of the remaining years of the Frei administration. In spite of what appeared at the outset to be a painful contradiction between land reform and other programs, the system once again displayed a remarkable capacity to muddle through its crisis of decision without really choosing either alternative.

Looking beyond the specific outcome of the land reform budget debate, however, the view seems less reassuring. Exposed in the readjustment controversy were many of the raw political nerves that lay just beneath the surface of Chile's constitutional order — a trade union movement disposed to guard its hard-earned prerogatives jealously, an increasingly disaffected business community, and a military establishment looking anxiously at developments within the civilian sector of the society. In this conflict-ridden context, the future of the reform government appeared highly problematical. Moreover, though the land reform problem itself had been temporarily settled, the failure of the forced savings proposals meant that the inflationary pressures which had originally led to the reductions in the reform budget were almost certain to recur — the next time perhaps without last-minute help from the United States. Finally, the agrarian program appeared all the more vulnerable when consideration is given to the fact that the peasant organizations had played only a marginal role in the crisis. Three years of

245

intensive organizational effort had not yet enabled the rural unions to attain a parity of influence with the more visible and strategically located urban organizations.

This did not mean that land division would necessarily come to a halt. Much of the weakness of the peasant unions stemmed from internal rivalries that could conceivably be smoothed over. Even if these rivalries were not eliminated, the strength of peasant organizations was on the increase, indicating that their role would also probably increase in the near future. Through land seizures, strikes, and demonstrations, these groups were still potentially capable of exerting considerable pressure on a sympathetic reform government. But to the extent that land division involved settlement expenditures and credit — as well as the simple expropriation of lands — it was unlikely that either peasants or a reform government could count on the active cooperation of city dwellers.

One reason for this was, as noted, that well before the 1960s, Chilean urban sectors had been able to displace the "oligarchy" politically without recourse to an alliance with peasants. But at least one additional potential basis for an urban-rural coalition — the presumed interest of both sectors in the developmental aspects of a land reform program — requires further discussion. Presumably, land reform would interest city dwellers no less than peasants, because in addition to providing land to rural workers, the reform would provide more food in the cities, more jobs for urban workers, wider markets for manufacturers, and greater price stability for all citizens. Yet although these very themes had been stressed by most political leaders since the inception of the land reform controversy, they had little apparent effect in mobilizing urban support. This apparent immunity of the urban population to the barrage of developmental appeals can be understood on three different levels.

The nature of relations between urban and rural societies. Perhaps the most immediate and obvious reason for the urban population's apparent disinterest in land reform was that key sectors of the city population were removed socially, as well as geographically, from the realities of rural life. This is not the case in some developing countries, where, for example, much of the urban population is dispersed in small towns that serve as centers for the larger rural surroundings. Social distance would also be relatively short in nations where all sectors of the urban population retain kinship ties with their families in the countryside, or where seasonal employment patterns encouraged actual movement back and forth between the city and the countryside. In this sort of situation, it is plausible to assume that much of the urban population had concretely experienced rural life and that, even after moving to the cities, it would find an issue like land reform far more than an abstract expression.

In Chile, where much of the nonagricultural population lived in large cities rather than in small towns, the countryside probably seemed far more remote. In 1959 almost one-half of the total Chilean population lived in cities with over 20,000 inhabitants. Almost one-third lived in the two major cities of Valparaiso and Santiago, the major political and social centers of the country. Data on the nature of linkages between the people who dwell in the cities and the countryside are sparse, but it is probable that among the white-collar and small business elements that comprise the big-city middle class these linkages were relatively few. In Chile, where there are very few medium or small family-sized farms, it is unlikely that many members of the big-city middle class come directly from farming communities, as is the case in some Mediterranean countries. More probably, these groups came initially from middle class backgrounds in the provincial towns, or they emerged, after several generations, from other urban classes.

At the top and the bottom of the urban social pyramid, direct relations with the countryside were much closer. The upper and upper middle strata were linked to the landholding class through marriage and direct ownership of land, while many slum dwellers were former peasants. However, neither group was likely to lend strong, active support to land reform efforts. The urban upper class was, if anything, inclined to oppose reform efforts, while the subproletarians — whatever their basic attitudes — remained essentially without influence in national politics.[32]

Proletarians can be located somewhere between the isolation of the white-collar classes and the relatively close rural ties of the urban marginals. In some Chilean mining areas, interaction between miners and peasants is intense, with miners moving back and forth from employment in the mines to work on the land.[33] Miners themselves, however, tended to be geographically remote from the urban working class as a whole. Given the scarcity of industrial employment in the large cities, it is likely that most factory workers were recruited from the urban marginals, perhaps in the course of the second generation, rather than directly from the peasantry. Those who have achieved high status within the factory working class — the shop stewards and unions leaders — moreover, appear to have enjoyed a lengthy tenure with the plant.[34]

Therefore, for the large, influential segments of urban society, from the middle class down to the blue-collar workers, interest in the countryside was likely to be distant and indirect. These groups might learn of the process of rural change through newspapers or magazines, through propaganda films, or perhaps through letters or visits to distant relatives. The landed upper class may be a convenient target for the frustration of these urban dwellers, and agrarian reform might be an attractive political slogan. It is unlikely, however, that the program would be viewed as a matter of intense, personal concern by individuals who had never directly experienced the hunger for land, the injustice of arbitrary rural authority, or the outright misery of rural life experienced by the peasants themselves.

Indirectly, of course, all of the urban population did suffer from these problems, for they were unquestionably related to the amount of food available to the cities. Food shortages or food price increases were sometimes the occasion for bitter urban protest, but the chain of reasoning that linked this problem to existing tenure relations was complex and highly debatable. It should be no surprise, then, that protests against food shortages were directed against local government authorities or merchants, who were close at hand, rather than against the landowners who were far away. Nor should it be any wonder that the measures demanded were price controls and food imports, which tended to work against any long-run solutions to the problem of productivity.

General problems of cooperation in Chilean society. Whereas interest in land reform remained relatively low, the tendency to pursue particular competing benefits was relatively high. This characteristic was not, however, the exclusive property of the urban white- and blue-collar organizations active in the readjustment controversy. From recently established asentados, who sought to exclude other peasants from their association, to large industrial entrepreneurial classes which sought to grab quick profits through short-lived and unproductive investments, Chileans of all social categories had historically tended to eschew cooperation and to engage in bitter, destructive competition. The assumption that the size of the total economic pie would remain constant, that one group's gain would be another's loss, appeared ubiquitous in the larger society.

The origins of this assumption — by no means unique to Chile — have been traced to different sources by different authors. Some have linked it to the mercantile traditions of the Spanish colonial empire.[35] Others have stressed the poor communications and the mutual suspicion characteristic of a stratified society.[36] It may also be argued that the assumption is based, more or less realistically, on objective conditions of scarcity that make mutual sacrifice difficult or even fatal. Whatever the beginning of the "fixed pie" notion, it has a self-sustaining and cumulative momentum of its own that increases the insecurity of each group and reduces to a minimum the trust and communication that are presumably necessary for a broad cooperative effort. These culture traits — if they are as pervasive as many writers argue — would be inhibiting factors at any level of development. It is likely, however, that they would become more destructive as urbanization multiplied the number of groups engaged in conflict with one another.

Among the white- and blue-collar wage earners, the logic of the fixed-pie assumption was reflected and exaggerated by the tendency to group into small, isolated, protective associations, which existed almost solely in order to enforce the particular claims of their membership. One illustration of the insecurity and the uncertainty which underlay the operations of these groups can be seen in a letter of protest by the leaders of the Postal and Telegraph Workers Association, published at the height of the readjustment controversy in 1968. The forced savings proposals, argued the letter, was only one of a long list of instances in which the government had attempted to undermine the well-being and position of the postal employees. All of this, it was suggested, meant that "someone must be interested in the destruction of this [administrative] division." [37] If the employees of a public postal service — presumably one of the more permanent undertakings of any government — could seriously entertain the possibility, it is no wonder that most of the rest of the salaried class might be skeptical of proposals that they undergo "temporary" sacrifices.

Viewed from the perspective of each group, this sense of insecurity was by no means irrational, for each had to be concerned with holding on to a constantly threatened share of the total available wealth and status. In a situation where inflation constantly eroded the gains painfully won, where competition for jobs was bitter and intense, and where another's gain might well come at one's own expense, prudence dictated the urgent necessity of clinging to whatever advantages were close at hand.

The "logic of collective action." The difficulties of promoting cooperation in order to achieve a general objective are not unique to Chile, to Latin America, or even to the underdeveloped world. One need go no further than the boundaries of the United States or Great Britain to discover that labor, business, and other interest group associations are only rarely, if ever, inclined to cooperate on developmental or price control measures that presumably would benefit everyone equally. Mancur Olson has argued that this difficulty is not the exception, but the norm — that "noncooperation" is not the result of individual irrationality, but of the pursuit of "enlightened self-interest." [38] His general theory provides a useful overall framework for concluding the more specific discussion of the factors underlying the behavior of the urban sector.

Olson argues that self-interested, rational individuals will not, *without compulsion,* cooperate to achieve a "collective benefit," for each would prefer that others pay the entire cost of such a benefit. The idea of a "collective benefit" — the concept central to Olson's theory — is defined as any product or service that can be enjoyed by each member of a collectivity regardless of whether he had borne part of its cost. In a national collectivity, for example, police and fire protection, public roads, public health services, and national security arrangements are goods of this sort, for normally they are enjoyed by taxpayers and nontaxpayers alike.[39] Similarly, higher wage levels or higher tariffs might be considered collective benefits for the workers or manufacturers in a given industry, for each worker or manufacturer would be able to enjoy the benefits of the wage or tariff increases whether or not he was a member of the organization which promoted it. The profits in a partnership, the facilities of an exclusive country club, or tax exemptions for members in certain types of organizations might, on the other hand, be considered "noncollective" benefits, which would accrue only to the individuals willing to pay the cost.

Using the concept of a collective benefit as his premise, Olson's chain of reasoning can be summarized as follows: (1) In a large collectivity, no one member can normally afford to pay the entire cost of a collective benefit. (2) Normally, a decision by one individual *not* to bear his share of the cost would not have a noticeable effect on other members, since their own costs would not be noticeably affected by his decision. (3) If each individual were permitted to choose, therefore, his most rational course of action would be to allow every other member to pay the cost of a collective good. (4) Thus, some degree of coercion is necessary to get people to cooperate to achieve collective group interests. For "even if all the individuals in a large group [were] rational and self-interested, and if, as a group, they acted to achieve their common interests or objectives, they still will not *voluntarily* act to achieve that common or group interest." [40]

This theory has some interesting applications to many features of Chilean politics. It sheds considerable light, for example, on the tendency of small cliques to undercut attempts by the government to generalize the burdens of anti-inflationary efforts by seeking special exemptions or by outright evasion, and it illuminates still further the earlier discussion of the nature and limits of the support for agrarian reform that might be expected to flow from the cities. Though the theory does not, of course, account for all of the variants of the Chilean situation, it does permit us to define more precisely the nature of alleged urban interests in the land reform program, to distinguish this interest from that of the peasants themselves, and to speculate about the conditions under which urban apathy might be expected to crystallize into more positive encouragement of reform efforts.

First, it seems clear that the structural arguments which associate land reform with such benefits as greater price stability, more jobs for urban workers, and wider consumer markets for manufacturers will not in themselves be enough to mobilize these groups in support of a land reform program. Quite apart from the merits of these structural arguments, which are questionable, and leaving aside the earlier observation that structural notions had not penetrated deeply within urban society, the appeal to the "enlightened self-interest" of urban dwellers invokes the very types of benefit which Olson describes as collective. Presumably, each worker would gain from expanded employment opportunities and each manufacturer would profit from wider consumer markets, *whether or not* he contributed to the costs of the programs allegedly necessary to achieve such conditions. Even in the best of circumstances, therefore, urban sympathy for land reform is likely to stop at the point where city dwellers are asked to bear its burdens. In the actual circumstance, the attempt to impose the burdens in the form of taxes or wage restrictions resulted in stiff opposition to the existing regime.

Second, only among peasants is there likely to be a source of active, organized mass support for land reform. In spite of the idea, implicit in arguments favoring reform, that there is a complementarity between the interests of the peasants and those of the city inhabitants, their interests are of a qualitatively different nature. For the peasants, the benefits of agrarian reform fall into the category of a private good. Unlike wider job opportunities, or markets, ownership of land is by definition exclusive to the owner himself. Insofar as the goal of a peasant organization is a parcel for each of its members, this organization might be expected to be cohesive and to press for land reform.[41] In the city, on the other hand, it is unlikely that similar organizational activity will take place. The formation of, for example, a Merchants and White Collar Association for Land Reform that really functions is almost impossible to imagine. For the same reason, it is unlikely to expect from any of the present urban organizations any more than vague, pro forma statements of sympathy for the land reform program.

Third, the risk that the noncooperation of urban groups could lead to an abandonment of reform efforts and thus to a frustration of developmental objectives is not likely to deter individual urban groups from continuing in their attempts to push the costs of reform onto others. Cooperation to achieve common objectives by supporting land reform may not materialize, even if the individuals or groups within the urban sphere come to realize that their noncooperation may result in a failure to achieve collective benefits.

The reasoning behind this proposition requires a further allusion to Olson's theory. According to Olson, the likelihood of voluntary cooperation increases as a group diminishes in size, and/or as its components become more unequal in influence.[42] The smaller the group, the more likely it is that the noncooperation of one member will be noticed and affect the actions of the others. Thus, in this situation it is also more likely that each member will be forced to consider that the failure of the group enterprise will be one of the consequences of his individual decision. In the second situation, where the members of the group are unequal in influence, a few large members may consider the collective benefit of sufficient importance to undertake the entire costs of the enterprise, even though smaller members, which did not share the costs, could also enjoy its results.

In large collectivities where resources are evenly divided (for example, an industry with many small producers), the chances of voluntary cooperation diminish. For one thing, the noncooperation of each member of the collectivity is not likely to affect the decisions of others, since his individual contribution to the collective good would constitute only a small fraction of its total cost. Moreover, even if the individual *were* to decide to shoulder his share of the burden, others would still be likely to evade the costs. Thus, since an individual decision will not in itself affect the expectations of others and since that decision cannot, by itself, determine the probability of group action, each individual's most rational choice is not to pay the cost of attaining the collective benefit *even when he realizes that similar decisions by everyone else will mean the frustration of the group's objectives.*[43]

The structure of Chilean urban society seems far closer to the last situation than it is to either of the other two types of collectivities. Its wage earning and professional sector is characterized by small, independent groupings associated only loosely within the larger trade union framework. Proprietors, similarly, are divided into large numbers of conflicting associations. Power is fragmented. In such a situation no single sector can, by itself, be expected to bear the entire costs of a developmental program.

And no sector can be sure that by bearing its share of the costs, it can induce others to do the same. As Olson has predicted, therefore, these small groups often aggressively pursue their own particular interests, even when they recognize that these actions are self-defeating in the long run. This seems to be the case even in instances where the collective benefits at stake are "obvious" to everyone. Urban groups have consistently refused to make the sacrifices necessary to halt inflation, for example, even though price instability was a condition from which all groups suffered. In the case of land reform, where the "collective benefit" at stake is in fact quite remote, where the groups involved are far from "rational and self-interested," and where mutual suspicions and rivalries reinforce specific disagreements, it is understandable that "national cooperation" would be even more unlikely.

Finally, Olson's theory casts further light on some of the conditions under which city dwellers might give active support to a land reform program. Rational, self-interested individuals will not cooperate voluntarily, if "all" that is at stake is prosperity. Urban support may conceivably be mobilized, however, through "nonrational" ideological and emotional appeals, or through the promise of some sort of "noncollective" benefit for each individual group — a redistribution of urban property, new social security benefits, or the like. It is precisely under these conditions that most revolutionary elites have managed, at least temporarily, to form alliances between peasants and one or more of the urban sectors. The struggle against a corrupt regime or against an oligarchy has been used as a symbol for the mobilization of large sectors of the population. The consolidation of peasant support through land reform was accompanied by dramatic redistributions of status or of income in the cities. Even in these revolutionary situations, however, the urban-rural coalition is usually temporary. When the euphoria dies down and when land has been redistributed, many revolutionary regimes are forced to turn their attention back to the cities, as in Mexico, or to confront permanent proletarian opposition, as in Bolivia. "Socialist revolutions" in the Soviet Union, China, and Cuba, on the other hand, have sought to shift their emphasis from redistribution to production by developing instruments of coercion and control that can squeeze investment from both the town and the country.

254

For a moderate government such as the Christian Democrats, the mobilization of urban support through an ideological appeal or through the promise of noncollective benefits was difficult to achieve. A land reform which was paced out gradually over time and which invited large landowners to collaborate in the process was unlikely to sustain the imagination of the middle class or to excite the class hatred of the lower class. The provision of noncollective benefits, such as new social security programs for special working class groups, would have worked against the objective of balanced, economic growth and would have stimulated the inflation the Christian Democrats had sought to control.

Chapter 8   The Vertical Brokerage System and the Process of Reform

This study has treated in considerable detail the evolution of one land reform effort in one country over roughly two decades. Its empirical scope is thus extremely limited in both time and space. It is limited in time, because the study ends just before the 1970 Chilean presidential elections — elections which brought defeat for the incumbent Christian Democrats, victory for the Marxist presidential candidate, and perhaps new directions for Chilean politics. It is limited in space, because it does not systematically compare what has occurred in Chile with similar phenomena in other countries. These very limitations, however, make it important for us to step back from the discussion of specific men and events and to attempt, at least speculatively, to place our observations in a broader perspective. One cannot, of course, generalize with confidence from a single case, and still less can one hope to predict the future. But this should not prevent us from moving cautiously beyond the data at our disposal. The processes we have described in the preceding pages do, after all, presumably reflect deeply entrenched Chilean social and political realities. A more general discussion of these realities should enrich our understanding, although not our foreknowledge, of what is to come in that particular country. More important, a discussion of the social and political forces which shaped land reform in Chile may provide a basis for sorting out the factors which have produced so many variations on the same theme in Latin America as a whole.

Land reform in Chile was the product of three interrelated factors: the structure of Chile's semideveloped society; the strategy of the reform leadership; and Chile's system of representative institutions — which have been termed the vertical brokerage system.

The structure of Chile's semideveloped society is in some ways the most important, for the conflicting social forces operating within that structure set the parameters within which Chilean politicians operated. A politicized peasantry, a large number of sizable and influential urban mass groups, and an articulate network of special publics — landowners, businessmen, and intellectuals — all served to set the limits of conflict and accommodation associated with the reform process.

The factor most directly affecting the system's specific response to the challenge of rural reform was the strategy of the Christian Democratic leadership, which resembled what Hirschman has called reformmongering.[1] The Christian Democrats attempted to forge a patchwork coalition, composed of heterogeneous elements unable to agree on a grand design for change but willing to join in support of specific reform measures. The land reform process which emerged from this coalition-building effort moved forward in relatively small incremental steps rather than in great dramatic leaps. From the passage of the authorizing legislation, to the initiation of expropriation, through the later conflicts between urban and rural social groups, each step was the rather modest product of the juggling of many conflicting interests, rather than the massive outcome of a clash between polarized social forces.

Finally, the Chilean parties and interest groups operated at an intermediate level, intervening between the aspirations and interests of the various social forces and the more immediate choices and decisions of top governmental leaders. Although the elites within these representative institutions reflected and represented contending forces in the land reform controversy, their shared interest in the preservation of the parliamentary order led them to restrain these forces and to divert disruptive tendencies. During the early phases of the reform, Chile's vertical brokerage system provided at least a minimum framework of conflict-control necessary for the establishment and maintenance of a reform coalition and for incremental adjustments in the land tenure system. Table 21 summarizes the relationship between broad social forces, the responses of the vertical brokerage agencies, and the resulting process of reform.

This chapter attempts to expand the discussion of the interrelations among these factors and to generalize from them. The first section surveys the general obstacles involved in evolving and implementing a reformmongering strategy in Latin America. The second summarizes the characteristics of the vertical brokerage system which permitted Chilean reformers to surmount these dif-

257

Table 21. Vertical brokerage system

	Social		Political Institutions	Governmental output
	Mass Publics	Special Publics		
Actors	Urban electorate Rural electorate	Landowners Business elites Intellectuals Military Peasant unions[a] Urban unions	Right: (PN, SNA) Center: (PDC, PR) Left: (PCCh, PS)	
Processes				
PHASE I (1958–1964)	Urban discontent directed against center-right coalition. Peasant voting for the left.	Articulation of structuralist position. Articulation of rightist counterpositions.	Organization of peasant unions. Adoption of land reform plank by middle class parties. Moderation in right's position.	Passage of Alessandri land reform laws.
PHASE II (1964–1967)	Election of Christian Democrats. Severe electoral defeats for right.	Debates among reform-oriented elements about the type of reform desired. Debates among opposition elements about the implications of reform.	Proposal of reform law by PDC. Strong support of law by left. Moderate opposition by right.	Passage of PDC Reform Law. Start of expropriation of land. Consideration of the financing problem.
PHASE III (1967–1970)	Urban electoral losses for PDC. Reaction of urban middle and lower classes against taxation and inflation. Continued peasant voting for the left and the PDC.	Continuing strategic debate within special publics. Increased visibility for military and urban unions within political process.	Proposal by PDC for new austerity measures as "price" of land reform. Defense by opposition of constituent interests against austerity. Acceptance by PDC of inflationary wage compromises.	Continuing land expropriations. Acceleration of inflationary spiral.

[a] Formed largely after 1964.

ficulties during the early phases of the reform. The third section turns to a broader discussion of the "social factors" involved in the reform process — particularly the new problems and obstacles that were raised as urban and rural interests began to diverge after 1968. The final section reevaluates the vertical brokerage system in terms of its relative capacity to cope with the new tensions associated with the emergence of the urban-rural cleavage.

The Reformmongering Process in Latin America

The models of incremental reform in Latin America that have been developed by A. O. Hirschman and Charles Anderson both attempt to map the many varieties of change that can occur between the conventionally stated alternatives of peaceful evolution and violent revolution.[2] Of the two, Hirschman's model is the more relevant at this stage of the discussion, since his work more or less explicitly directed strategic recommendations to prospective reformers and since the actions of the Christian Democratic government during the early phases of the reform followed many of these recommendations.

Two basic postulates seem to be most important to the reform-mongering strategy. First, to maximize his strength at any one time, a reformer should frame his overall objectives as vaguely as possible, in the hope that groups with quite different ultimate aims might be brought to support the same specific proposals. Second, the reformer should assume that the total power resources available to him, especially at the early stages of the reform, cannot be a match for the combined resources of the opposition. Guile and manipulation must thus supplement the use of coercion as important tools for dealing with actual or potential opposition elements. Reform is seen as an act of contrivance, in which "some of the hostile power groups are won over, others are neutralized and outwitted, and the remaining diehards (are) often barely overcome by a coalition of highly heterogeneous forces."[3]

In Chile, within the context of the early 1960s, both assumptions seemed plausible. The landowners and their upper class allies within the cities had, for decades, enjoyed a veto over government agrarian policy, while the social forces which tended to promote rural change were weak and disorganized.[4] Until 1967, peasant unions lacked both numbers and legality, while the urban dissatisfaction which swept the Christian Democrats to power was an uncertain and undependable source of support for land reform efforts. From 1958 to 1967, broad mass dissatisfaction was more or less a backdrop against which the drama of reform was played out. The more immediate battlegrounds were the social clubs, the universities, the legislature, where the many special publics reviewed the situation and considered how their interests might best be protected. In this arena, the weight of organization, prestige, wealth, personal connections, and communications skewed power heavily to the right. It seemed prudent, therefore, for the Christian Democrats to seek to keep potential opponents on the sidelines as much as possible, accepting confrontations only with isolated elements of the opposition. In this way, as Hirschman argued, the reformers maximized the possibilities of pushing through at least limited change and minimized the dangers of being ousted or stalemated by more conservative elements within the Christian Democracy, the rightist parties, and perhaps the military.

Yet, as Hirschman himself readily admits, in the tense and conflict-ridden societies of Latin America even the best conceived strategies may often backfire or prove disappointing. For an understanding of how the vertical brokerage institutions contributed to the relative success of reformmongering in Chile, it is necessary to summarize and elaborate some of the *problems* the reformmonger faces, both in the Chilean situation and in Latin America as a whole, as he attempts to patch together a supporting coalition.

As already pointed out, perhaps the most important assumption underlying the reformmongering strategy is that the reformer can manipulate the behavior of special publics by the way in which he himself uses governmental power to raise and frame political issues. Clearly, however, neither the individual reformer nor the government can determine completely what issues will be raised and how they will be viewed by the competing forces within the political arena. One of the basic aspects of almost any process of social change is the ambiguity which surrounds the definition of special interests and the behavior of individual groups and political actors. As traditional authority relations break down, as instances of local violence increase, as new or old political leaders emerge to articulate demands for change, the "facts" of the social struggle do not speak for themselves. They are subject to interpretation and reinterpretation by the social elites and special publics operating at the apex of the political order. And though a skillful reformer may at times exploit this uncertainty to his own advantage, ambiguity may work against his objectives.

In situations of flux and uncertainty, for example, it is possible (and indeed many persons would argue, probable) that landowners, industrialists, military men, and various parts of the middle class will overreact to the pressures emerging from below, and that they will profoundly mistrust the motives of reformers whose plans were quite limited in scope. There is little reason why anxious and beleaguered conservatives should be reassured by moderate reformers who claim that they can "channel" the forces of change. In many circumstances it is probably no less rational to take just the opposite view — that the reformer is an unwitting accomplice of revolutionaries, and that his "limited" reform is a dangerous stimulus to rising aspirations which should be "nipped in the bud," rather than encouraged. At the other end of the political spectrum and within the ranks of their own supporters, reformers might expect similar pressures from those who, in their mistrust of a conservative opposition and in their anxiety for change, seek to clarify issues through an immediate and perhaps disastrous confrontation. In many cases mutual distrust and the uncertainty of each side about the others' motives may exacerbate the conflict between contending groups far beyond what might appear merited by the substantive issues that divide them.

Conflict of this sort does not, of course, stem simply from mistrust and confusion between "men of good will." Compounding the reformers' difficulty is the behavior of the "diehard" conspirators of the left and the right, who seek actively to polarize the situation. From the diehards of the right there will come, almost invariably, the charges of communism and anarchy designed to drive wavering conservatives into active opposition. On the left, the jacobins will, with equal certainty, seize upon any move by the reformer toward moderation or compromise as a sign that he is about to sell-out on his promises of reform.

The bargaining process through which the reformer seeks to

mold his coalition is, thus, fraught with peril. The atmosphere of suspicion and rivalry, nurtured by the disruptive behavior of "extremist" elements, works strongly against an attempt to promote lasting cooperation between the various elites dissatisfied with the status quo. Regardless of the skill of the reformer in bringing together these dissident elements, such negative factors may well reinforce and expand what are otherwise rather mild disagreements over specific issues. In this situation it should not be surprising that the reformer is not infrequently crushed between the social groups he is attempting to juggle. A tendency toward escalation, which is built into many political contexts in Latin America, subjects the reform coalition to profound strain and often leads to stalemate on the specific reforms being proposed. These tendencies could be perceived in Chile itself, where such right-wing groups as FEDAGRI and the Coordinating Committee attempted to draw business groups directly into the struggle over land reform, and where left-wing elements within the Christian Democracy attempted to expand land reform efforts into an all-out attack against the "oligarchy." In other countries, similar processes have led to the overthrow of the reform governments well before the proposed reforms had been begun. One account of the collapse of the Goulart regime in Brazil illustrates this point quite well:

Goulart's basic government policies favored wealthy urban and rural interests . . . [Faced with popular impatience], he made a jog to the left with . . . presidential decree laws . . . The first gave the president the right to expropriate uncultivated land in holdings of over 500 hectares located within ten kilometers of federal roads, railroads, or waterways . . . The second law expropriated the remaining oil refineries . . . These reforms were not so radical in themselves, but conservatives saw that Goulart could no longer control the forces he had unleashed and feared what other reforms might follow.[5]

This is not to say, of course, that reformmongering strategies do not work in some situations. But the relative success of a reformongering effort, no matter how skillfully contrived, cannot be taken for granted. The reform coalition is bound to be inherently unstable; without institutionalized patterns of behavior to counter the tendency toward general antagonism and polarization, it is almost certain to collapse.

The Vertical Brokerage System and the Rural Breakthrough

In Chile the institutions operating within the vertical brokerage system appeared to be the mechanisms which contained this tendency toward escalation of conflict. They did not perform this role perfectly, for they reflected as well as refined the tensions emerging in the larger environment. But the very presence of these representative agencies helped to stabilize expectations in a variety of ways. The existence of identifiable and relatively large Marxist parties, for example, did much to promote the reform effort, both by adding to the pressure for change and by clarifying the distinction, so often blurred by established elites, between the essentially limited and constitutionalist aims of the democratic left and the more sweeping objectives of jacobin elements. Speaking more generally, it is likely that the competition between relatively cohesive and disciplined organizations of left, center, and right facilitated bargaining by providing each side with cues regarding the intentions and strength of the others. And in funneling the interests of dissident groups into the parliamentary arena, both reform and opposition parties regulated and controlled the behavior of groups which, elsewhere in the hemisphere, have often interacted and clashed without institutional restraints.

The Christian Democrats as a coalition-building agency. The most important agent of change within the vertical brokerage system was the Christian Democratic party. Since the leaders of this party were similar in their social origins, in age, and in ideology to the leaders of democratic reform movements which have emerged elsewhere in the hemisphere, it is useful to begin with some propositions about the political factors which may have led to variations in the behavior and in the relative success of these movements. Political factors cannot explain everything, since these groups emerged in countries with widely divergent socioeconomic characteristics and with highly distinctive kinds of developmental problems. Nevertheless, the leaders of these different national movements were recruited into widely different kinds of political systems, which offered quite different options and experiences. The fact that in Chile during the 1930s and 1940s the Falangist leaders moved into a relatively open political system may have had much to do with their relative success during subsequent decades in forging a coalition of elites oriented toward change.

The Falangist leaders' admission into parliamentary politics offered them at least two kinds of advantages. Through this experience, the Falangists were able to acquire an aura of respectability that tended to protect them from the charges of Marxism or crypto-communism which have sometimes been instrumental in bringing down leaders elsewhere in Latin America. More important, it was at least in part through their activity within the parliamentary arena that they acquired the sense of timing and finesse that became so evident after 1964. Admittedly, Latin American reform leaders have also acquired this capability in other ways. As Charles Anderson and others have pointed out, the Venezuelan Democratic Action party's abortive period in power from 1945 to 1948 provided the party's leaders with valuable lessons which they put to advantage when they returned to power in 1958.[6] This type of learning experience, however, seemed considerably more costly than that acquired by the Christian Democrats, for it subjected the AD leaders to a decade of repression, and Venezuela to a ten-year period of misrule. Certainly, when one compares the adroit political performance of a Frei with the more erratic behavior of a Bosch, a Frondizi, or of others who come to power from prison, exile, or the university, the contrast in political skills is striking.

But the options provided by the Chilean system encouraged more than the emergence of individual reformmongers. They appeared also to have influenced the formation of a broader, relatively coherent reform coalition — the Christian Democracy. The relative openness of the system tended to encourage the electoral activity of individuals who might otherwise have sought other means of acting in the political arena. At the same time, the possibility of competing within a multiparty rather than a one- or two-party framework may well have encouraged elites with a variety of interests and orientations to come together in a single reform movement.

These propositions are supported by the general patterns of behavior of democratic left movements elsewhere in Latin America noted by Charles Anderson. He states that in systems which were "hermetically sealed" during the 1930s (Guatemala, Nicaragua, El Salvador), "great difficulties were encountered in finding cohesion, structure, and common purpose" among reform elements.[7] Another pattern predominated in Colombia, Honduras, Uruguay, and Ecuador, where traditional two-party systems "provided the established organizations with a preemptive bid in the recruitment of new political talent." [8] In such systems, as might be expected, anti-status quo elements were often absorbed by the traditional parties — a phenomenon that may well have diluted their reformist identity and commitment. Finally, it was in the systems which were relatively open during the 1930s (Costa Rica, Venezuela, Bolivia), Anderson argues, that reform movements acquired a "nucleus of organization, leadership, and continuity . . . that carried over into the post-war period." [9]

When placed within this final grouping of countries, the Chilean Christian Democratic party represents an extreme case of a more general phenomenon, since, in Chile, the electoral and parliamentary system was far more entrenched than in the countries Anderson mentioned. Even in these other, relatively open systems, elections operated intermittently and uncertainly. In such systems it might be expected that individuals who might otherwise have joined reform movements would turn instead to other power resources — technical skills, student support, or conspiracy — to gain changes within the system. But in Chile the initial group of Falangist reformers was able to recruit a relatively broad range of dissident elites which added their strength to Christian Democratic leadership ranks as the prospects for electoral victory increased. Although these groups were never completely assimilated into the internal structure of discipline and authority formerly characteristic of the old Falange, their entry into the Christian Democracy started more than a decade before the party's rise to power. By 1964 the party framework had jelled sufficiently to provide the Christian Democratic government with at least a minimum of assured support once it had arrived in office.

Owing largely to the permissive characteristics of the electoral and parliamentary system, the Christian Democratic party came to office having already accomplished many of the tasks of coalition-building at the leadership level. This did not mean that the contingent of Christian Democratic leaders who filled governmental posts and who occupied congressional seats formed a united cadre. The reformist government shaped policy within the context of bitter factional struggle, and the process of intraparty bargaining was framed by the ever-growing possibility of splintering and schism. Clearly, however, the Christian Democracy had far greater unity of purpose than coalitions which had been temporarily brought together in support of a single candidate.[10] The common loyalties and interests shared by party leaders with divergent policy predispositions helped to mute the bitterness of the factional struggle and to increase the possibility of support for reform. Intraparty bargaining not only strengthened governmental leaders in their efforts to deal with the outside opposition, but for most of Frei's term harnessed the commitment and energy of more radical Christian Democrats to the purposes of moderate reform.

The role of the opposition sectors. The parties and interest groups of the left and the right also played important and positive roles in the process of reform. Not only were these organizations instrumental in establishing and supporting the parliamentary context in which the reform party emerged but, even after 1964, when the left and the right were in opposition to the Christian Democratic government, they contributed to the reform effort. The Marxists, as mentioned earlier, served as an important link between the government and the most dissident segment of the Chilean peasantry. Rightist organizations operated during the first three years of the Frei administration to restrict and moderate the opposition of the upper classes. Therefore, although relations between the reformist leaders and the opposition elites were not without bitterness or controversy, the latter in many ways acted to ease the pressure on the reform coalition.

A variety of factors must be taken into account in explaining the moderation of these opposition leaders. The limited availability of revolutionary mass support is of clear importance in explaining the behavior of the Chilean Socialists, while the action of the Communists seemed relatively closely attuned to the general caution of the Soviet line. On the right, an alleged historical tradition of relative enlightenment is sometimes cited to account for the flexibility of the Chilean aristocracy.

At least to some extent, however, the moderation of the opposition elites — like the skills of the reform party leaders — appeared to be related to the elites' long participation within the parliamentary system. The extent to which Chilean leftists had been permitted to participate in elections, to hold positions within the bureaucracy, within municipal councils, and even to join in cabinet coalitions was without precedent in the rest of Latin America; and the respectability acquired through these long years of participation appeared to have been of considerable value — even to those Socialist politicians who were most critical of Chilean "democracy." However much their rhetoric may have suggested to the contrary, the leftists' ties to the constitutional order appeared to stem from something far more durable than tactical expediency. This point is perhaps even more important, and perhaps less noted, in the case of the Chilean right. Contrary to conventional notions, it is not the norm in Latin America for aristocratic elements to participate actively or extensively within a parliamentary framework.[11] In Chile the rightist "aristocrats," like the leftist "revolutionaries," appear to have been "domesticated" by participation within such a framework. Rightist groups elsewhere in Latin America, when challenged by new social forces, are without the means or inclination to defend their interests through constitutional channels. In Chile rightist politicians continued to define their options and to take their cues from within the parliamentary system, even though the landowners' position was seriously threatened by the rise of the PDC and even though persuasive cases were made for more hard-line and disruptive modes of opposition.

A final point to be considered is the capacity of the representative elites to place restraints on the behavior of rival elites and constituent special publics advocating a more radical course of action. Here there are some important differences between the left and the right, for the elites of each sector were tied to quite distinct constituencies which varied greatly in social status, cohesiveness, and general aspirations.

The right's constituency was the traditional Chilean upper class which, because of its strategic position at the apex of major economic institutions, its internal social cohesion, and its controls over various nonconstitutional power resources and capabilities, could enjoy a broad, diffuse influence within the formal political system *with or without* formal political representation. The capacity of the rightist leaders to control the behavior of other members of the upper class thus depended in part on the development of more or less "modern" agencies of representation — with more or less clearly defined lines of authority, with explicit means of resolving internal conflicts, and with established patterns of internal recruitment that could regulate and direct the more diffuse means of influence enjoyed by members of the upper class over the system as a whole. The internal organization of both the rightist parties and the SNA were weapons which the leaders of those institutions could wield against fellow conservatives who relied on other, nonconstitutional bases of power.

On the left, the bases of regulatory activity were somewhat more complex. Clearly some organizational structure was necessary if leftist leaders were to reach the traditionally apolitical and apathetic peasant masses and to serve as a communications link between these masses and the system. Whereas the organization of representative agencies on the right tended to channel *existing* claims on the system, extensive organization by the left threatened to mobilize *new* demands, often in ways that could be profoundly destabilizing for the system as a whole. The operation of the Chilean left as a safety valve thus depended on the fact that leftist efforts to mobilize mass groups were tempered by organizational divisions and by particularistic patterns of representation which whittled down the claims of dissident strata to a size at which they could be handled by the reform government. Whereas on the right, conflict-control required the evolution of modern representative structures which could partially offset the traditional power bases of the upper class, on the left just the opposite was necessary: the evolution of traditional ties between leftist politicians and peasant followers, which counterbalanced a tendency toward mass organization.

Appropriate analogies to both situations can be found in both Europe and in other parts of Latin America, and these might offer a useful empirical focus for further research. Parallels to the behavior of the Chilean left may be found in continental Europe, and perhaps especially in Italy, where the Communist party has also been said to play a brokerage function.[12] On the right, analogies with the Chilean case might be drawn from Mexico and Venezuela, where right-wing parties and interest groups, ostensibly in opposition to governing parties, may actually have done much to control the behavior of dissident conservatives.[13] Appropriate contrasts might be sought in countries like Argentina, the Dominican Republic, and Cuba, where traditional aristocratic elements abandoned the formal political arena and relied on non-constitutional bases of power to keep governmental leaders within acceptable limits.[14]

That the parliamentary system in Chile could accommodate both the left and the right was undoubtedly one of the major bases of its stability and perhaps the outstanding characteristic of the vertical brokerage system. This, of course, has also meant that the system was not particularly dynamic in responding to the crisis of agricultural production or peasant mobilization, since the presence of the right and the moderation of the left may have slowed as well as channeled the process of rural change. These problems will be discussed further in the final section of this chapter. What should be noted at this point is that the system as a whole was able to respond to rural challenges, at least in an incremental fashion, and that the leftist and rightist organizations were an important part of this response, defining cues and expectations on the right and regulating the entry of new peasant groups on the left.

The Emergence of the Urban-Rural Cleavage

Historically, the representative institutions operating within the Chilean vertical brokerage system found their major bases of social support from voters who were not directly involved in the rural subsystem; and although the emergence of land reform as a political issue corresponded closely to the emergence of peasants as a new voting mass, Chilean political elites remained most responsive to urban mass elements. Thus, the shifts (or perceived shifts) in the attitudes of the latter groups were crucial variables in determining the manner in which the various political elites responded to the issue of land reform.

To understand the role of urban social forces, it is important to distinguish between the pre- and post-1967 phases of the reform. During the pre-1967 phases, urban discontent provided a favorable climate for a rural reform effort not only by contributing directly to the Christian Democratic victory but also by promoting the belief among Chilean politicians of all ideological persuasions that land reform was a popular program. From the early 1950s, when rural change first became a major political issue, to 1967, when major land legislation was finally passed, the interests of the peasants and those of a broad majority of the city population appeared to converge.

After 1967, however, the role of urban social forces within the land reform controversy changed in two ways. First, with the municipal elections of March 1967, the erosion of Christian Democratic strength within the large cities indicated that urban discontent was beginning to be directed against the reformist government, and this tended to increase the degree of competition among Chilean political elites. Second, with the passage of the land reform legislation and the need to find financing for the land reform program, the behavior of urban mass groups (and particularly of the white- and blue-collar unions) became more directly relevant to the land reform process itself. Strong resistance to governmental calls for sacrifice and savings made it clear that most urban elements were opposed to paying the costs of reform, even though most continued to give lip service to the idea of reform. This undertow of discontent, far more than the direct opposition of the landed classes, may prove to have been the most important obstacle placed in the way of the Chilean system's efforts to respond to rural demands.

Chapter 7 detailed the emergence of the urban-rural cleavage and suggested some of the reasons for it. Two related issues warrant additional comment. One is the extent to which an increasingly politicized and well-organized peasantry might eventually counterbalance the competing pressures of urban society. The other is the chance that urban discontent — which is in many ways unfocused and diffuse — can be directed toward targets other than the land reform itself.

The Vertical Brokerage System and Reform

Peasant Politicization versus Urban Resistance

Through electoral participation and increased organization, mass groups can acquire considerable influence within the political process. The Chilean peasantry is no exception to this rule. In focusing on the importance of urban social forces, it should not be forgotten that peasant votes for the left and the Christian Democrats made important contributions to the general pressures for change, and that the future growth of peasant syndicates in Chile may increase the visibility of the land problem regardless of what occurs within the cities. However, it is important to distinguish between various "base-line" criteria that can be employed in judging the degree and nature of prospective peasant influence. Viewed from the perspective of the peasants' previous exclusion from the Chilean polity, about the only direction they can go is "up." Land seizures, marches on neighboring towns and cities, strikes and petitions may well increase the likelihood of governmental action in rural areas, and, at a higher level of collective action, rural union organizations may provide important links between the peasant masses and the political elites.

However, it is less certain that Chilean peasants can achieve a parity of political influence and importance with competing elements operating within the urban context. The voices of peasant union leaders were virtually inaudible at many important points of the land reform struggle. Rivalries within the union movement and within the governing party itself can account for some of this weakness, but there were probably broader and more permanent underlying factors at work as well. Although Chilean peasants had, by 1968, acquired considerable strength in bargaining with local landowners, their minority status within the national voting population reduced their importance as a source of electoral support; illiteracy, geographic dispersion, and isolation from strategic national centers of decision worked against their capacity to rival the white- and blue-collar unions as independent sources of political pressure.

To put the matter somewhat more generally, we would suggest that there are broad upper limits on the degree of influence peasants can hope to attain in a highly urban national society. As the arena in which they seek to exert influence expands from the immediate rural locale to the wider, national environment, and as the objectives which they seek become less particularistic and more programmatic in content, their capacity to command the attention of even relatively sympathetic decision-makers can be expected to diminish. And although this weakness may be partially offset by the ideological commitments of the decision-makers or by the nature of alliances formed by peasant leaders, the peasants' relative political importance is likely to remain secondary to that of urban social forces in a highly urbanized society. As an elaboration of this point, the following series of ideal-typical political contexts may be useful in illustrating the nature and probable limits of the peasants' power to promote a favorable governmental response:

Peasants versus landowners (*local level*). Peasants might be expected to be strongest in this situation. In part this is because the degree of peasant organization at this level need not be highly sophisticated to obtain results. At the local level, peasants clearly constitute the majority of the population, and, given the existence of sympathetic officials, collective effort to present wage petitions, to go on strike, or even to seize a fundo are likely to involve few risks and considerable payoffs. Peasant organization can be effective because the issues at stake can often be resolved without reference to the national ideological debate — employers' compliance with welfare legislation, higher wages, and even petitions for particular pieces of land are all questions which need not involve national political forces.[15]

Peasants versus radical intellectuals (*local and national levels*). In several parts of Latin America,[16] the mobilization of peasant masses by relatively moderate political elites has enabled them to contain the activities of more radical leaders attempting to foment guerrilla warfare and rebellion within the countryside. It may be hypothesized that, at both the local and the national level, as the peasants become organized, governmental authorities will be likely to heed the voices of peasant leaders over intellectuals. To the extent that government leaders can count on a deliverable bloc of peasant votes, the support of the more radical intellectual critics becomes less valuable to the governing party and their defections become less costly.

Peasants versus right-wing civilian and military elites (*national level)*. Even relatively well-organized peasant syndicates have only rarely proven able to survive in confrontations with nationally organized right-wing and military elites. Peasants, by themselves, lack the education, geographical concentration, and wealth necessary to compete as a cohesive national organization. Much the same weakness might be postulated in less extreme circumstances, in which reformist authorities attempt to establish some sort of equilibrium between peasant leaders and upper and middle class groups in national policy decisions. Aside from the threat of the actual execution of a coup d'etat (which peasant syndicates may be powerless to prevent), conservative groups have at their disposal a variety of weapons (information about national economic conditions, personal contacts, and bribery) which peasant organizations are rarely able to match. Even when the government is sympathetic to reform and even when peasants have national representation, therefore, prolonged confrontations between peasants and the right over national policy questions are likely to end with the co-optation of national peasant leaders or with repressive measures against peasant organizations.[17]

Peasants versus urban workers and middle class associations (national level). Peasants are also weak in competing for the resources of the state when their claims come into conflict with the claims of the organized wage-earning and salaried strata of the urban population. Against local landowners, intellectuals, and even against conservative national elites, peasants might use their votes as weapons, especially if they supplement their numerical advantage with collective political action. Against urban workers, peasants are deprived both of an organizational advantage (assuming that urban workers tend to be more organizable, to have better strategic location, and so forth) and of their numerical importance. They can neither out-vote nor out-riot their working class competitors.

Urban Indifference as a Permissive Factor in Rural Change

Fortunately, the form in which urban resistance to land reform expenditures emerged in Chile indicates that the conflict between the countryside and the city is rarely direct. Few strata of urban society actively supported land reform, and most made claims which competed with that program. But the disaffection that re-

273

sulted from the government's inability to meet those claims was directed against the *government,* rather than against land reform or against peasants. It is probably fair to say that unlike the landed opposition, most city dwellers remained either indifferent to the agrarian problem or were vaguely in sympathy with the objectives of land reform.

In spite of strong urban resistance to the diversion of resources from the city to the countryside, the immediate context in which the reformer operates is thus still a relatively permissive one. Over the short run, reformers may well find it politically expedient to give in both to urban welfare claims and to demands for land reform, risking inflationary pressures that may bring negative political repercussions in the long run. Moreover, as long as city dwellers do not explicitly come to feel that the peasants' gain must be at their expense — as long as their diffuse dissatisfaction does not crystallize into a more explicit opposition to land reform — urban voters who oust a reformer in one election may return to support him in the next. There may be a "pendulum effect" in the political allegiances of urban mass groups, which would permit reformist or radical elites to come to power at irregular intervals, to engage in spurts of redistributive activity, and gradually to absorb at least some peasant groups into the political system.

In Chile the intermediate institutional arrangements discussed in the preceding section should help to increase these possibilities. The tendency to rely on inflationary settlements as a means of averting more serious confrontations between social and political groups is characteristic of the vertical brokerage system. This method was used during 1967–68 by the Christian Democrats to avoid immediate urban resistance to land reform. Finally, although the prospects for the reelection of a Christian Democratic government appeared to be growing considerably dimmer during the later years of the Frei regime, the existence of a relatively well-entrenched electoral system maximized the possibility that, sooner or later, a new reformist or radical regime would rise to power in the future.

In such a situation the process of land reform in Chile is likely to occur as a more or less extended affair, stretching out perhaps over a number of decades, and occurring in bursts of energy, activity, and controversy, as various parties and elites decide to promote or reward peasant followers or as various peasant groups acquire sufficient strength to make their voices heard at the local level. Though it would clearly be foolhardy to attempt to speculate about the exact outcome of such a process, the study of Chile would suggest that a combination of urban indifference, peasant protest and organization, and the conflict-averting potential of the vertical brokerage mechanisms should permit a gradual and uneven, but significant, absorption of at least some peasant groups into the political system.

The Chilean case also serves as a reminder, however, that Latin American societies may reach a threshold of urbanization above which the city, rather than the countryside, becomes the logical focus of political attention. Although concerted efforts to promote rural change remain possible in such situations, the decline of peasants as a potentially important national political force and the expected conflicts of interest between urban and rural social forces may work to restrict the scope and impact of a land reform process below levels that might seem desirable from a social or economic point of view.

Viewing these conflicts from the perspective of the decision-maker, it is easy to see why even relatively reform-oriented elites are constantly confronted with the temptation to postpone the land reform, to reduce its size, or to reorient priorities away from the redistributive and social aspects of reform and toward the objective of increasing agricultural productivity. For while the peasants' decline in political importance diminishes the incentive to press forward with redistribution, the expansion of the urban sector makes productivity goals far more important and increases the political costs of a collapse in agricultural production.

Ironically, however, the same urban pressures which tend to impede land redistribution also work against planned, concentrated efforts to increase agricultural production. This is so not only because land reform may be an essential part of a productivity drive, as the structuralists claim, but because efforts to increase production also require the diversion of resources from the city to the countryside. Therefore, governments which cut back on redistributive priorities are likely to find themselves in no better shape than those which push forward with the goal of giving land to peasants. Those which do press forward with redistribution are likely to find themselves unable to follow through with sufficient credit, social services, and extension facilities. Either way a large number of peasants are likely to be short-changed.

Viewing the politics of land reform from the perspective of the system as a whole, urbanization and the emergence of the urban-rural cleavage diminish the possibility that land reform can serve as a vehicle for centralizing and expanding political power within the system. In less advanced societies, where peasants continue to comprise a large majority, land reforms may be more "explosive," but their potential outcomes are more clear-cut. A government which succeeds in mobilizing the rural majority is also in a position to overcome urban opposition, and to construct a new and perhaps more viable political framework. Although land reforms may have similar results in urbanized societies (as the Cuban case clearly shows), these results appear far less likely. While spurts of land reform, along with extensive peasant unionization, may attract peasant groups into the system, reform governments are likely to be faced with erosions in their urban strength; and the system as a whole, with alternations of quite different types of governments in office. In an urbanized society, land reform may help to pacify the countryside but not to stabilize the system.

The Vertical Brokerage System and the Urban-Rural Cleavage

It is not entirely clear whether the obstacles outlined above can be overcome either in Chile or in other semideveloped societies, where urban resistance might also be expected to deter rural change and to impede the emergence of more centralized and stable political systems. Massive land reforms were undertaken in both Cuba and Venezuela — two countries with approximately the same demographic composition as Chile. But special circumstances in both cases — oil wealth in Venezuela and an atomized and confused middle class in Cuba — facilitated governmental efforts to promote rural change and minimized the chances that these governments would be brought down by an urban-based reaction. Even in these situations, however, the outcome of the land reform process depended at least in part on the strategic predispositions of the governmental elites and on the nature of the intermediate political structures within which they operated; and it seems useful to return to a more explicit discussion of the role of these factors in Chile as well.

Strategic Options

The approach employed by the Christian Democratic government was, in many ways, an extension of the reformmongering strategy it had employed to guide the reform bills through the Congress during the earlier phases of the reform. Just as in the Congress emphasis was placed on playing off the left against the right, in the post-1967 phase of the reform emphasis was placed on avoiding polarization and on striking a balance between urban and rural social forces. The government adopted a permissive posture toward rural unions, continued its moderate redistribution program, and appealed broadly to all groups in the society for support of the reform. It also spread out the costs of the reform as thinly as possible among the many groups competing within urban society, and it was willing to give in to inflationary pressures when it appeared that inflation was the only alternative to a choice between urban and rural programs. The advantages of this approach were that the government minimized the dangers of confrontations that might eject it from office and that it provided time in which the reform could inch forward.

But there were important disadvantages as well. For the problems posed by the urban-rural cleavage were in many ways different from those of the earlier period, and in some ways they pointed to the limitations of the reformmongering approach. In the pre-1967 phases the major problems facing the reformers were those involving elimination of the veto power of the landowning class, the establishment of the legal and administrative apparatus necessary for reform, and gaining acceptance for the emerging peasant unions. The government's allies and adversaries during these periods were, for the most part, established elites and special publics of both the left and the right, for whom the issue of land reform had a direct ideological, social, and political salience. Since the Christian Democrats and the leftist parties had already managed to organize a large number of these established groupings in support of land reform legislation, the most prudent course of action for the government appeared to be one of reducing the reaction which threatened to annul this legislation, both by convincing potential adversaries among the urban industrial, financial, and military circles that land reform would not harm them and by encouraging landowners to believe that moderate opposition would be the best way to minimize their losses. Since much of the rest of urban society appeared to be mildly in favor of land reform, it seemed pointless and risky to draw these groups more directly into the controversy by raising the issue of which of them would be forced to pay for the reform.

In the post-1967 phase, however, the central problem confronting the reformers became one of extracting resources to pay for the expropriation and redistribution of land, and in this new, more difficult context, the question of costs obviously became more difficult to evade. This change had two important strategic implications. First, as the struggle over who should pay for the reform intensified, the earlier differences between the left and the right became blurred; and the government could not rely, as it had in the past, on the relatively unequivocal support of existing leftist groups and elites. It was thus perhaps more necessary than before for the government to engage directly in the mobilization and organization of new, more active, and more centrally directed peasant support; to supplement this activity with the extension of private benefits to at least some urban groups; and to strengthen its mechanisms of coercion and control. A second strategic implication concerned the distribution of the costs themselves. After 1967 it became clear that the government could not avoid urban opposition by relying simply on the way it articulated its objectives in the countryside, for costs, rather than objectives, were now the dominant issue. Instead of attempting to spread the burdens of the reform thinly among all groups in the population, therefore, it might have been more useful to impose the costs of expropriation more selectively — to free some urban groups entirely and to concentrate on others more directly.

These observations are highly tentative, and extreme caution is warranted in the evaluation of this alternative strategy. Redistributive measures directed toward the forging of a coalition between peasants and specific sectors of the urban population are bound to invite a bitter reaction from the others, thereby clearly increasing the possibility of a military intervention. More important, the confrontations which such a strategy would involve would risk severe economic contractions, and in this situation a reform government could well dissipate the support of the very groups whose allegiance was being sought. An attempt to weigh the relative merits of the strategic choices confronting Chilean decision-makers thus encounters many imponderables — the degree to which dramatic redistributive measures would attract support from urban as well as from rural groups, the relative capacity of governmental authorities to organize this support, the nature and strength of the reaction, and so forth.

In retrospect, however, it is tempting to suggest that perhaps the Frei regime would have fared better in coping with the urban resistance if it had concentrated more on the building and expansion of mass support, both urban and rural, and less on the neutralization and division of special opposition groupings. A more aggressive effort to use governmental resources for organizing the peasantry, for example, might have increased the regime's advantages in the countryside, while the extension of concrete redistributive benefits to key urban groups might have enabled the government to gain the allegiance of at least some city groups. In distributing housing benefits to slum dwellers, large welfare benefits to organized labor, and massive wage increases to military officers, the government might have obviated at least some of the problems discussed in the preceding chapter. For in such a situation the joint support of the Christian Democrats by the peasants and by some urban sectors would not have rested on common efforts to win a collective benefit, but on complementary interests in the distribution of private goods. By attempting to strike a relatively even balance between the various contending groups, the Christian Democrats in fact won few loyal friends but acquired many enemies. As the 1970 presidential elections drew near, the party found it had lost the support of much of the middle sector, had dissipated its strength within organized labor, and had incurred the opposition of most of the business community.

The Vertical Brokerage System and Horizontal Mobilization

Precisely because the selection of strategic options involved so many imponderables, it is difficult to evaluate fully the role of

Chilean representative institutions in dealing with the changing social situation. The system did, after all, continue to manage tensions and to permit change, even during the post-1967 phase of the reform. Nevertheless, the critique of the Christian Democratic policy given above is important if only because it helps to highlight some of the possible limitations of Chile's highly institutionalized vertical brokerage structures as the Chilean society entered the new phase of the reform. As the term vertical brokerage implies, Chilean representative institutions were not likely to promote the integration of society along horizontal lines. The decentralized, multiparty structure, the urban bases of social support for the competing parties, and the absorption of change-oriented leaders into the parliamentary framework — the very characteristics which had worked to mediate conflicts during the earlier phases — tended after 1967 to work against governmental efforts to impose the burdens of reform selectively and to organize a broad basis of popular support. To the extent that such efforts became more necessary with the emergence of the urban-rural cleavage, the conflict-averting mechanisms built into the system appeared less appropriate than in earlier stages of the reform for promoting change, and the system as a whole appeared more subject to internal strain.

The altered relation of the multiparty structure to the problems of change illustrates some of these larger difficulties. During the pre-1967 phases of the reform, the availability of a new rural electorate and the apparent shift of urban voters to the left provided a strong incentive for the leaders of all the major political parties to adopt a more reformist position. And in bidding for the support of "popular forces," the well-defined party organizations each played important roles in policing the particular special publics associated with its point of view.

As the interests of peasants and the competing urban groups began to diverge, however, some of these structural assets became liabilities. The very division of the party system into separate Marxist, centrist, and rightist sectors inhibited the formation of a genuine elite consensus on the reform issue itself. And, more important, as urban voters defected from the Christian Democracy, these divisions tended to increase the tensions involved in a prospective alternation of parties in office; for no genuine centrist alternative had appeared on the horizon to replace the Christian Democrats.

Finally, with the emergence of the urban-rural cleavage, the focus of competition between the political elites shifted from the countryside back toward attempts to mobilize their older, more established, electoral constituencies. The right redirected its appeal from the "progressive" voters to more conservative middle class elements. The left and the radicals redoubled their efforts to protect their mining, proletarian, and white-collar clienteles. This pattern is common within multiparty systems. As Huntington has put it:

In multiparty systems where the parties are more solidly rooted in social forces, each party normally has its own constituency and makes intensive efforts to mobilize that constituency, but party competition for the support of the same groups is less than in the two-party or dominant party system. Each party tends to have a fixed block of voters who support it regularly, are firmly identified with the party, and are generally impervious to the appeals of other parties. Assimilation of a new social force into the multiparty system hence normally requires the creation of a new party.[18]

The urban roots of the Chilean leftist and center-leftist parties complicated matters still further. For by the time the peasants began to appear on the scene as a potent electoral force, the political sectors which were ideologically most attuned to the need for rural change had already acquired large, established, nonrural constituencies. In this respect the Chilean system can be distinguished from other multiparty, as well as single-party systems, in which the governing party or coalition acquired its initial base of support in the countryside. In Venezuela the leaders of the Democratic Action party began in the early 1930s to recruit its mass base in rural areas; this pattern persisted during later decades, even though the peasants were rapidly becoming a minority of the population. When AD came to power in 1959, therefore, it had already acquired a relatively well-organized base of peasant support, and this permitted the party to predominate over an urban majority which divided its vote among many splinter parties. After ten years, the AD lost its predominance within the Venezuelan system, but not before the party had engineered a relatively massive land reform, which provided for a new, peasant-based power structure in the rural regions.[19]

The sequences involved in the emergence of the Chilean parties, in contrast, make this type of outcome less likely. Unlike the Democratic Action party, the Christian Democrats were carried into office by middle and lower class urban voters, rather than by peasants. For the Christian Democrats, land reform was a device for attracting new supporters, rather than for consolidating existing ones. In focusing their attention on the countryside, AD leaders could at least temporarily afford to write off the votes of Caracas. The Christian Democrats' attempt to move from the city to the countryside, on the other hand, involved far more difficult and costly choices; for the outflow of Christian Democratic city voters to well-organized opposition parties threatened to offset whatever gains the party might make within the peasantry. Land reforms may thus be more extensive in those societies (Cuba, Venezuela, Mexico) where the politicization of the peasantry coincides with, rather than follows, the organization of the party system, as was the case in Chile.

The same factors may also make it easier for a rural-based party system to avoid defections as it shifts the flow of governmental services to other groups within the population. Here the case is on admittedly shaky ground, since in the Venezuelan example used above, the Democratic Action party was unable to expand from the countryside into the city. Nevertheless, the matter is worth exploring. Once granted land, peasants do appear to give relatively unconditional allegiance to their benefactors, especially if the granting of land is followed up by measures of organization and control designed to mobilize the rural vote. This may give the rural-based party system, if not the governing party itself, considerable flexibility in dealing with the urban-rural cleavage. In Mexico, for example, the PRI was able to absorb most of the middle sector, after having consolidated its support within the peasantry. In Cuba, an admittedly far different case, land reform was a base from which the Castro regime could establish control over *both* the urban and rural sectors and to shift its attention from one to the other with relative ease. In Venezuela, the replacement of the AD by the more urban-oriented COPEI party may signal a process in which the urban-rural gap is being bridged by the system as a whole, rather than by a single party. In contrast, the urban social forces on which the Chilean system rested were far more vigilant than the peasants and much more demanding on their political representatives. The constraints which this placed on a party in power were made painfully evident by the Christian Democratic experience, and it is a problem which is likely to recur for the successors of the Frei regime.

A final factor to be considered in evaluating the capacity of the vertical brokerage system to cope with the challenges of the urban-rural cleavage is the skills and training of the Chilean political elites. It is likely that through participation in the parliamentary framework the political representatives of Chilean social forces had acquired orientations often associated with the reformmongering approach. Chilean politicians of all sectors were at their best in the art of bargaining with other elite elements within the society. These skills, however, were not necessarily the kinds of leadership qualities that were important during the later phases of the reform. The reformmongering strategy stressed, in Hirschman's words, the reformer's need to "spread his net as wide as possible," and to avoid stantial size . . ." [20] The demands of the post-1967 phase appeared to call for more decisive choices, bidding for the support of some groups and accepting the more or less permanent opposition of others. The primary (though by no means the exclusive) emphasis of the reformmongering strategy was maneuvering among existing power groups, while the problems of the urban-rural cleavage called in part for the mobilization of new ones.

These, however, were qualities not notably apparent among the Chilean political elites. Although Christian Democratic governmental leaders adopted a permissive policy toward the organization of rural unions, for example, the actual tasks of organization were generally left to others — left-wing party elements, Catholic-sponsored educational institutes, and individual lay Catholics, loosely affiliated with the PDC. The task of organizing urban workers, both proletarian and marginal, received a still lower priority. Marxist orientations, moreover, ran along similar lines. Although the politicians of the left engaged in some effort to organize rural workers, most of their attention and priorities appeared to be directed to other activities — operating within the parliamentary arena, acting as spokesmen for the organized urban workers, and competing with rival leftist leaders within the existing party and trade union framework.

Yet the long years of activity within the system were probably not responsible for these weaknesses. Although participation within the system may have been partially responsible for the leaders' flexibility and moderation, the converse is not necessarily true: struggle against the system does not always lead to the capacity to attract and organize large-scale mass support. The more frequent phenomenon is one of sterile conspiracy, isolated acts of terrorism, or perhaps long and frustrating periods of exile. However, Chilean politicians were equipped, by earlier training, to deal with the problems of change in some ways but not in others. As experienced brokers within a well-established institutional framework, they were prepared to articulate and refine the interests of established groups in a way that would be compatible with that framework. To bolster their positions within the system, they were prepared to act as spokesmen for new groups as they emerged. Chilean political elites were not, however, prepared to foster the emergence of these groups or to aggregate these claims with those of older elements already operating within the political arena.

Concluding Comments

Having made this point, we have now come almost one hundred eighty degrees in our discussion of the vertical brokerage system. At the beginning of the chapter, we suggested that reformmongering was a useful strategy for initiating the rural breakthrough and that the brokerage activities of Chile's representative institutions tended to encourage such efforts. Toward the end of the chapter, we suggested tentatively that the urban-rural cleavage might be dealt with most effectively through an abandonment of some of the tenets of reformmongering, and that the vertical brokerage system tended to discourage the implementation of new, potentially more effective, courses of governmental action.

We have not, however, reversed position entirely. What prevents such a reversal is that in spite of the tensions encountered during the post-1967 period, the Chilean system displayed at least a minimum responsiveness to peasant demands and at least some capacity to continue with the process of reform. This raises further questions which cannot be answered entirely within the framework of this volume.

We now know, for example, that reform was possible within the Chilean parliamentary framework — something that was by no means certain in 1964. In this study we have pointed out some of the strains involved in the pursuit of this reform, and the strengths and weaknesses of the system in withstanding these strains. But we still cannot say with any certainty whether Chile's constitutional order will survive. Few would deny the probability that limited violence, considerable unrest, and bitter conflict will continue to be a part of the Chilean political scene, or that institutional discontinuities of a more serious nature are a distinct possibility. Yet, as we have attempted to show in the preceding pages, Chilean representative institutions are deeply entrenched parts of the political process and have demonstrated the capacity to protect themselves and the system as a whole from profound social tensions. As in the past, therefore, they may well emerge from temporary breakdowns stronger than they were before. It will thus take a far longer perspective than we now have to determine whether we have witnessed the birthpangs of a new sociopolitical adjustment, or the beginning of the ultimate deterioration of the system as a whole.

A more intriguing question, perhaps, is whether alternative institutional arrangements might have promoted more desirable patterns of change. It is clear, of course, that in the final analysis the answer to this question turns on the meaning and priorities one attaches to such values as stability, constitutionality, economic growth, and social equality. It would also depend on a more careful investigation of the similarities and differences between the relatively institutionalized systems of Latin America. Efforts to compare such systems as Chile, Mexico, Uruguay, Costa Rica, Venezuela, and Cuba in terms of the origins, social bases, and structure of their institutional development might yield considerable insight into the capacity of various party systems to promote social reform.

The *strength* of political institutions as well as their *form*, however, should clearly be a factor in evaluating this capacity. Chile may prove more or less effective in managing social change when compared to some of the other systems mentioned above. In many ways, however, the very existence of well-defined structures of political authority is a factor which gives Chile much in common with these otherwise quite different systems, and it serves to distinguish Chile from the brittle military dictatorships and fragile constitutional orders in most of the rest of its sister countries. At least in the long run, this factor appears to have been responsible for that modest degree of success which Chile has enjoyed in facing its agrarian problem. *Some* political institutions, therefore, are probably better than *no* institutions, and the latter is a distinct alternative within the Latin American setting. From an alternative perspective, the *limits* of political institutions and organizations in promoting social change and development should also be stressed. It was suggested that perhaps Venezuela, Cuba, and Mexico will be more successful than Chile in welding the urban and rural sectors into a single national community. The suggestion should clearly be tempered by the awareness that the problems of the urban-rural cleavage are possibly ones which no set of institutional arrangements, however strong, is capable of solving in a satisfactory manner.

The emphasis on the strength and limits of political institutions raises a final set of questions — which must ultimately be dealt with by those individuals who operate within the Chilean arena itself and who are daily confronted with decisions concerning the politics of reform. Granting the imperfections of the vertical brokerage system, can a new, more viable institutional framework be constructed to replace it? Clearly, it is possible that Chile may someday see in power a regime which, dissatisfied with the difficulties of bargaining within a pluralistic order, attempts to move outside of it. The dissolution of Congress, the outlawing of rival parties or movements, the issuance of massive reform decrees — all of these moves are possible. In taking these actions, however, such hypothetical revolutionaries would have working against them much of the weight of Chile's institutional system, as well as the more serious risks of reaction from the social groups which this system has traditionally restrained. Although dissident elites may indeed destroy the system, there is no guarantee that they possess the ruthlessness, unity, and organizational capacity which presumably would be required to build anything better. Is, therefore, the alternative to the admittedly frustrating and slow process of incremental change actually a more violent, but ultimately more progressive revolutionary process? Or is the alternative anarchy, reaction, and stalemate?

Notes

Introduction

1. Albert O. Hirschman, *Journeys Toward Progress* (New York: The Twentieth Century Fund, 1963).

2. Charles W. Anderson, *Politics and Economic Change in Latin America* (Princeton, N.J.: Van Nostrand, 1967).

3. In 1960 Chile ranked fourth among the Latin American countries in urbanization, with 46.3 percent of its population living in towns of more than 20,000. Chile had the third highest literacy rate, with 80.1 percent of its population classified as literate in 1952. Bruce M. Russett et al., *World Handbook of Political and Social Indicators* (New Haven and London: Yale University Press, 1964), pp. 51 and 222. According to one estimate, in 1950 the middle and upper sectors comprised 22 percent of the Chilean population, and manufacturing and construction workers constituted 24 percent of the economically active population. On these measures Chile ranked third and fourth respectively among the twenty Latin American countries. José Nun, "A Latin American Phenomenon. The Middle Class Military Coup," in James Petras and Maurice Zeitlin, eds., *Latin America, Reform or Revolution?* (Greenwich, Conn.: Fawcett Publications, Inc., 1968), p. 158.

4. See especially, Samuel P. Huntington, *Political Order in Changing Societies* (New Haven, Conn.: Yale University Press, 1968); Eric A. Nordlinger, "Political Development Time Sequences and Rates of Change," *World Politics,* col. XX, no. 3 (April 1968), pp. 494–520; and Joseph LaPalombara and Myron Weiner, eds., *Political Parties and Political Development* (Princeton: Princeton University Press, 1966).

5. Huntington, *Political Order*, pp. 39–59.

6. Ibid., pp. 78–92.

7. Ibid., p. 398.

1 Chilean Politics and Agrarian Reform

1. Charles W. Anderson, *Politics and Economic Change in Latin America* (Princeton, N.J.: Van Nostrand, 1967), p. 104.

2. See, for example, John J. Johnson, *Political Change in Latin America, The Emergence of the Middle Sectors* (Stanford, Calif.: Stanford University Press, 1958).

3. Claudio Veliz, ed., *Obstacles to Change in Latin America* (Lon-

don, New York, Toronto: Oxford University Press, 1965), esp. Claudio Veliz, "Introduction," pp. 1–9, and Osvaldo Sunkel, "Change and Frustration in Chile," pp. 116–145. Also, Seymour M. Lipset and Aldo Solari, eds., *Elites in Latin America* (New York: Oxford University Press, 1967), esp. Seymour M. Lipset, "Values, Education, and Entrepreneurship," pp. 3–61.

4. Frederick Pike, "Aspects of Class Relations in Chile, 1850–1960," in James Petras and Maurice Zeitlin, eds., *Latin America, Reform or Revolution?* (Greenwich, Conn.: Fawcett Publications, Inc., 1968), pp. 202–220.

5. Veliz, *Obstacles to Change in Latin America,* pp. 1–9.

6. Anderson, *Politics and Economic Change,* pp. 89–93.

7. Robert E. Scott, "Political Elites and Political Modernization," in Lipset and Solari, *Elites in Latin America,* p. 127.

8. For a discussion of this process, see David Felix, "Chile," in Adamantio Pepelasis, Leon Mears, and Irma Adelman, eds., *Economic Development: Analysis and Case Studies* (New York: Harper and Brothers, 1961), pp. 288–326.

9. Ibid., p. 318.

10. James O. Morris and Roberto Oyander C., *Afiliación y Finanzas Sindicales en Chile, 1932–59* (Santiago de Chile: Instituto de Organización y Administración, INSORA, Editorial Universitaria, 1962), p. 37.

11. Sunkel, "Change and Frustration," p. 131.

12. Ibid., p. 129.

13. See Felix, "Chile," and Sunkel, "Change and Frustration in Chile."

14. See Henry A. Landsberger, "The Labor Elite: Is It Revolutionary?" in Lipset and Solari, eds., *Elites in Latin America,* pp. 256–301.

15. Samuel P. Huntington, *Political Order in Changing Societies* (New Haven, Conn.: Yale University Press, 1968), pp. 192–264. For similar discussions, related more specifically to Latin America, see: Anderson, *Politics and Economic Change,* pp. 87–115, and Scott, "Political Elites and Political Modernization," pp. 117–146. For an illustration of "praetorianism" in one country, see Kalman H. Silvert, "The Costs of Anti-Nationalism: Argentina," in Kalman H. Silvert, ed., American Universities Field Service, *Expectant Peoples, Nationalism, and Development* (New York: Random House, 1963), pp. 345–373.

16. Huntington, *Political Order,* pp. 12–24.

17. It should be emphasized that in spite of the fact that Chilean political institutionalization has occurred along constitutional lines, there is no theoretical reason why institutionalized systems must be "democratic" systems. On the contrary, the Communist regimes of the Soviet Union, Eastern Europe, and perhaps also of Cuba should be considered no less institutionalized than the political systems of the United States and Western Europe. Both types of system share in common the fact that "political" institutions and procedures are "strong"

in relation to social forces and organizations. Although the competitiveness of the Chilean system played an important role in the land reform process, the dimension of institutionalization is intended to distinguish that country not only from weak military dictatorships in Latin America, but also from the brittle constitutional regimes that are found in the area.

18. To my knowledge, reliable cross-national data systematically measuring Huntington's concept of institutionalization have not yet been developed. However, some of the judgmental rankings developed by Arthur S. Banks and Robert B. Textor in *A Cross-Polity Survey* (Cambridge, Mass.: The M.I.T. Press, 1963) provide the means for an indirect comparison between Chile and the other Latin American countries. I selected ten Banks and Textor variables, each of which groups the countries according to some aspects of the functional importance of their representative institutions. An index was then created by giving each Latin American country one point each time that its ranking suggested a significant role for its political institutions in the political process. On this admittedly tentative measure, Chile and Uruguay scored eight out of a possible ten points, while only two other Latin American countries (Costa Rica and Venezuela) scored more than five. The variables selected and Chile's score on each are given below:

Variable	*Score for Chile*
1. Polities where autonomous groups are fully tolerated in politics (Variable 107)	1
2. Polities where the electoral system is competitive (Variable 105)	1
3. Polities where interest articulation by associational groups is significant or moderate (Variable 116)	1
4. Polities where interest articulation by institutional groups is moderate or limited (Variable 119)	1
5. Polities where interest articulation by non-associational groups is limited or negligible (Variable 122)	1
6. Polities where interest articulation by anomic groups is occasional, infrequent, or very infrequent (Variable 124)	1
7. Polities where interest articulation by parties is significant (Variable 127)	1
8. Polities where interest aggregation by parties is significant or moderate (Variable 131)	0
9. Polities where interest aggregation by the executive is significant (Variable 133)	0
10. Polities where interest aggregation by the legislature is significant (Variable 136)	1
Total score for Chile	8

19. See especially James O. Morris, *Elites, Intellectuals, and Consensus: A Study of the Social Question and the Industrial Relations System in Chile* (Ithaca, N.Y.: New York State School of Industrial and Labor Relations, Cornell University, 1966). Morris summarizes a brilliant and well-documented study of the rise of the Chilean labor movement by stating on p. 100: "In the relatively short span of thirty years (1890 to the 1920s), industrial violence had rocked the country from end to end and the blood of those who rebelled lay in the desert, in the streets, and on the barren and windswept plains of the south."

20. Quoted by Donald William Bray, "Chilean Politics During the Second Ibañez Government, 1952–58," (Unpublished Ph.D. dissertation, Political Science, Stanford University, 1961), pp. 177–78.

21. Computed from the *New York Times* Index.

22. Peter G. Snow, "The Chilean Multiparty System," in Robert D. Tomesak, ed., *Latin American Politics, Studies of the Contemporary Scene* (Garden City, N.Y.: Doubleday & Company, Inc., 1966), pp. 399–413.

23. Computed from the Dirección del Registro Electoral, Santiago, Chile.

24. Arend Lijphart, "Consociational Democracy," *World Politics,* vol. XXI (January 1969), pp. 207–226.

25. Computed from data provided by the Oficina de Informacion, Congreso de Chile.

26. George M. McBride, *Chile: Land and Society* (New York: American Geographical Society, 1936), p. 144.

27. Bruce M. Russett, "Inequality and Instability: The Relation of Land Tenure to Politics," *World Politics,* vol. XVI (April 1964), pp. 87–95.

28. Solon Barraclough, "Agricultural Policy and Strategies of Land Reform," in Irving Louis Horowitz, ed., *Masses in Latin America* (New York: Oxford University Press, 1970), pp. 136–37. The figures for the other five countries were: Argentina (1960), 36 percent; Brazil (1950), 60 percent; Colombia (1960), 45 percent; Ecuador (1954), 42 percent; Guatemala (1950), 40 percent.

29. For a discussion of this early period see, CIDA, *Chile, Tenencia de la tierra,* pp. 1–38, and McBride, *Chile: Land and Society,* pp. 61–146. Much of the forthcoming discussion will also be based on these works.

30. In 1955, 61.5 percent of all rural properties in Chile consisted of parcels of less than twenty-five hectares. CIDA, *Chile, Tenencia de la tierra,* p. 10.

31. *III Censo Nacional Agrícola Ganadero, Republica de Chile,* Abril 1955, Vol. I–XXX, VI.

32. McBride, *Chile: Land and Society,* p. 166.

33. Ibid., p. 170.

34. See, for example, Zeitlin's comments on the differences between

the Chilean and Cuban prospects for a worker-peasant alliance: "Dispersion of these (Chilean) centers of working class strength served as sources of countervailing power without posing a real threat to the power of the ruling class, because local and regional struggles tended to remain confined to (and to be dissipated in) these areas rather than grow into national struggles between the classes as a whole. In Cuba, in contrast, the sugar *centrales* were scattered throughout the country and located in the midst of the countryside; there was regular contact between agricultural laborers and mill workers, and coordination of strikes in the nation-wide industry inevitably became a national struggle." Maurice Zeitlin, "The Social Determinants of Political Democracy in Chile," in Petras and Zeitlin, eds., *Reform and Revolution*, p. 230.

35. Federico G. Gil, *The Political System of Chile* (Boston: Houghton Mifflin Company, 1966), p. 148.

36. McBride, *Chile: Land and Society*, p. 170.

37. Pike, "Aspects of Class Relations in Chile," p. 214.

38. Ibid., p. 215.

39. McBride, *Chile: Land and Society*, p. 144.

40. Markos Mamalakis and Clark W. Reynolds, *Essays on the Chilean Economy* (Homewood, Ill.: Richard D. Irwin, Inc., 1965). Writing of Latin America as a whole, Rodolfo Stavenhagen also notes the exploitative relation between the growth of cities and the deterioration of peasant wages: "The struggle of the urban working class . . . for high wages, more and better public social services, price controls, etc. finds no seconding in the peasant sector because benefits obtained in this way are usually obtained at the cost of agriculture — i.e., the peasants . . . In other words, the urban working class in our countries is also a beneficiary of internal colonialism." Rodolfo Stavenhagen, "Seven Fallacies about Latin America," in Petras and Zeitlin, eds., *Latin America, Reform or Revolution?*, p. 29.

41. Mamalakis and Reynolds, *Essays on the Chilean Economy*, p. 144.

42. McBride, *Chile: Land and Society*, pp. 164–65.

43. *III Censo Nacional Agrícola.*

44. McBride, *Chile: Land and Society*, p. 164.

45. See below, Chapters 4 and 6.

46. Dirección del Registro Electoral.

47. James Petras, "After the Chilean Presidential Election: Reform or Stagnation?", *Journal of Inter-American Studies*, vol. VII, no. 3 (July 1965), p. 380.

48. Felix, "Chile," p. 317.

49. Albert O. Hirschman, *Journeys Toward Progress* (New York: The Twentieth Century Fund, 1963), p. 160.

50. Gil, *The Political System of Chile*, p. 29.

51. CIDA, *Chile, Tenencia de la tierra*, p. 23.

52. Comisión Económica para America Latina/Organización de las naciones para agricultura y la alimentación (CEPAL/FAO), *Análisis de algunos factores que obstaculizan el incremento de la Producción Agropequaria. E/CN. 12/306* (Santiago, 1953), pp. 85–6. My italics.

53. Hirschman, *Journeys,* esp. "Inflation in Chile," pp. 159–227.

54. Mamalakis and Reynolds, *Essays,* p. 132, give an excellent critique of the structuralist thesis.

55. For a definitive and inclusive summary of these data, see CIDA, *Chile, Tenencia de la tierra.*

56. Robert Scott, "Political Elites and Political Modernization," p. 128.

57. Mancur Olson, *The Logic of Collective Action* (Cambridge, Mass.: Harvard University Press, 1967), p. 7.

58. Hirschman, *Journeys,* and Anderson, *Politics and Economic Change.*

59. See Oscar Delgado, ed., *Reformas agrarias en la America Latina, procesos y perspectivas* (Mexico-Buenos Aires: Fondo de Cultura Economica, 1965), esp. Benno Galjart, "Estructuras de podér y reforma agraria," pp. 177–184; Andrew Gunder Frank, "Tipos de reformas agrarias," pp. 184–189; and Oscar Delgado, "Las elites del podér versus la reforma agraria," pp. 189–232.

60. Hirschman, *Journeys,* pp. 272–73.

61. David E. Apter, *The Politics of Modernization* (Chicago and London: University of Chicago Press, 1965), pp. 210–212.

2 The Alessandri Reform, 1962–63: A Redefinition of Rightist Interests

1. For example: Joseph Grunwald, "Some Comments about the Chilean Economy," in *Survey and Perspectives of Chile's Economic Development, 1940–65* (Santiago, Chile: Instituto de Economia de la Universidad de Chile, 1957), pp. 5–6; Markos Mamalakis and Clark W. Reynolds, *Essays on the Chilean Economy* (Homewood, Ill.: Richard D. Irwin, Inc., 1965), pp. 117–148.

2. *El Mercurio,* Editorial, April 6, 1957, p. 3.

3. Computed from data provided by Dirección del Registro Electoral, Santiago, Chile.

4. It was to decline still further — to less than 5 percent in 1964.

5. Computed from data provided by the Dirección del Registro Electoral.

6. Source: *Diccionario Biográfico de Chile* (Santiago de Chile: Empresa Periodista Chile, 1962–1964). For a complete breakdown of the economic backgrounds of the party congressional delegations, see Chapter 3, Table 5.

7. Sources: *El Mercurio,* March 10, 1957, p. 25; Federico G. Gil,

The Political System of Chile (Boston: Houghton Mifflin Co., 1966), p. 228.

8. Source: *Diccionario Biográfico de Chile* (1962–1964).

9. See José Luís de Imáz's comments on the Argentine landowners: "In the Argentine case, many liberal and rightist conservative groups have visualized the party as something instrumental for coming to power; as a means and not an end. For many conservatives, the party is not valued in itself, but only insofar as it is an operational instrument. In some instances, it can be useless. Thus, the armed forces or other pressure groups might appear to conservative eyes as channels of access to power . . . which are functionally more useful than the party. Thus, it might not be necessary to waste energy to become greatly involved in the leadership of something that can only be useful in limited circumstances." José Luís de Imáz, *Los que mandan* (Buenos Aires: Editorial Universitaria de Buenos Aires, EUDEBA, 1964), p. 204.

10. Celso Furtado, "Political Obstacles to Economic Growth in Brazil," in Claudio Veliz, ed., *Obstacles to Change in Latin America* (London, New York, Toronto: Oxford University Press, 1965), p. 154.

11. Source: Dirección del Registro Electoral.

12. Ibid.

13. Source: Oficina de Informaciones, Congreso de Chile.

14. Source: *Diccionario Biográfico de Chile* (1962–1964).

15. Source: *Diccionario Biográfico de Chile* (1942–1944).

16. Directiva Conservadora de Aconcagua, Letter to the Editor, *El Mercurio,* March 7, 1962, p. 27.

17. Ibid.

18. Letter signed by backers of Luís Valdés Larraín, *Diario Ilustrado,* April 16, 1961, p. 8.

19. Francisco Bulnes Sanfuentes, "Discurso a la Dirección General," *Diario Ilustrado,* June 13, 1963, p. 2.

20. Ernesto Noguera, Provincial Secretary of Valparaiso, Letter to the Editor, *Diario Ilustrado,* March 11, 1962, p. 12.

21. Francisco Bulnes Sanfuentes, "Discurso a la Dirección General."

22. Departamento Gremial Liberal, quoted in *La Nación,* May 7, 1961, p. 13.

23. Source: *Diccionario Biográfico de Chile* (1962–1964).

24. Ibid.

25. Interview, June 3, 1966.

26. Domingo Godoy Matte, Letter to the Editor, *Diario Ilustrado,* December 12, 1961, p. 2.

27. "Informe sobre la reforma constitucionál," *El Campesino,* XCIV, No. 1 (January 1962), pp. 9–19.

28. Ibid.

29. Ibid.

30. See, for example, the charges of Carlos Bulnes Correa: "Payment that is disguised under the euphemism of deferred payments is not payment . . . The Liberal and Conservative parties abandon thus, at a stroke, one of the basic principles of their existence: respect for private property." Letter to the Editor, *Diario Ilustrado,* November 23, 1961, p. 3.

31. C.A.S., Letter to the Editor, *Diario Ilustrado,* December 22, 1961, p. 7.

32. Carlos Bulnes Correa, Letter to the Editor, *Diario Ilustrado,* December 27, 1961, p. 3.

33. Javier Echevarría Alessandri, Letter to the Editor, *Diario Ilustrado,* December 27, 1961, p. 3.

34. Fernando Coloma Reyes, Letter to the Editor, *Diario Ilustrado,* December 30, 1961, p. 3.

35. Source: Charles H. Daugherty, ed. *Chile Election Factbook* (Washington, D.C.: Institute for the Comparative Study of Political Systems, 1963).

36. FEDAGRI, Letter to the Editor, *Diario Ilustrado,* May 17, 1962, p. 3.

37. Asociación de Agricultores de Maule, Letter to the Editor, *Diario Ilustrado,* January 16, 1962, p. 6: "The lack of opportune and adequate information moved us to take a precipitate stand in the [last] session. After more extensive discussion our organization agreed in yesterday's session to give its full support to the formula which is provided in the constitutional reform for deferred payments for expropriations . . ."

38. Source: Corporación de la Reforma Agraria, Departamento de Planificación y Control.

39. Sociedad Nacional Agraria del Peru, quoted in Oscar Delgado, ed. *Reformas agrarias en la America Latina: procesos y perspectivas* (México-Buenos Aires: Fondo de Cultura Económica, 1965), p. 329.

40. Salomon Corbalán, Speech, *Discursos del Senado de Chile,* 25th session, July 26, 1962, p. 1920.

41. Source: Corporación de la Reforma Agraria, Departamento de Planificación y Control, CORA.

42. Interview, April 18, 1966.

43. Anthony Downs, *An Economic Theory of Democracy* (New York: Harper and Brothers, 1957).

44. Javier Echevarría Alessandri, Letter to the Editor, *Diario Ilustrado,* October 10, 1964, p. 3.

3 The Christian Democratic Factional Struggle and Agrarian Reform, 1964–1967

1. This view was set forth most systematically in Jorge Rogers's *Dos Caminos para la Reforma Agraria en Chile: 1945–1965* (Santiago de Chile: Editorial Orbe, 1966).

2. Frei's published volume of speeches, *Pensamiento y Acción* (Santiago de Chile: Editorial del Pacífico, 1958), ranges over a broad variety of topics and includes detailed statements on inflation, the balance of payments problem, and economic growth. There are only a few brief and vague passages on land reform.

3. In 1965 Frei introduced the land reform law in the following manner: "In the agrarian reform which we are going to undertake we will not take away the right to property but complete it . . . We intend to carry out that task with a profound sense of justice and liberty, creating thousands of new property holders, strengthening the role of the small and intermediate property holders already in existence, and encouraging those who are farming their land efficiently today." Excerpt from *Primer Mensaje del Presidente de la República de Chile al Congreso Nacional* (May 21, 1965), published by the Presidential Department of Publications, Santiago, Chile, translated by Paul E. Sigmund, ed., *The Ideologies of the Developing Nations* (New York, Washington, London: Frederick A. Praeger, 1967), p. 392.

4. Federico G. Gil, *The Political System of Chile* (Boston: Houghton Mifflin Co., 1966), p. 273.

5. The reform of the American-owned copper industry was considered by Frei to be the most important measure of his administration, and typified this moderate reformist approach. One aspect of the copper plan committed the Chilean government to purchase from 25 to 51 percent of stock in various American mines. The other held out the promise of broad tax reductions, designed to encourage new investments. Thus, while the plan sought to place controls on the American companies, it was also presented as an alternative to nationalization. For this very reason, it was roundly condemned by Marxists and by the Christian Democratic left-wingers as a "sell-out" to American imperialism.

6. Julio Silva, a leading Christian Democratic ideologist, was typical of the left-wing leaders. In his middle thirties at the time of the 1964 elections, Silva had been active in student politics at the University of Chile. As a journalist and writer he acquired strong personal and ideological ties with the Marxists, and sought to incorporate Marxist concepts into the framework of Christian values. In the years preceding the elections, he had been a columnist for the Socialist newspaper, *Ultima Hora.*

7. "The Non-Capitalist Road to Development," P.E.C. No. 239 (July 28, 1967), p. 3.

8. The major exception to this rule was Rafael Augustin Gumucio — one of the founders of the Falange — who was the successful left-wing candidate for the party presidency in 1967.

9. Jacques Chonchol, "El Desarrollo de America Latina y la Reforma Agraria," *Ciclo para Funcionarios de la Corporación de la Reforma Agraria* (Santiago: Instituto de Capacitación e Investigación en Reforma Agraria [ICIRA], Documento No. 2, n.d.). Chonchol especially stressed the conflict of interests between expropriated landlords and the peasants. The more the latter were compensated for their land, the less possibility there would be of a radical agrarian reform. Therefore, bitter resistance was to be expected as the reform progressed, and the "affected minorities" were to be placed in a "position where they could no longer oppose," (p. 75).

10. Ibid., p. 77.

11. Luís Corvalán, "Adelante con la Reforma Agraria," *Principios, Revista Teórica y Política del Comité Central del Partido Comunista de Chile* (Santiago), vol. XXVII, no. 112 (March–April 1966), p. 13.

12. Interview, April 21, 1966.

13. Alberto Jeréz, as quoted in *El Mercurio* (Santiago), November 6, 1965, p. 21.

14. Luís Hernandez Parker, "Aguas Bravas para Barco DC," *Ercilla*, No. 1588 (October 27, 1965), p. 13.

15. See below, Chapter 7.

16. Interview, April 21, 1966.

17. See below, Chapter 7.

18. Interview, March 11, 1966.

19. Interview, May 10, 1966.

20. Interview, May 24, 1966.

21. Although the meeting was held in secrecy, the fact that it had taken place and some of the details eventually leaked to the press. Referring to the meeting over a year later, in May 1967, one SNA councilor quoted Leighton as having "promised to amend the bill during its passage in the Chamber of Deputies." Hector Rios Igualt, Letter, *El Mercurio* (Santiago), May 17, 1967, p. 23.

22. *Boletín P.D.C., Organo Oficial del Partido Demócrata Cristiano,* Año 2, Nos. 7, 8, 9 (January and February 1966), p. 3.

23. Interview, May 3, 1966.

24. Source: Oficina de Planificación Agrícola de los Balances Presupuestarios, Ministerio de Hacienda. The figures for the year 1967 are official estimates.

25. Tomás Cox, as quoted in *Diario Ilustrado* (Santiago), March 27, 1965, p. 7.

26. Source: Oficina de Planificación, CORA. Other expropriated areas also tended to be in heavily populated regions. The south central

province of Cautin, for example, was the most heavily populated province in Chile, after Santiago, Valparaiso, and Concepción. A bulwark of Christian Democratic voting strength, this province also received considerable attention from the reform administration.

27. Source: Economic Commission for Latin America, *Economic Survey of Latin America, 1969* (New York: United Nations Publication, 1970), p. 154.

28. For more details on these parliamentary rules, see below, Chapter 5, at Table 15.

29. See below, Chapter 5, at n. 36.

30. See below, Chapter 6, at n. 25.

31. Albert O. Hirschman, *Journeys Toward Progress, Studies of Economic Policy-Making in Latin America* (New York: The Twentieth Century Fund, 1963), p. 285.

32. Ibid., p. 286.

33. Ibid., p. 287.

34. Alberto Jeréz H. and Julio S. Silva, Letter to *El Siglo* (Santiago), March 18, 1966, p. 8.

35. Anthony Downs, *An Economic Theory of Democracy* (New York: Harper and Brothers, 1957).

36. Bosco Parra, quoted by Luís Hernandez Parker, "En Cartegena dio Examen de Madurez la DC," *Ercilla*, No. 1609 (April 6, 1966), p. 8.

37. "The Non-Capitalist Road to Development," p. 3.

4 Effects of the Christian Democratic Reform, 1964–1967: The Problem of Mobilizing Peasant Support

1. Elias H. Tuma, *Twenty-Six Centuries of Agrarian Reform: A Comparative Analysis* (Berkeley and Los Angeles: University of California Press, 1965).

2. Data obtained from the Oficina de Planificación, Corporación de la Reforma Agraria, CORA.

3. Ibid.

4. Ibid.

5. Organización de las Naciones Unidas para la Agricultura y la Alimentación y el Instituto de Capicitación e Investigación en Reforma Agraria, (ICIRA), *Evaluación preliminar de los asentamientos de la reforma agraria en Chile* (Santiago de Chile, 1967), p. 7. The land area was 30.4 percent of all land incorporated into the agrarian reform during 1965–66.

6. Ibid., p. 35.

7. Ibid., p. 30.

8. Some of Aldunate's analysis appears in *El Mercurio* (Santiago), March 5, 1968, p. 23.

9. Interview, March 1968.

10. "Evaluación de la reforma agraria," *El Mercurio* (Santiago), July 6, 1968, p. 25.

11. Between 1960 and 1969, the index of per capita agricultural production (based on 1957–1959 = 100) was as follows:

Year	Output	Year	Output
1960	96	1965	95
1961	95	1966	94
1962	90	1967	94
1963	96	1968	96
1964	97	1969	87 (preliminary estimate)

Source: Agency for International Development, *Summary Economic and Social Indicators for 18 Latin American Countries: 1960–69.* (Prepared by the Office of Development Programs, Bureau for Latin America, June 1970), p. 42.

12. *Evaluación preliminar* . . . , pp. 28–30. The tendency for land reform to produce higher peasant incomes is also supported by independent studies. See William Charles Theissenhusen, "Experimental Programs of Land Reform in Chile," Ph.D. dissertation (University of Wisconsin, 1965).

13. *Evaluación preliminar* . . . , p. 18.

14. Thirty-eight percent of the asentados in the ICIRA study said housing conditions had improved; 58.5 percent said they were the same. Medical care was considered bad, or only "so-so" by over 80 percent of the peasants. Ibid., pp. 47–48.

15. Ibid., p. 58.

16. Ibid., p. 18. After 1967, various rightist politicians turned to this sector in the attempt to mobilize peasant opposition to expropriations, see below, Chapter 5, at n. 43.

17. *Evaluación preliminar* . . . , p. 56.

18. *La Nación* (Santiago, January 16, 1967), p. 23.

19. *Evaluación preliminar* . . . , p. 57.

20. Ibid.

21. *Ley 16.640,* as published in *Diario Oficial de la República de Chile,* No. 26.804, viernes 28 de Julio, 1967. Article 72, p. 9.

22. *Evaluación preliminar* . . . , p 23.

23. Interview, March 1968.

24. *III Censo Nacional Agrícola Ganadero,* República de Chile, April 1955, Vols. I–VI.

25. Female voters were excluded from the calculation, because they have traditionally displayed special ties to the Christian Democrats. These ties should be considered as separate variables from those related to region and class. For somewhat the same reasons, the communes of the five provinces from the far north and far south were also excluded from the calculations. Their geographic isolation and special economic interests have given them voting traditions which are re-

moved from national politics; their sparse populations, moreover, have little impact on the total national vote.

26. Samuel P. Huntington, *Political Order in Changing Societies* (New Haven and London: Yale University Press, 1968), p. 371.

27. Ibid., p. 376.

28. Communes with 50 percent or more agricultural workers in the total labor force.

29. See below, Chapter 6, at n. 31.

30. Data obtained from the Oficina de Sindicatos Rurales, Ministerio de Trabajo.

31. Much of what follows is based on interviews during March 1968, with personnel of ICIRA and of the Centre de Desarrollo de America Latina (DESAL), another study group which was also doing sociological research in the agrarian reform area.

32. For an account of the first of these large-scale strikes and settlements, see James Petras, "Chile's Christian Peasant Union," *News Letter,* The Land Tenure Center, University of Wisconsin (Madison, Wis., July 1966), No. 23, pp. 23–26.

33. About one-half of the 1571 union members on whom background data was available were classified as afuerinos. The assertion that the social composition of most unions came from a mixture of peasant substrata is also supported by the impressions of various field observers with whom the author spoke in March 1968.

34. For the Communist version of this struggle, see the account by Cipriano Pontigo, "Los Comités de Asentamiento en el Valle de Choapa," *Principios,* XXVII, No. 112, Año (March–April 1966), pp. 49–63.

35. Declaration of the CNC, *El Mercurio,* March 7, 1968, p. 21.

36. *Evaluación preliminar . . . ,* p. 62.

37. Enrique Astorga and Enrique Contreras, "Bases Precooperatives en Asentamientos del Valle del Choapa," Departamento de Cooperativas y Crédito, ICIRA (January 1967), p. 76.

38. Interview, June 15, 1966. One highly articulate leader of the Christian unions, of middle class origin, spoke in the following manner about the asentamientos:

They are doing everything they can to stop us from organizing. On one asentamiento, we tried to have a meeting in the house of one of the peasants. Two CORA functionaries came up to me and said, "Do you have permission to hold this meeting?" I turned to the mistress of the house and said, "I don't know, do I have your permission?" When she said yes, I turned to the CORA people and said, "I have the permission of the duena de la casa. Do you have permission to come in here?" After that, they left, but they make things very difficult.

39. Declaration of the Colchagua congress. *La Nación,* January 17, 1967, p. 23.

40. The Christian unions' emphasis on individual property and "pluralistic" rather than government-controlled unions can also be explained at least in part in terms of their financial ties to agencies of the United States government. These agencies, and the privately run International Development Foundation which dispensed U.S. government funds, were clearly committed to such a position. However, it is uncharitable and probably inaccurate to view the union leaders simply as the paid spokesmen for the Americans. Rather, the CNC's ideological position seems to have developed quite independently of its American financial backers, well before American aid was distributed to the union movement. Although the correspondence between the CNC's views and those of the American agencies undoubtedly contributed to the Americans' decision to support the unions, I could see no strings attached to the aid money or any evidence that the Chilean union leaders were not acting more or less autonomously.

41. Interview, June 2, 1966.

42. Along with some rather spectacular struggles within the provincial congresses, this rivalry was also reflected at the communal level. Data from the ministry of labor shows that in Nuble, for example, each of the eleven communal unions, originally affiliated with the CNC, came under the control of INDAP in 1966–67.

43. Emilio Lorenzini, Speech to the Chamber of Deputies, quoted in *El Mercurio* (Santiago), May 25, 1966, p. 29.

44. Terry L. McCoy, "Chile's Campesino Strike," *News Letter*, no. 25, The Land Tenure Center, University of Wisconsin (Madison, Wis., November 1966–March 1967), p. 12.

5 The Right and the Christian Democratic Reform

1. Aníbal Correa Ovalle, letter, *La Nación*, December 23, 1964, p. 3.

2. Editorial, *La Nación*, June 9, 1965, p. 4.

3. Editorial, *El Campesino*, official journal of the SNA, vol. SCVIII, no. 14 (April 1966), p. 15.

4. Ibid.

5. Interview No. 24, May 17, 1966.

6. Even on the ideologically explosive issue of asentamientos, Larraín tended to be cautious in his language. In a major press conference held after the presentation of the land reform bill, Larraín objected only to CORA's power to extend the asentamiento indefinitely. He argued that in the case of land farmed "cooperatively," the bill gave no protection to the rights of individual peasants, or even to the collective as against the state. These criticisms were identical to those made by the Christian unions, whose leaders also feared the potential power of CORA and mistrusted the men who directed it. Rather than condemning asentamientos as a whole, moreover, Larraín criticized only

aspects of this provision. And though these aspects were characterized as "dangerous" or "totalitarian," Larraín made it clear that he did not apply such adjectives to the government as a whole: "With this law an agrarian reform can be realized with free citizens . . . and it can also be made a collectivist reform where the new retainers are slaves of the State. The President has been clear that his road is the first of those named, but the possibility that others, with the same law, might follow the second road puts the agrarian reform bill and the future of the Republic in the darkest shade." (As reported in *El Mercurio,* December 3, 1965, p. 21.)

7. Luís Larraín Marín, press conference, *El Mercurio,* December 3, 1965, p. 21. A more detailed summary of Larraín's criticisms is given in an earlier published version of this chapter, *The Chilean Political Right and Agrarian Reform: Resistance and Moderation* (Washington, D.C.: Institute for the Comparative Study of Political Systems, 1967), pp. 30–32.

8. Interview, March 11, 1966.

9. Luís Larraín Marín, Interview, March 17, 1966.

10. This was the group that led the opposition to the deferred payments amendment during Alessandri's tenure. It is of interest to note the effect of the passage of this amendment on the position of these leaders. None of the men interviewed felt it was possible to challenge what had already been established in the old law. Many did feel, however, that their earlier predictions were coming true, and they expressed frustration at being hemmed in by the previous commitments of the parties and the SNA. As one leader stated: "They [the parties and the SNA] supported the constitutional reform because they wanted to win the election. But now that they have lent their support to one law, none of us can oppose this law as it should be opposed." (Interview No. 5, April 1, 1966.)

11. Interview, June 3, 1966.

12. Interview, March 3, 1966.

13. Interview, March 10, 1966.

14. Interview, April 1, 1966.

15. Interview, March 3, 1966.

16. Dale L. Johnson, "The National Progressive Bourgeoisie in Chile," *Studies in Comparative International Development,* vol. IV, no. 4 (1968–69), p. 76. There were, of course, some important individual exceptions to this rule among industrialists. A few industrial and commercial leaders had initially supported the Christian Democrats as the best defense against Communism, and several served in the Frei cabinet. On the other side, a handful of wealthy industrial leaders were counted among the most vocal opponents of the land reform program.

17. Interview, June 13, 1966.

18. See Donald Bray, "Chilean Politics During the Second Ibañez Government," Ph.D. dissertation, Political Science, Stanford University, 1961.

19. See Samuel P. Huntington, *Political Order in Changing Societies* (New Haven and London: Yale University Press, 1968), pp. 192–264.

20. Ibid., p. 216.

21. Interview, March 3, 1966.

22. Comando Coordinador de Organizaciónes Agrícolas, *El Mercurio,* October 12, 1965, p. 27.

23. Ibid.

24. Ibid.

25. *El Mercurio,* March 26, 1966, p. 25.

26. Interview, April 23, 1966.

27. Pedro Enrique Alfonso, press conference, *El Mercurio,* March 26, 1966, p. 25.

28. Hector Ríos Igualt, letter, *El Mercurio,* May 17, 1967, p. 31.

29. José Pablo Lopez, "Reforma Agraria sin macetero," *Ercilla,* No. 1615, May 18, 1966, p. 6.

30. Interview, April 18, 1966.

31. Ibid.

32. El Partido Nacional y la Reforma de Propriedad, *El Mercurio,* May 28, 1967, p. 35.

33. Pedro Ibañez Ojeda, quoted in *Diario Ilustrado,* April 18, 1966, p. 3.

34. Interview, May 23, 1966.

35. Interview, April 20, 1966.

36. Pedro Ibañez, Senate speech, quoted in *Diario Ilustrado,* April 2, 1966, p. 3.

37. Interview, May 23, 1966.

38. Interview, May 17, 1966.

39. Francisco Bulnes Sanfuentes, Senate speech, text in *El Mercurio,* April 13, 1966, p. 1.

40. Originally the conversion tables had distinguished only between irrigated and nonirrigated soil, giving a smaller reserve area to lands in the latter category. The amendment inserted a third category — partially irrigated land — giving to the owners of this type of property a somewhat larger area of reserve than they would have had if their land had been classified simply as "irrigated."

41. Litigation concerning whether the owner was entitled to reserve lands, for example, could now be taken to the special appellate tribunals.

42. In the original bill the designation of the reserve lands was left entirely to the discretion of CORA. With the amendment, the owner could choose his own reserve territory, provided (a) that the land selected was composed of contiguous territory, (b) that it was equal in quality to the soil expropriated, (c) that it included the owner's house and a reasonable proportion of his capital investment, and (d) that it was susceptible to rational cultivation.

43. SNA insertion, *Diario Ilustrado,* February 28, 1968, p. 5. Their italics.

44. *El Mercurio,* June 11, 1966, p. 23.

45. Among the additional criticisms levied by the SNA were: that no provisions exist which would permit properties that fulfill the requisites of efficiency to be declared inexpropriable; that "the secure and peaceful possession of the 80 hectares reserve has not yet been sufficiently safeguarded"; that the government should eliminate the provision that the 30 percent of the value of the bonds paid in compensation for expropriations would not be readjusted to account for inflation; and that the law did not require the government "to formulate periodic plans that might define the limit of the action to be carried out in the near future." Ibid.

46. Interview, March 17, 1966.

47. Source: Dirrección de Registro Electoral.

48. Ibid.

49. Hector Ríos Igualt, letter, *El Mercurio,* May 17, 1967, p. 31.

50. Ibid.

51. Jacques Chonchol, "El Desarrollo de America Latina y La Reforma Agraria," (Santiago: Instituto de Capacitación e Investigación en Reforma Agraria (ICIRA), n.d.), Documento No. 2, p. 75.

6 The Chilean Left and Agrarian Reform

1. See, for example, Seymour M. Lipset's characterization. Along with other "totalitarian" movements, Communists "do not see themselves as contestants in a give-and-take game of pressure politics but as partisans in a mighty struggle between divine or historic truth on one side and fundamental error on the other . . . Totalitarian organizations, facist and Communist alike, expand the integrationist character of political life to the furthest limit possible by defining the world completely in terms of struggle." *Political Man: The Social Bases of Politics* (Garden City, N.Y.: Anchor Books, Doubleday and Co., Inc., 1963), pp. 74–75.

2. For an excellent discussion of this general ideological debate between the Chilean Communists and Socialists, see Ernst Halperin, *Nationalism and Communism in Chile* (Cambridge, Mass.: M.I.T. Press, 1965). The Socialists, Halperin concludes, are a party of "militant nationalism with a record of participation in conspiracies and coups; its policies have always been determined by a leadership of middle class intellectuals, even though the party membership is of working class stock. The Chilean Communists, on the other hand, lack a revolutionary tradition, and in spite of their totalitarian mentality, they have a history of collaboration with non-Marxist groups." p. 229.

3. Oscar Nuñez, "Enfoque Socialista del Gobierno Actual," *Arauco,* No. 59, Año V (December 1964), p. 11.

4. Osvaldo Sunkel, "Change and Frustration in Chile," in Claudio Veliz, ed., *Obstacles to Change in Latin America* (London, New York, Toronto: Oxford University Press, 1965), p. 132.

5. James O. Morris, *Elites, Intellectuals and Consensus: A Study of the Origins of the Industrial Relations System in Chile, 1900–1938* (Ithaca, N.Y.: New York State School of Industrial and Labor Relations, Cornell University, 1966), p. 46.

6. Carlos Contreras Labarca, "La Gran Experiencia del Frente Popular," *Principios*, No. 120, Año 28 (July–August 1967), p. 40.

7. Maurice Duverger, *Political Parties, Their Organization and Activities in the Modern State* (London: Methuen and Co., Ltd.; New York: John Wiley and Sons, Inc., 1954), pp. 168–205.

8. The change in the percentage of congressional leaders over time should also be noted. In 1941, only one of the seven-man Central Committee was also serving in the Congress.

9. *Diccionario Biográfico de Chile* (Santiago de Chile: Empresa Periodista Chile, 1962–1964).

10. Sigmund Neumann, "Toward a Comparative Study of Political Parties," in Sigmund Neumann, ed., *Modern Political Parties, Approaches to Comparative Politics* (Chicago: The University of Chicago Press, 1956), pp. 400–405.

11. Alejandro Chelán Rojas, quoted in *Arauco*, vol. II, no. 15 (January–February 1961), p. 12.

12. Writing in the Socialist newspaper, *Ultima Hora,* the Christian Democratic left-wing leader, Julio Silva, notes the Communist "zeal for stifling debate, for avoiding the most minimal mental contamination . . ." He accuses that party of a "narrow and timid dogmatism of which the official Communist mentality cannot rid itself. As long as it does not command state power, this strict ideological vigilance is limited to the party members, but once it has obtained this power, it is extended to the entire community." Quoted in Ernst Halperin, *Nationalism and Communism in Chile*, p. 100.

13. See above, Chapter 3, Table 5.

14. James O. Morris, *Elites, Intellectuals and Consensus*, p. 46.

15. Sunkel, "Change and Frustration in Chile," p. 132.

16. See Maurice Zeitlin, "The Social Determinants of Political Democracy in Chile," in James Petras and Maurice Zeitlin, eds., *Latin American Reform or Revolution* (Greenwich, Conn.: Fawcett Publications, Inc., 1968), pp. 220–235.

17. James O. Morris and Roberto Oyander, *Afiliación y Finanzas Sindicales en Chile, 1932–59,* Instituto de Organisación y Administración (INSORA), Publicaciones INSORA (Santiago de Chile: Editorial Universitaria, 1962), p. 37.

18. For an account of this early unionization effort by Christian Democratic-oriented groups, see Henry A. Landsberger, "A Vineyard Worker's Strike: A Case Study of the Relationship between Church, Intellectuals, and Peasants in Chile," unpublished paper, n.d.

19. During the debate on the Alessandri reform, the right and the Radicals charged that the FRAP's opposition was part of a plan to prevent peaceful adjustment, in the hope that worsening conditions in the countryside would eventually lead to revolution. This charge had little merit. The FRAP was joined in opposition by the Christian Democrats, whose motives could not be so easily called into question. From the point of view of both the FRAP and the PDC, the Alessandri measure was a "fraud" which would bring only minimal rural change. It was probably for this reason that neither grouping was willing to endorse the measure by giving it their votes. Yet the FRAP's general opposition to the bill did not prevent it from attempting to improve it by working for the inclusion of amendments. Joining with the Christian Democrats and with some Radicals, the left attempted (unsuccessfully) to incorporate a provision establishing a parity between the then unequal minimum wage levels of the peasants and the urban workers.

20. Clodomíro Alméyda, "El Socialismo Chileno y la Reforma Agrarian," *Arauco,* No. 31, Año II (July 1962), p. 23.

21. José Gonzalez, "Hacia una verdadera reforma agraria, *Principios,* no. 100, vol. XXV (March–April 1964), p. 25.

22. Statement of the Central Committee of the Communist Party, *El Siglo* (Santiago), November 26, 1965, p. 1.

23. Senate speech by Salomon Corbalán (Session 11a, esp. Oct. 19, 1966), quoted in *Arauco,* No. 81, Año VII (October 1966), p. 59.

24. Corbalán's speech in support of the project was reported as follows by *Arauco:* "The Executive will not carry out a truly revolutionary reform, due to the social composition of the governing party . . . At bottom, there only exists a reformist intention directed toward strengthening the present system . . . To create 100,000 new proprietors means to extract these persons from the peasant masses and to transform them into a propertied sector which will defend the present capitalist system and private enterprises . . ." ibid.

25. Interview, March 1968.

26. Sunkel, "Change and Frustration in Chile," pp. 133–34.

27. One Socialist leader put the problem this way: "If we had opposed the measure, the repudiation of the people would have been enormous. We would never have recovered electorally." Interview March 1968.

28. *El Siglo,* April 1, 1966, p. 1.

29. Interview, April 21, 1966.

30. James Petras and Maurice Zeitlin, "Miners and Agrarian Radicalism in Chile," in Petras and Zeitlin, eds., *Latin American Reform or Revolution?,* p. 247.

31. Ibid., p. 246.

32. Interviews, March 1968.
This includes one Socialist Central Committee member, one senator, and one Communist leader of the FCI.

33. José Campusano, "El papel de las organizaciónes campesinas en la lucha por la Reforma Agraria," *Principios,* No. 112, Año XXVII (March–April 1966), pp. 30–31.

34. Luís Corvalán, "The Communists and Agrarian Reform," in T. Lynn Smith, ed., *Agrarian Reform in Latin America* (New York: Knopf, 1965), p. 141.

35. Data taken from the files of the Ministry of Labor.

36. Terry L. McCoy, "The Seizure of 'Los Cristales': A Case Study of the Marxist Left in Chile," *Inter-American Economic Affairs,* vol. 21, no. 1 (Summer 1967), p. 77.

37. Ibid., p. 89.

38. Ibid.

39. For an account of this see Cipriano Pontígo, "Los Comités de Asentamiento en el Valle del Choapa," *Principios,* No. 112 (March–April 1966), pp. 49–63.

40. Enrique Astorga and Enrique Contreras, "Bases Precooperativas en Asentamientos del Valle de Choapa," (Departamento de Cooperativas y Crédito, ICIRA, January 1967), p. 10.

41. Sidney G. Tarrow, *Peasant Communism in Southern Italy* (New Haven: Yale University Press, 1966), p. 293.

42. This move was accepted by the PDC government on the condition that the headquarters did not attempt any revolutionary activity. Through 1968, at least, this condition was accepted.

43. Ernst Halperin, *Sino-Cuban Trends: The Case of Chile* (Cambridge, Mass.: M.I.T. Center for International Studies, 1964) C/64–13, p. 68.

44. Ibid.

45. The former Socialist Secretary General, Raul Ampuero, stated: "We are categorically against terrorism. Every Marxist is. The incident last night (a bombing attempt) is only an indication of the lack of unity and organization of the Chilean left . . . It is a question of idealists without political maturity, who because they lack leadership, fall into these errors." *El Mercurio,* March 23, 1968, p. 28.

46. *El Siglo,* November 28, 1965, p. 3.

47. *El Siglo,* November 30, 1965, p. 3.

48. *Boletín PDC, órgano oficial del Partido Demócrata Cristiano,* Nos. 8 and 9, Año 2 (January–February 1966), p. 4.

7 The Urban Radicals and Land Reform

1. Elias Tuma, *Twenty-Six Centuries of Agrarian Reform: A Comparative Analysis* (Berkeley and Los Angeles: University of California Press, 1965), p. 176.

2. Frederick B. Pike, "Aspects of Class Relations in Chile, 1850–1960," in James Petras and Maurice Zeitlin, eds., *Latin America: Re-*

form or Revolution? (Greenwich, Conn.: Fawcett Publications, Inc., 1968), p. 216.

3. "The Non-Capitalist Road to Development," *P.E.C.*, no. 239 (July 28, 1967), p. 3.

4. See E. J. Hobsbawn, "Peasants and Rural Migrants in Politics," in Claudio Veliz, ed., *The Politics of Conformity in Latin America* (London, New York, Toronto: Oxford University Press, 1967), pp. 43–66. Daniel Goldrich, "Toward the Comparative Study of Politicization in Latin America," in Dwight B. Heath and Richard N. Adams, eds., *Contemporary Cultures and Societies of Latin America* (New York: Random House, 1965), pp. 361–379. Joan M. Nelson, *Migrants, Urban Poverty, and Instability in Developing Nations* (Cambridge: Occasional Paper No. 22, Center for International Affairs, Harvard University, 1969). Wayne A. Cornelius, Jr., "Urbanization as an Agent in Latin American Instability: The Case of Mexico," *American Political Science Review*, vol. LXIII (September 1969), pp. 833–858.

5. Henry A. Landsberger, "The Labor Elite; Is it Revolutionary?" in Seymour Martin Lipset and Aldo Solari, eds., *Elites in Latin America* (New York: Oxford University Press, 1967), pp. 275–76.

6. Ibid.

7. Ibid., pp. 272–73.

8. Ibid., p. 274.

9. Source: Dirección de Trabajo, Departmento de Conflictos. Compiled by Henry A. Landsberger for "Labor under Christian Democracy: The First Two Years." Paper presented at the Colloquium on Overall Development in Chile. (Indiana: University of Notre Dame, March 8–10, 1967).

10. James Petras, *Politics and Social Forces in Chilean Development* (Berkeley and Los Angeles: University of California Press, 1969), p. 325.

11. Federico G. Gil, *The Political System of Chile* (Boston: Houghton Mifflin Co., 1966), p. 265.

12. Kalman H. Silvert, as quoted in Gil, *The Political System of Chile*, p. 76.

13. Anselmo Sule, Secretary General of the PR, quoted in *El Siglo*, January 25, 1964, p. 5.

14. Edison Perez Rojas, Regional Secretary of San Felipe and Los Andes, quoted in *P.E.C.*, no. 234 (June 23, 1967), p. 3.

15. Gil, *The Political System of Chile*, p. 273.

16. Statement of Juventud Radical, *La Nación*, May 14, 1966, p. 2.

17. Radical leaders did not, however, withdraw from their sub-cabinet posts in the agrarian reform administration or from the electoral coalition itself. Although the withdrawal from the cabinet placed strains on the center-right coalition, the coalition did not break up until the defeats at Curicó in 1964.

18. *Exposición sobre el Estado de la Hacienda Pública.* Presentada por el Ministro de Hacienda don Sergio Molina Silva a la Comisión Mixta de Presupuestos el 7 de Noviembre de 1967. Dirección de Presupuestos, Folleto No. 112, Noviembre de 1967, pp. 7 and 10.

19. Ibid., p. 61.

20. "The Non-Capitalist Road to Development," section on Reajustes, pp. 33–37.

21. Raul Saez, Radio address to the nation. Text reprinted in *El Mercurio,* March 13, 1968, p. 21.

22. Ibid.

23. Ibid.

24. Interview, March 1968.

25. Ibid.

26. Source: *Exposición sobre el Estado de la Hacienda Pública.* Cuadro No. 8, Ingresos del Sector Fiscal, 1963–1967, p. 73. *Direct* taxes had almost doubled in real currency from 1,471 million escudos in 1964 to 2,593 million in 1967. *Indirect* taxes increased from 1,988 million escudos to 3,386 million.

27. Interview, March 1968.

28. *Ultima Hora,* March 12, 1968, p. 2.

29. For a fuller account see "El 'gremio' uniformado," by Luís Hernandez Parker, *Ercilla,* No. 1716 (May 8–14), 1968, pp. 10–13.

30. Speech of José Cademartori, as printed in *El Siglo,* March 22, 1968, p. 3.

31. Statement of Communist leader of CUT, *El Siglo,* March 22, 1968, p. 3.

32. In one study, Henry Landsberger, Manuel Barrera, and Abel Toro found that "far from being a malcontent," the union leader "is a stable element in the plant community and is recognized as such by management." (p. 403). Sixty-four percent of that sample had served more than eight years in the same plant. "The Chilean Labor Union Leader: A Preliminary Report on His Background," *Industrial and Labor Relations Review,* vol. 17, no. 3 (April 1964).

33. James Petras and Maurice Zeitlin, "Miners and Agrarian Radicalism," in Petras and Zeitlin, eds., *Latin America; Reform or Revolution?,* pp. 235–249.

34. There is some evidence that even the ties between the urban marginals and the peasants may be somewhat more attenuated than in other countries. In his study of migration into Chilean cities, Bruce Herrick notes a "wave" pattern of movement, from the countryside, to small towns, to provincial cities, and then to one of the large cities. If this is correct, it means that even many of the migrants are at least one step removed from the land. Bruce Herrick, *Urban Migration and Economic Development in Chile* (Cambridge, Mass.: M.I.T. Press, 1966).

35. Richard M. Morse, "The Heritage of Latin America," in Louis

Hartz, ed., *The Founding of New Societies* (New York: Harcourt, Brace, and World, Inc., 1964), pp. 123–178.

36. Albert O. Hirschman, *Journeys Toward Progress* (New York: The Twentieth Century Fund, 1963), p. 208.

37. Statement of the Postal and Telegraph Workers Association, *El Siglo,* March 15, 1968, p. 4.

38. Mancur Olson, *The Logic of Collective Action* (Cambridge, Mass.: Harvard University Press, 1967).

39. There is, of course, a voluntary aspect to the payment of taxes which finance roads, defense, etc. Governments would be helpless if all citizens sought to evade taxes, as the cases of many European and Latin American countries suggest. But the threat of sanctions clearly underlies the decisions of most individual taxpayers to pay taxes, and without such sanctions the citizens' contribution to the establishment and maintenance of various governmental services is almost unimaginable.

40. Olson, *The Logic of Collective Action,* p. 21.

41. In Mexico during the 1930s, membership in the Mexican peasant union was required for any rural worker desiring to be given *ejido* lands and government credit. Gerrit Huizer, "Peasant Organization in Agrarian Reform in Mexico," in Irving Louis Horowitz, ed., *Masses in Latin America* (New York: Oxford University Press, 1970), p. 468.

42. In a small, single-industry town or in an alliance between one large nation and many small ones, for example, the individual company or nation may feel that it is in its interest to contribute to public security arrangements, even though it realizes that the smaller merchants or the weaker nations can benefit without paying for these arrangements.

43. The best example is in the agricultural industry, where the farmer invariably decides to produce as much as possible, even though he realizes that if all others do the same, the price he receives for his product will go down. Some cooperation, of course, may occur in situations of this sort. Farmers form associations, or — to take another example — workers organize trade unions. Often, however, private benefits (extension services, the publication of specialized information, or social facilities), or government compulsion (legislation compelling union membership or the reduction of cultivated acreage) are necessary for the formation of such groups.

8 The Vertical Brokerage System and the Process of Reform

1. Albert O. Hirschman, *Journeys Toward Progress* (New York: The Twentieth Century Fund, 1963).

2. Ibid. Charles W. Anderson, *Politics and Economic Change in Latin America* (Princeton, N.J.: D. Van Nostrand Company, Inc.,

1967); see also Samuel P. Huntington, *Political Order in Changing Societies* (New Haven: Yale University Press, 1969), pp. 344–362.

3. Hirschman, *Journeys Toward Progress,* p. 272.

4. The growth of a large middle class and the expansion of urban power groups have not, in themselves, proved a particularly strong deterrent to military interventions. José Nun, for example, finds no relationship between the size of the middle class and the frequency of military coups in Latin America. "The Middle Class Military Coup," in Claudio Veliz, ed., *Politics of Conformity in Latin America* (London, New York, Toronto: Oxford University Press, 1967), pp. 66–119. Similarly, Martin Needler finds only a slight correlation between social modernization and political stability. *Political Development in Latin America: Instability, Violence, and Evolutionary Change* (New York: Random House, 1968).

5. Thomas F. Harding, "Revolution Tomorrow: The Failure of the Left in Brazil," *Studies on the Left,* vol. IV, no. 4 (Fall 1964), pp. 40–41. Thomas E. Skidmore provides a similar interpretation of the events leading to Goulart's ouster in *Politics in Brazil, 1930–64: An Experiment in Democracy* (London, Oxford, New York: Oxford University Press, 1967), pp. 205–322. Martin Needler's model of the dynamics of a coup d'état suggests a similar process of escalation, *Political Development in Latin America,* pp. 66–76.

6. Charles W. Anderson, *Politics and Economic Change,* pp. 87–115; John D. Martz, *Acción Democratica* (Princeton, N.J.: Princeton University Press), Part I.

7. Anderson, *Politics and Economic Change,* p. 233.

8. Ibid.

9. Ibid.

10. Compare this to Brazil where, as Skidmore notes, "there was no organized political base" to sustain the program of the "positive left" in 1963. "The PTB remained in the hands of unresponsive manipulators, and the "progressive wings of the PSD and the UDN were but ineffectual minorities within their own parties. There was neither time nor leadership to organize a new party of the left. Furthermore, the center, representing middle-class opinion which wanted both honesty and reform, was also debilitated by disorganization," *Politics in Brazil,* p. 305. Compare this also with Anderson's description of the situation in Guatemala in 1944: "No cohesive reformist movement existed . . . to give coherence and impetus to a program for change. Rather, the plethora of groups that emerged from the dark recesses of Ubico's Guatemala found agreement only in their candidate, Juan José Arévelo, and left to him the task of determining what that agreement implied." *Politics and Economic Change,* p. 290.

11. Anderson's discussion of Latin America suggests, for example, that national governments and formal parliamentary institutions have normally been the arena of competition for middle groups—"misfits"

who did not fit comfortably into the status niches provided by the traditional economic and social institutions. Ibid., pp. 3–87. Merle Kling's famed thesis about the causes of Latin American instability carries with it similar implications. "Toward a Theory of Power and Political Instability in Latin America," *Western Political Quarterly*, vol. IX, no. 7 (March 1956), pp. 21–35.

12. See Sidney Tarrow, *Peasant Communism in Southern Italy* (New Haven: Yale University Press, 1967).

13. In Venezuela, for example, it might be useful to study the role of the COPEI part in this respect. For a discussion of a possibly similar role for the Mexican *Partido de Acción Nacional,* see Kenneth F. Johnson, "Ideological Correlates of Right Wing Political Alienation in Mexico," *American Political Science Review,* vol. LIX (September 1965).

14. On Argentina, see José Luís de Imáz, *Los que Mandan* (Buenos Aires: EUDEBA, Editorial Universitaria de Buenos Aires, 1964); on the Dominican Republic, see Abraham F. Lowenthal, "The Dominican Republic: The Politics of Chaos," in Arpad von Lazar and Robert R. Kaufman, eds., *Reform and Revolution: Readings in Latin American Politics* (Boston: Allyn and Bacon, Inc., 1969). For a suggestive comparison between Cuba and Chile, see Maurice Zeitlin's discussion: "Since [in Chile] the old aristocracy had itself participated directly in party politics, entered government service, and elective office, so too did newer elements in the ruling class. Men of ability and energy, therefore, of whatever social origins, looked on politics as a respectable career . . . In Cuba respect for elective office was lacking, fundamentally because such office carried with it little real authority over the nation's destiny, controlled as it was by a foreign power. "Politics" was a dirty word; opportunism, corruption, and gangsterism were identified with public office; and men of quality either spurned politics as a career or were deformed in the process of becoming seasoned politicians." "The Social Determinants of Political Democracy in Chile," in James Petras and Maurice Zeitlin, eds., *Latin America: Reform or Revolution?* (Greenwich, Conn.: Fawcett Publications, Inc., 1968), p. 231.

15. It is at this local level that the peasant syndicates seem to have acquired their greatest influence in Chile. Although at the level of national policy the unions appeared to have only a marginal impact, in several local regions of the country their power as bargaining agents exceeded that of some urban unions. In Venezuela, John Powell has argued, rural unions have provided a similar basis for peasant predominance at the local level. See "Agrarian Reform or Agrarian Revolution in Venezuela?" in Arpad von Lazar and Robert R. Kaufman, eds., *Reform and Revolution,* pp. 267–290.

16. Bolivia, Venezuela, Mexico. Referring more broadly to Asia and Africa, as well as to Latin America, Huntington has argued that po-

litical stability depends in part on a coalition between two of three social forces: the relatively conservative military, which "has the guns," the intelligentsia, which "has the brains," and the peasants which have "the numbers and the votes." A coalition "between the intelligentsia and peasants . . . usually involves revolution." *Political Order in Changing Societies,* pp. 240–241.

17. In Brazil, for example, the quite sizable Peasant Leagues which operated during the early 1960s were rather quickly suppressed by the Brazilian military government. In Venezuela, from 1948 to 1958, right-wing governments were also able to suppress with relative ease the peasant organizations that were built up during the first Democratic Action regime from 1945 to 1948.

18. Samuel P. Huntington, *Political Order in Changing Societies,* p. 428. Also, Anthony Downs, *An Economic Theory of Democracy* (New York: Harper and Bros., 1957).

19. See John D. Powell, "Agrarian Reform or Agrarian Revolution in Venezuela?", pp. 288–290.

20. Hirschman, *Journeys Toward Progress,* pp. 274–275.

Persons Interviewed

In the course of this study, informal interviews of varying length were conducted with over sixty persons active in Chilean political life. Because most of these persons are still involved deepy in a sensitive political process, they were not cited directly when they were quoted in the text. A partial, alphabetized list of these people is presented below, however, along with the relevant roles they played during the reform controversy. Where necessary, the governing name has been italicized.

Amino Afonso, Member of the staff of the Instituto de Capacitación e Investigación en Reforma Agraria (ICIRA).

Hector Alarcon, Leader of the Confederación Nacional de Campesinos (CNC).

Mario Alarcon, Leader of the Confederación Nacional de Campesinos (CNC).

Pedro Enrique Alfonso, Leader of the Radical Party; Director of the Comité Coordinador de Asociaciones Agrícolas.

Rodrigo *Alvarado* Moore, Secretary of the Asociación de Viticultores; Founder of the Federación Agrícola (FEDAGRI).

Gonzalo Arroyo, S.J., Economist.

Mario Astorga, Secretary General of the Consorcio Agrícola del Sur (CAS).

Jorge *Bentjerodt* Becker, Liberal politician; Staff member of Comité Coordinador de Asociaciones Agrícolas.

Francisco Bulnes, Conservative Senator, President of the Partido Conservador Unido (PCU).

Juan *Bulnes* Aldunate, Founder of the Federación Agrícola (FEDAGRI).

Fernando *Cancino* Téllez, Christian Democratic representative in the Chamber of Deputies.

José Campusano, Leader of the Federación de Campesinos e Indigenas (FCI).

Jaime Castillo, Christian Democratic Cabinet Minister of Land and Colonization.

Alejandro *Chelén* Rojas, Socialist Senator.

Jacques Chonchol, Executive Vice President of the Instituto de Desarrollo Agropecuario (INDAP).

Fernando *Coloma* Reyes, Vice President of the Partido Conservador Unido (PCU).

Persons Interviewed

Eugenio *Correa* Montt, Founder of Federación Agrícola (FEDAGRI).

Maria Elena Correa, Socialist Senator.

Renato de la Jara, Christian Democratic representative in the Chamber of Deputies.

Sergio Diez, Conservative representative in the Chamber of Deputies; Vice President of the Partido Conservador Unido (PCU).

Ramon Downey, Head of the Planning Office of the Corporación de Reforma Agraria (CORA).

Hernan Errázuriz, Leader of Liberal Youth Division.

Ladislao Errázuriz, Liberal Senator; President of the Partido Liberal (PL).

Angel Faivovich, Radical Senator.

Carlos Garcés, Christian Democratic representative in the Chamber of Deputies.

Domingo *Godoy* Matte, Liberal representative in the Chamber of Deputies.

Eugenio Heiremans, President of the Sociedad de Fomento Fabril (SFF).

Pedro Ibáñez, Liberal Senator.

Alberto Jerez, Christian Democratic representative in the Chamber of Deputies.

Julio César Jobét, Socialist historian and writer.

Miguel Lavanchy, Vice President of the Consorcio Agrícola del Sur (CAS).

Jorge Lavandero, Christian Democratic representative in the Chamber of Deputies.

Luís *Larraín* Marín, President of the Sociedad Nacional de Agricultura (SNA).

Jorge *Larraín* Valdivieso, Founder of the Federacíon Agrícola (FEDAGRI).

Alcides Leal, Member of the National Executive Committee of the Radical Party.

Emilio Lorenzini, Christian Democratic representative in the Chamber of Deputies; Leader of the Confederación Nacional de Campesinos (CNC).

Luis Maira, Christian Democratic representative in the Chamber of Deputies.

Jorge Mardones, Christian Democratic activist.

Héctor Millán, President of the Consorcio Agrícola del Sur (CAS).

Rafael Moreno, Executive Vice President of the Corporación de Reforma Agraria (CORA).

Guillermo Moore, Founder of the Federación Agrícola (FEDAGRI).

Recaredo Ossa, Independent spokesman for industrialists and agriculturalists.

Roberto Oyander, Staff of Instituto de Organisación y Administracion (INSORA).

Andrew Pearse, Staff of Instituto de Capacitación e Investigación (ICIRA).

Carol Pinto, National Secretary of the Christian Democratic Youth Organization.

Luis Quiroga, Staff of Instituto de Desarrollo Agropecuario (INDAP).

Alonso Quintana, Minister of Agriculture during Ibáñez regime.

Aniceto Rodríguez, Socialist Senator, Secretary General of the Partido Socialista (PS).

Jorge Rogers, Former Christian Democrat in opposition to the Frei administration.

Juan Ramon Samaniego, General Manager of the Sociedad de Fomento Fabril (SFF).

Plinio Sampaio, Staff of Instituto de Desarrollo Agropecuario (INDAP).

César Sepúlveda, Secretary General of the Sociedad Nacional de Agricultura (SNA).

Alfonso Silva, Secretary General of the Union Social de Empresarios Cristianos (USEC).

Julio *Silva* Solar, Christian Democratic representative in the Chamber of Deputies.

Stephen Smith, Director of the International Development Fund (IDF).

David Stitchkin, Member of the National Executive Committee of the Radical Party (PR).

Anselmo Sule, Secretary General of the Radical Party (PR).

George Wheelright, Director of the International Development Fund (IDF).

Federico Willoughby, Activist in the Conservative party youth movement.

Arturo Venegas, President of the Radical Party Youth Division.

Abel *Valdés* Acuña, Former Minister of Agriculture under Ibáñez; Leader of regional agricultural interest group.

Enrique Zorilla, Christian Democratic representative in the Chamber of Deputies.

Index

317

Index

land reform, 45–60 *passim,* 68, 71, 72; outlook of, 53; and deferred payments debate, 61–65; support for, 71
Consociational democracies, 19
Consortium of Agricultural Societies of the South (CAS), 158–159, 163
Coordinating Committee of Agricultural Associations, 162–166, 262
COPEI, 282
Copper reforms, 91–92, 99–100, 106–110; dispute over, and agrarian reform, 171–177; dispute over, and the FRAP, 204–206, 213–218
CORA, *see* Corporation for Agrarian Reform
Corbalán, Salomon, 199, 203
Corporation for Agrarian Reform (Corporación para la Reforma Agraria, CORA), 69, 90–91, 128, 211–212; Chonchol appointed head of, 87, 92–93; functions of, 90–91, 102–103; budget expenditures of, 99; and impact of asentamientos, 115–118, 120; and struggle for control of reform, 137–143; officials, lockout of, 178; and readjustment bill, 240, 242
Correa, Aníbal, 153
Correa, Hector, 57–58, 59
Corvalán, Luís, 210
Coups d'etat, 17
Cuban revolution, impact of, on land reform, 47
CUT, *see* Central Confederation of Workers

Deferred payments debate, 58–61; and the parties vs. the landowners, 61–66; rightest party experience and, 73–76
Democratic Action Party (AD), Venezuelan, 125, 142, 264, 281–282
Diario Ilustrado, 215
Diez, Sergio, 59
Durán, Julio, 233
Duverger, Maurice, 190

Economic Commission for Latin America, 87
Economy: difficulties within, 14, 30–31, 32; growth of, 222; and readjustment, 235–244
El Campesino, 151, 153, 154
Elections of *1967:* and asentamientos, 123–128; opposition gains and losses in, 129–132; and the urban vote, 228
El Mercurio, 47, 215
El Siglo, 206
Encomienda, defined, 23
Ercilla, 166
Errázuriz, Ladislao, 61

Falange, Falangists, *see* National Falangist party
FEDAGRI, *see* Agricultural Federation
Federation of Peasants and Indians (FCI), 132–134, 138, 141, 209–210; first congress of, 196
Food and Agricultural Organization (FAO) of the United Nations, 87
FRAP, *see* Popular Action Front
Frei, Eduardo, 72, 80, 83, 177, 264; and CORA and INDAP, 69, 87, 92; and election of *1964,* 79; and land reform, 81, 93–97, 103; policies of, 84; on the peasants, 90; and copper reform, 91, 100, 174–175; CNC support for, 141; and NSA, 149, 156, 158; criticism of, 164–165
Fuenzalida, Gilberto, 153
Furtado, Celso, 54

Garcia, Victor, 167
Garrido, José, 60
Gil, Federico G., 30, 229
Godoy, Domingo, 63
Gonzalez, Gabriel, 230
Goulart regime, 262

Hirschman, Albert O., 1, 183; and reformmongering, 1, 37, 40, 257, 259–260, 283; and logrolling, 108–109
Horizontal mobilization, and vertical brokerage system, 279–284
Huntington, Samuel P.: on modernization process, 3; on Chilean political organization, 4; his four criteria for political development, 14–15, 42; on city as center of unrest, 125; on multiparty systems, 281

318

Publications Written under the Auspices of the Center for International Affairs, Harvard University

Created in 1958, the Center for International Affairs fosters advanced study of basic world problems by scholars from various disciplines and senior officials from many countries. The research at the Center focuses on economic, social, and political development, the management of force in the modern world, the evolving roles of Western Europe and the Communist block, and the conditions of international order. Books published by Harvard University Press are listed here in the order in which they have been issued. A complete list of publications may be obtained from the Center.

Books

The Soviet Bloc: Unity and Conflict, by Zbigniew K. Brzezinski (jointly with the Russian Research Center), 1960. Revised and enlarged edition, 1967.

Rift and Revolt in Hungary: Nationalism versus Communism, by Ferenc A. Vali, 1961.

The Economy of Cyprus, by A. J. Meyer, with Simos Vassiliou (jointly with the Center for Middle Eastern Studies), 1962.

Entrepreneurs of Lebanon: The Role of the Business Leader in a Developing Economy, by Yusif A. Sayigh (jointly with the Center for Middle Eastern Studies), 1962.

Communist China 1955–1959: Policy Documents with Analysis, with a foreword by Robert R. Bowie and John K. Fairbank (jointly with the East Asian Research Center), 1962.

In Search of France, by Stanley Hoffmann, Charles P. Kindleberger, Laurence W. Wylie, Jesse R. Pitts, Jean-Baptiste Duroselle, and Francois Goguel, 1963.

Somali Nationalism: International Politics and the Drive for Unity in the Horn of Africa, by Saadia Touval, 1963.

The Dilemma of Mexico's Development: The Roles of the Private and Public Sectors, by Raymond Vernon, 1963.

The Arms Debate, by Robert A. Levine, 1963.

Africans on the Land: Economic Problems of African Agricultural Development in Southern, Central, and East Africa, with Special Reference to Southern Rhodesia, by Montague Yudelman, 1964.

Public Policy and Private Enterprise in Mexico: Studies, by M. S. Wionczek, D. H. Shelton, C. P. Blair, and R. Izquierdo, edited by Raymond Vernon, 1964.

Democracy in Germany, by Fritz Erler (Jodidi Lectures), 1965.

The Rise of Nationalism in Central Africa: The Making of Malawi and Zambia, 1873–1964, by Robert I. Rotberg, 1965.

Pan-Africanism and East African Integration, by Joseph S. Nye, Jr., 1965.

Germany and the Atlantic Alliance: The Interaction of Strategy and Politics, by James L. Richardson, 1966.

Political Change in a West African State: A Study of the Modernization Process in Sierra Leone, by Martin Kilson, 1966.

Planning without Facts: Lessons in Resource Allocation from Nigeria's Development, by Wolfgang F. Stolper, 1966.

Export Instability and Economic Development, by Alasdair I. MacBean, 1966.

Europe's Postwar Growth: The Role of Labor Supply, by Charles P. Kindleberger, 1967.

Pakistan's Development: Social Goals and Private Incentives, by Gustav F. Papanek, 1967.

Strike a Blow and Die: A Narrative of Race Relations in Colonial Africa, by George Simeon Mwase, edited by Robert I. Rotberg, 1967. Second printing, with a revised introduction, 1970.

Development Policy: Theory and Practice, edited by Gustav F. Papanek, 1968.

Korea: The Politics of the Vortex, by Gregory Henderson, 1968.

The Brazilian Capital Goods Industry, 1929–1964 (jointly with the Center for Studies in Education and Development), by Nathaniel H. Leff, 1968.

The Process of Modernization: An Annotated Bibliography on the Sociocultural Aspects of Development, by John Brode, 1969.

Taxation and Development: Lessons from Colombian Experience, by Richard M. Bird, 1970.

Lord and Peasant in Peru: A Paradigm of Political and Social Change, by F. LaMond Tullis, 1970.

The Kennedy Round in American Trade Policy: The Twilight of the GATT?, by John W. Evans, 1971.

Korean Development: The Interplay of Politics and Economics, by David C. Cole and Princeton N. Lyman, 1971.

Development Policy II – The Pakistan Experience, edited by Walter P. Falcon and Gustav F. Papanek, 1971.

Peasants Against Politics: Rural Organization in Brittany, 1911–1967, by Suzanne Berger, 1972.

Transnational Relations and World Politics, edited by Robert O. Keohane and Joseph S. Nye, Jr., 1972.

Latin American University Students: A Six Nation Study, by Arthur Liebman, Kenneth N. Walker, and Myron Glazer, 1972.

The Politics of Land Reform in Chile, 1950–1970: Public Policy, Political Institutions, and Social Change, by Robert R. Kaufman, 1972.